Oh crap, oh crap, oh crap, this all got way out of hand and now I have to write a 4th book!

By

Paul Tompkins

B is for Bottle, the kind you uncork.
He's kind of a grumpy old know-it-all dork.

E is for Editor, we call him Skip,
He once was an intern but we have no ship.

S is for Sandra, the mistress of D,
The princess of human resources is she.

BB for Bridbrad our public relations,
He photogs and narrates and sends salutations.

M is for Milton whom no one invited,
He manages finances, boy, we're delighted.

GREGORY's GREGORY, no bones about it.
That screech from the closet was him, don't you doubt it.

C is for Compy, collector of stuff,
He brings me more records when I don't have enough.

G is for Gladys knitting away
In the front office keeping the riffraff away.

Join our media empire, more like a tomb,
We are Bottle of Beef in the Bunker of Doom.

© Paul Tompkins/Bottle of Beef 2022

Typeset in 11pt Palatino

Interpretation is not inherent truth, but rather the path to mutual enlightenment.

Once Upon A Time…

"Cap'n, we're gliding. We've lost lateral thrusters, the gyroscopes keep reorienting themselves, the 3D printers are making what appear to be inch-thick butcherings of cow flesh..."

"Are they T-Bones?"

"I hate you so much right now, Cap'n."

"Kelis can't save us. Any way to reroute the windbags to blow port and starboard rather than out our back end?"

"I could duct tape two drier vents to a bucket, Cap'n."

"Shame to waste a perfectly good bucket, but give it a try. If that doesn't work, I guess we'll just 'ave to 'ope for a nice squishy P-class planet to crash into."

"P-class, Cap'n?"

"P is for pillow. A nap sounds good right about now. Wake me up whenever whatever 'appens 'as already 'appened."

"Aye, aye, Cap'n"

… several hours later…

CRASH! KAPOW! ZZZZZZZIP! CLANG.

"Welp, guess that qualifies. Pants around 'ere somewhere… [ziiiiip]

…

"'Ardly qualifies as a soft landing, Commander. Still, at least it's over, and nobody I know appears to be scattered in multiple locations. Where are we?"

"Earth, Cap'n"

"Is that the one with the lizard people?"

"No, Cap'n. Oddly enough, some of the inhabitants think there are secretly lizard people, but not the ones you're thinking about."

"Oh, ok. The one where Apes are in charge?"

"Noooo, but again, oddly enough they've imagined that possibility. They call themselves 'Human.'"

"Why are you putting so much emphasis on the 'H'?"

"Because they do. Quite a lot of their H-es are aspirate."

"'H'onestly 'orrible. Still, making the rules is well above my pay grade, did The Shovelers survive your delightful divot-dive approach to this golf ball in the sky?"

"Yes, Cap'n. We let 'em play in the bouncy castle while we handled the crash landing."

"Good, send 'em out all willy-nilly, I need 'allways in all ways for the think-walking."

"Aye aye, Cap'n. Permission to hand out the skittles as well?"

"The after-amnesias? I'll never understand why you guys hate remembering the future so much. Fine, whatever. I personally don't see the fun in forgetting, but if it makes you less agitated, forget away. I'll make up some ridiculous backstory like always."

Uriah Heep – Demons and Wizards

The books are done! Time to reboot this franchise.

Everybody who has a basis for comparison says Demons & Wizards is Uriah Heep's best album, and now I can say I'm no exception. This thing is phenomenal. There's prog, there's some heavy metal, there's a whole lot of bluesy endings to musical phrases, there's Dio style falsetto ridiculousness, everybody sings lead at some point, and it all just rocks.

Yes, it's all kind of fantasy magic characters and stuff, but no it's not really a concept album. And wow is it fun. David Byron's vocals are dramatic and engaging, Gary Thain's melodic bass lines are just gorgeous, Ken Hensley is bloop-bleeping on every available keyboard, and there are legitimate moments of everyone spastically flailing their picks at an acoustic guitar. If nothing else it sounds like a group of people having fun, and that's a recipe for awesome in my book.

Huey Lewis and the News – Sports

Cool is often objectively subjective, but sometimes good doesn't need to be qualified. I adore Huey Lewis and the News. There's a really interesting history of lawsuits about I Want a New a Drug, but I'll let you go read the little bit about his dust ups with Ray Parker Jr. on your own. I'm more interested in the fact that it's the only album named after an actual segment of "the news." You don't even want to know how many different ways he tried spelling his stage name. Half-right-ipedia is half right as usual, they got the Rock and New Wave part correct, but it's serious old-school Rock & Roll, saxes and harmonica style.

Absolutely true that Back to the Future was the reason people went out to find this album, but how could they be disappointed? It's like 38 years later and though this old man's barely breathing, the heart of Rock & Roll is indeed still beating. I'm perfectly happy with small amounts of the old-drugs. As an adult I fully understand the underlying problem with the 80s, but I was an actual kid, and this is just pure happy-time in my brain. Not that you actually could, but don't spoil it for me.

FM – Surveillance

B: Why so glum, Mz. D?

S: Hmm? Oh, sorry, I guess I'm just bored. We finished GREGORY's album, but I can't really do the cover for the book until Skip tells me the actual page count; they're sticklers about the spine width. What about you? I figured you'd be all over farcebook after today's outage. Didn't you write anything?

B: Sure, yeah, a dozen of the little buggers. One about Lars Vilks's car crash on Sunday, the mutual benefits of cooperative business structures, Proudhon's erratic version of anarchy, funny blurbs about the album, not funny blurbs about the album, today's DNS failure (which is like the 9th or 10th this year alone because decentralization and redundancy are the foundation of the internet as we know it, but corporatization doesn't have a brain to understand why centralization and monopoly are points of failure rather than security), the weird idea that giving addicts a platform for honest expression is actually worse than telling them they are horrible people, all sorts of crap. It's what I do. I don't need to publish any of it, though.

S: Oh, I thought that was part of the reason you did.

B: No, no, no, I do it because it's fun, to show people the inside never stops. I don't care if people read them or not. I like it when they do, but I'm not chasing them down and demanding a reply. I'm just giving a voice to ideas that can't speak for themselves.

S: So, what are you going to do next?

B: I was thinking about listening to FM's 3rd album, Surveillance; it picks up the space-rock weirdness from where the first album leaves off. Surveillance was also their first mass-market release. Plewman left after the first album, so Ben Mink has electric violin duty on this one.

S: I thought you hated the space exploration stuff.

B: No, not at all. Why? Oh, the Musk and Bezos and Branson thing? Ok, you have to understand, SpaceX is doing truly amazing things, advancements NASA couldn't even dream of if they all went on a week-long LSD bender. That stuff is totally fascinating, and I'm all for it. The catch is that they think you and I should pay for it by not having any money for stupid things like food and clothes and record collections and education. Musk wants to own space travel, and pass that ownership down to Gx-Delta%, or whatever they named that poor kid. That's the part that wads my panties.

S: Ooooooh, I get it now.

B: Welcome home. Same problem I have with field corn and soy beans. We're growing animal feed that's terrible for animals and subsidizing gasoline additives instead of planting edible, nutritious crops we can eat. Musk is like the human embodiment of Monsanto, just evil incarnate when it comes to minion power. Think about it, forests worked pretty good for millions of years until we chopped 'em all down to make toilet paper. Before you even start, yes, I'm exaggerating.

S: I know that, Bottle. I guess I just assumed you really were a grumpy old man.

B: Only if I need to be. If it's "at the expense of...," then yeah, I'll rain on every parade. If I had an ulterior motive, it would be teaching everyone that it's exposing the exploitation that matters; you can go to the moon and presumably Mars in a decade or so, if you're willing to exploit enough people to make it happen. More than half of them will cheer you on and call you a role model while you do it. That's not jealousy talking, by the way. 90 hours a week and board meetings at 2am is not my idea of fun, whatever the outcome. I'm a generalist, not a professional nail sharpener. I'd rather listen to a skeleton play Russian piano music, or Canadians sing about space travel, than measure plate thickness in micrometers for 14 hours every day. A great achievement for mankind is not the same as *my* great achievement at the expense of mankind, it's just not.

S: But are you going to review it?

B: No. It's lovely. Goofy, but lovely. Disagree?

S: No, I suppose not. Way better than the 80s English Hair band also named FM.

B: No argument from me. 70s Canadian Space-Prog wins. Even has tubular bells hiding in there. Plus, it ends with the Star Council giving us a few more years to figure out how to stop killing each other before totally banning us from the rest of the universe.

S: 40 years might be pushing our luck.

B: Oh, yeah, we're totally screwed if they catch us Florida-ing up the place now.

The Association

You'll like this. I did a totally Bottle thing. I had this gigantic essay where I intertwined a serious discussion about Anarchy and The Association's 5th album. All sorts of calamities could happen at that point, so I try to copy them as a backup, but this time I hit delete as I was trying to copy it. It's fine, I don't care. We'll just hit the salient points.

1) The Association is one of those bands that completely surprises me.

2) You might think a self-titled 5th album goes against Bottle's Taxonomy, but it's their first proper album, not just a singles collection, so that totally works.

3) It's Stonehenge on the moon and Earth is a cube. This is half PP&M style folkstravaganza, half Psych-Rock pastiche, including a critique of Vietnam, a song about Dubuque, one called Broccoli, and a whole lot of "the trappings of the modern world are garbage." No, seriously, it's about "turning you on to broccoli," the actual vegetable. It grows in the ground and he likes to eat it with his mouth. None of it makes any sense, as only The Association could really pull off. They might be the most sarcastically cynical Sunshine Pop band ever.

You'll just have to imagine the ingenuity I brought to that first draft. All I can really say is that The Association is completely unpredictable, and totally wackadoodle in their unique way. Banjos and pedal steel and trumpets and tons of la-la-la-las. I love 'em, but then again you know how weird I am, so plan accordingly.

You seriously have to hear Broccoli by The Association. Go find it now, it's ridiculous. How can you take anything serious after that? No choice but to put it in the "what the hell am I listening to" crate. This album is pure insanity. No, really, really go look at that lyric insert band photo. 'Nuff said.

Fleetwood Mac – Rumours

Today on Bottle of Beef, we find out if Germany is good at pressing records for Target. This one's gold-dust colored, apparently.

I've heard lots of rumors that people don't like the singing voice of Stevie Nicks. You know me, as long as it's not Petula Clark or Barbara Mandrell, I don't care what barnyard animal they compare you to. Beeflieve it or not, I've never actually heard the entire British spelling. So, in that spirit, let's kick Mick in the toilet chains and ask him to cough up an album of mystical sagas about not 1, not 2, but 3 simultaneously failing relationships, and an amount of cocaine to rival David Bowie, Miles Davis, and Rick James combined. It's the undeniably classic album, Rumours.

Daaaamn. No, really, people say this is a pretty flawless album, and except for Lindsay's terrible chorused vocals on Never Going Back Again, I have to agree. The story goes that they'd show up at The Record Plant Sausalito (which looks more like a horror movie cabin in the woods than a recording studio), have a huge feast and get wasted, then start recording completely blitzed around 1 or 2 am. 6 other studios were involved as well, so about a million 1977 dollars in production costs. Afterward, they all looked at each other and asked "did we just make an album about our divorces and subsequent dating experiences. Oh, well, time to extensively tour it."

    The only creepy song is Oh Daddy, and with a name like Smuckers.... Doesn't matter that it's simultaneously about the reconciliation of Mick's marriage and his leadership of the band. It's creepy, Christine. The most surprising track is Buckingham's Never Going Back Again. Just an awesome piece of acoustic Folk-Rock guitar work, that one. Yeah, it's got all the super-hits, but it is a pretty spectacular album to contain them. And yes, Optimal Media GmbH knows how all the setting knobs and levers on their pressing machines work. This is the nicest piece of 21st-century vinyl I own.

    Is Rumours worthy of 25th best album ever recorded? I suppose so. I mean they intended to make a Pop album, they succeeded big time, the songs are actually enjoyable to listen to, it is a bit mysterious with a tinge of whimsy, you got weird sound effects all over the place, and that iconic bassline to guitar solo from The Chain to open Side B. It's their 11th, so they've had a fair bit of practice. Yeah, everything about this album is great. I guess the rumors are true; it's lovely. As many times as I've referenced it over the last two years, you'd think I'd own a copy before now. Nope, and if Target had a better selection, I might not have bought it today either. I am a mystery, wrapped in a conundrum flavored tortilla. Maybe if Kellogg's decides to pay their American employees properly, we'll turn it into a breakfast cereal. Bottle o' Beeflets - Malted Flakes: Makes its own gravy, just add milk! See? I knew I could work in some relevant social commentary if I just blabbered long enough. Enjoy.

Spirit – Clear (Revisited)

It's been a couple years, maybe I can learn to like Clear. I love 1, 2, & 4, it seems such a shame to hate it. Spoiler alert, no, I can't.

It's not the band or the songs, though. It's the engineering and mixing. The first time around I said it sounds muddy, and it does, but that's not really all that's bugging me. Randy's vocals are fine, and most of the lead guitar parts are ok if really, really dark, it's everything else that sounds like oatmeal. You can totally disagree, but I hate drums panned left, bass panned right. Next, things like background vocals, horn, strings, all that kind of sonic middle-ground sounds 30+ feet away from the mics. There're basically no high frequencies, so it only sort of sounds like someone might be playing a piano in a different room and you can't hear any attack on the synthy sounding guitar parts, but the hard left hi hats are so distracting it's hard to actually concentrate on anything else. The reverb isn't helping either. Half the time it sounds like they are literally around the next corner and you're hearing it bounce off a brick wall.

On top of that, the quiet sounds are almost always louder than the loud sounds, and a harp being louder than a tube saturated guitar lead sounds totally wrong. The EQ is so totally whack, I had to run it through an analyzer. You guys can't see them because this is a word book, but the first photo is a snapshot of the title track, Clear. The second photo is a snapshot of Fat Old Sun from Atom Heart Mother. I know you're gonna be like "Bottle, those look basically the same," but in real life that difference around 1k is like night and day. Clear sounds anything but.

Like I said, the songs are great, the slightly sloppy playing is gorgeous, the compositions are fantastic, the album sounds like I'm wearing ear muffs with walkmans glued to each side. Spirit doesn't sound like this, The Band that Plays

Together doesn't sound like this, Dr. Sardonicus doesn't sound like this, no wonder they told Lou Adler "smell you later." I said Seventh Sojourn deserved a time-travel type re-recording, but so does Spirit's 3rd album. It's certainly not as painful to listen to as any Rolling Stones album, but it's not particularly enjoyable.

So, there you have it. I wish I liked listening to it, but I probably never will. Clear could have been a great album, but it sounds too much like crap for me to ignore even when I'm trying. Sad, but true.

Edit: I was bummed after writing this, so I gave it yet another shot. This album actually sounds good played out loud through the speaker of your cell phone. That's not a win in my book, but there you go.

STP – Core

I was naughty and bought some records earlier this week. Hopefully they ship out tomorrow or Saturday. It's like there's a shortage of packaging materials or something. Oh well, it's not like I didn't wait months for Guiot's l'Univers de la Mer to get from Sweden to Iowa, let's just go back to albums I didn't write about in my 3 books (I also told you the collection is over a thousand, didn't I?).

Core. What an album. Invisible Purple is of course my favorite STP album, but wowzers that debut is smack you in the face awesome. Supposedly it's Core, as in the apple core left behind after Adam and Eve did that Bob James/Rasheeda Azar impression that made Skip blush like "well, I never!" Fun fact, the actual fruit is unspecified. Some random guy decided it should be "apple" so he could copyright his version of the bible. The internet told me that, so grain of salt, you know?

The important point is these are all character pieces from the mindset of "a sinner." Eve apparently called him a creep.

It's a fantastic album, but it's Brendan O'Brien. The acoustic guitar stuff is incredible, the electric alternative rock parts are a homogeneous cacophony of indistinguishable incomprehensibility. Everything that isn't vocals or snare drums sounds like garlic mashed-potatoes. That's a shame, because on the rare occasions when only two or three sounds are happening the tones are gorgeous.

I made it sound like that was a bad thing. It's not, really. Nothing is muddy or obnoxious. Everything works for the song at hand, it's just a shame that the album is flat-line as far as dynamics are concerned. A few of these songs deserve the added meaning of being slightly softer/louder, but nope, brick wall everything.

What is worth noting is that there is a fair amount of metal hiding in here. It quickly goes back to harmonically complex Alt-Rock, but some of these riffs are metal AF. On the other hand, I don't think I'm making up the feeling that their future music can only diffuse out into multiple less-coherent or interconnected musical avenues. Core sounds like the pinnacle and it's all downhill from here. Purple is by far my favorite, but Core is basically perfect and thus sadly cannot be improved upon. Like it or not, they got it right the first time.

Cloudkicker – Solitude

Well, today was a special brand of suck. Please excuse me while I go kick a cloud. We'll try again tomorrow.

Bottle's Favorites - Marcy Playground

It's true, I love albums. Look, if you took the time to deal with the hassles of practice and corporate executives and studio time, then someone needs to appreciate that effort. I do. Still, I can't help but have nuanced preferences. I have a very cultured and diverse palette. I'm an aficionado. So, here are some of my genuine favorites. I guess if I were like your little league record listening coach, these are the ringers I'd invite to teach you something. No particular order, though.

Parts & Labor - Mapmaker
Mastodon - Crack the Skye and Leviathan
Spirit - Twelve Dreams of Dr. Sardonicus
Supertramp - Breakfast in America
The Cars - The Cars
MCR - Black Parade
Pink Floyd - Dark Side of the Moon

And, believe it or not, the self-titled debut from Marcy Playground. Sadly, my copy is no longer with us, we'll have to youtube it today.

Sex and Candy was their biggest hit, but I'm happy to tell you that it just sits here as the unobtrusive track 2 it really is. It's not even in the top half as far as songs on this album go. The important thing is that all John Wozniak has is an acoustic guitar with a sound hole pickup and some generic effects pedals, and that is a very distinct post-grunge sound even though grunge is an adjective not a genre.

No critic likes this album, and that's because they hate how not a facade it is. This is the 90s, and this album is straight out of the loser side of town. The point I'm trying to make is that critics don't care about the album at all, they are criticizing the people who made it, the people who like it, and intentionally ignoring the fact that they themselves are part of the establishment that created the disenfranchised generation in the first place. I understand Christgau's point of view, but he and I have opposite taste in music. He likes the sound of the machine filtering out all humanity of an artist or band.

Chuck Eddy called it "icky" and "callow." I mean, it's named after John's alternative elementary school. It's an attempt to depict being a child in a world full of drugs, depression, loneliness, and suicide. This is one of those "how dare you hate all this marvelous garbage I shoved down your throat" situations. I bet I know what set them off. I bet it was Vampires of New York.

Now, you can hate all the same things the critics hated (his emotionally flat-line delivery, "sloppy" playing in the cautionary-est of quotation marks, the overt opioid references, the sarcasm even Bob Newhart might feel is a tad heavy-handed), but it's tough to argue that this isn't an amazing album. If I had to give the concept a one sentence synopsis, here it is:

The kings and queens hand you both literal and metaphorical opiates, they get richer while us plebes ironically languish and die defending it, and that's New York City; gee isn't that swell [baaaarf].

But can you see the difference? John's saying "look at what we've created; it's garbage." The critics respond, "no you're garbage."

Who's being callow?

KMFDM – WWIII

C: Holy hell, Bottle. You look like you've been through a Jack LaLanne power juicer.

B: It's been a rough couple weeks.

E: I was starting to get worried; you've barely reviewed anything since we finished the book.

B: No joke, this time of year is rough, everybody magically wants their houses and hotels and office buildings and crap finished before official winter sets in. Nevermind the covid and flu and all the wildlife fleeing the fields. And those rats on stilts. Fun fact, yes, you're supposed to just hit the deer and let your airbag do its job. Yeah, no, I'll pass. Everybody already hates me for driving the speed limit, 5mph slower at dawn and dusk isn't gonna cramp my style any.

S: So, should we expect a Halloween spectacular, or not?

B: I dunno. I was planning to do White Zombie or maybe have Compy do a real mixtape, but the world is right back to not having a clue how anything actually works, and I just can't care. I'm half tempted to do the official anti-W albums from the collection. Sure, why not? We'll start with WWIII.

KMFDM is part of the firmament of Industrial Rock/Metal. They started out as the kind of performance art that involves vacuum cleaners, and still exist. This isn't a band history though, so we'll just say that there are 3 kinds of people in this world: 1) people who have never heard of KMFDM, 2) people who only know of KMFDM in relation to Columbine, and 3) people who actually listen to KMFDM. I am the 3rd type of people. Musically, they are "ultra-heavy beat."

They are also highly political, maybe like 1 or two steps down from Rage Against The Machine. Anti-authoritarian, anti-violence, anti-hate, anti-war, anti-fascism. You'd have to have a severe lack of understanding of sarcasm and self-deprecating humor to misconstrue what they are saying. Yes, it's highly critical of US political policy, but so am I and we're still friends, right? All I'm advocating for is a whole lot less authoritarian nincompoopery. I don't want to "retire" on the backs of future generations of the working class. I want to be paid now for being me and die when it's my turn.

E: But the Demonrats are trying to steal from private retirement funds.

B: I love you Skip, but that's moron talk. Yes, there are rules and regulations that keep the balance of your 401ks and IRAs assigned to you, but it's double-spent money. Every penny you contribute to your retirement fund is reallocated to working capital, and only the ledger entry remains. Your retirement payout comes from the retirement contributions of future people. I'm 41 and my 401k is sitting at 1 year's salary. If I don't find 7 times that much money before I'm 60, it'll just go straight to whomever owns my student loan debt. I'll be working the day I die of old age, so I cannot possibly care. The cost of my caring is $200,000.

I suppose I could sit down and do the math to find out if it's better to cash out now and use it to start my own business, but I don't want to just walk away from the people I'm trying to help. I like where I work, but some days I get the unpleasant feeling that everyone else is actually a useless moron and my job is to prevent them from figuring that out. I can't function like that, I need to believe people are malfunctioning from bad instructions, not hiding from their own ineptitude.

Man, I'm way off track. The official translation of KMFDM is "no majority for the pity" with the German grammatical genders reversed (it was assembled from newspaper headline clippings and Sascha thought it was funny). That's some delicious wordplay right there. Critics say this album is blah, call it butt-rock, and generally act like I care what they think. That's a tough one because KMFDM is not a mainstream band, they just found some tangible mainstream validation in the mid-90s. WWIII is interesting because it's war on war.

Well, Beefettes, this was not a great review. I'm gonna chalk it up to being sore in muscles I didn't know I had and not feel too bad about it. Plus, the 3rd book of better reviews becomes officially available next Monday, so we should reserve some of what's left of my brain for hyping the crap out of that. There're records in the future too, they're just taking their sweet time getting here. Imma go to sleep, you guys do you. Oh, yeah, I almost forgot. Compy, we gotta do something about the website. Maybe a proper shop page or something.

I do feel a bit better, though. That moonshine pouring banjo intro punctuated by gunshot is a real wake-you-up gesture, and putting the intro as the last track never gets not enjoyable for me. Yeah, we'll try again tomorrow. Cheers.

Ministry – Rio Grande Blood

Rio Grande Blood is the second of Ministry's anti-Bush trilogy, sandwiched between Houses of the Molé and The Last Sucker. All their album titles are parodies of other famous titles and/or humorous slogans. Ministry began as terrible synthpop with a fake British accent, then morphed into much better industrial metal and thrash.

I have a conspiracy theory that the quality of a Ministry album is inversely proportionate to the amount of heroin Al is injecting at the time. He has a conspiracy theory that the Bush administration was complicit in the 9/11 attacks. This is not one of my favorite Ministry albums, and that's because it transcends hyperbole and invades completely inaccurate territory. Underlying sentiment yes, truthfulness not so much. It's a "truthiness" album.

Lots of parodized and reassembled Bush samples, some funny some not. Criticisms of the motivations for various wars in the Middle East. Oil played a big part, sure, but the illogic of staging a series of multi-national terrorist attacks in order to further empower the federal government so that they can weaken the federal government is a terrifying taxi ride through crazy town. I know everybody hasn't read my 3rd book yet, but understand that it's the CEOs and majority investors in major Corporations who now represent the Marxian middle-class. Most every store is a franchise at this point, the owner/operator is petit-bourgeois. What is completely true is that Bush was elected by this modern day ultra-conservative corporate middle-class. Point being, we got where we are today by completely normal status quo, exactly the way Marx said we would. Now unbristle those tail-feathers, I'm not yaying or booing one side or the other, I'm just describing the part of his imaginary story that looks hella-accurate.

Al was born in Cuba at the dawn of the overthrow of Batista by Castro, and his family fled to America around 1962. Reminds me of John Kay's family fleeing the erecting of the Berlin Wall, not to mention all those Brazilian emigres.

My real argument is that there is an underlying theme here. First, Cuba, Uruguay, all these 20th-century social revolutions didn't start out as Leninist movements, that's what they two-facedly became after the actual seizing of power took place, and there were massive protests and emigration as a result of the lies. Second, Marx has been dead for decades. Third, Lenin completely misunderstood Marx; dove head first into the empty swimming pool that Marx said was stupid and pointless, took the word "revolution" literal and tried to murder his way back to the other side of the cycle as quickly as possible.

Remember how Aaron Lewis didn't break the cycle, just waited for the elephant to circle back around so he could hop on at cruising speed? Same difference. Why is that? Well, no one is making decisions and no one is actually doing anything. It's all just reaction to the reaction to the knee-jerk reaction to the reaction to the misunderstanding of pointing out how stupid the whole thing actually is. You can't elect a bully to defend you then get upset at how much of a bully he turns out to be. You have to define what you will and won't do, then actually do and don't do it, respectively.

So, while I'm in agreement that W was an evil puppet of the personification of corporate incompetence, I find it a little tough to quantum leap over the invisible bridge to the bizarro universe where he masterminded anything. I'm with Marx on this one, it's just complete shortsightedly dumb philosophical optimism, and it's yet another part of the underlying stupidity of being a dizzy sheeple on the secret payroll of Haliburton. How do you even get into a situation where your hunting buddy is on the receiving end of a shotgun blast to the face, Dick? Making it all about money is the actual conspiracy, because it diverts you from the fact that privilege is the actual prize they're hoarding at the end of the unflamboyantly monochrome rainbow of doom.

So, in terms of Ministry albums, I'd much rather listen to The Mind is a Terrible Thing to Taste, The Land of Rape and Honey, or Psalm 69, but I get where Al's coming from.

Saosin – Along The Shadow

You don't even know how happy I am this record arrived today. I was not looking forward to revisiting eMOTIVe or American Idiot, or explaining how net worth is more like collateral and the "billionaires" are the actual buffer between government spending and general circulation, or that nonsense idea that congresspeople walk away millionaires. Instead, we'll say welcome back Anthony Green, and revel in the post-hardcore gorgeousness of Saosin's 2016 Along The Shadow.

The whole album is phenomenal, but Alex Rodriguez deserves special mention. No baseball jokes, the drumming on this album is out of this world. Not standout, though, every individual part is stellar, as is the overall songwriting. This is a maximum score album.

It's also a throwback to the good part of the early 2000s, because Green left to be the singer of Circa Survive after their debut EP. So, their first two LPs with Cove Reber are like a completely different band. This is original Saosin's actual debut album. I suppose you could call it Screamo, but that's a nonsense designation because the first thing you'll notice is that this is incredibly melodic, lushly orchestrated, and HEAVY. And wow is it beautiful, just a joy to listen to. There isn't a single awkward or incoherent moment. Instead, all the little glitches and stutters and swells and textural changes feel completely intuitive, clever, and coherent. Anthony's screaming comes across as a duality; like we're hearing both the outward expression and the inner context at the same time.

I know I don't evaluate albums the way most people do, but this is an album you could listen to for the 100th time and enjoy it more than the previous 99 listens. Seriously, give Along The Shadow some undivided attention. Really feel it, it's phenomenal.

Halloween 2021

B: Alrighty, kids. You know what today is?

Chorus: HALLOWEEN!

B: It's always Halloween in my head, why's today special? No, it's Bottle's 3rd Book Officially Gets Published Eve. Special day, it only happens once a lifetime. Or, deathtime if you're living that Nac McFeegle reverse chronology thing. Let the festivities commence!

Chorus: mumble, mumble, mumble.

B: I think I heard a "shut up" and possibly a "Bottle sucks" in there. Awesome. Alright, we'll compromise. You guys do Burger King, I'll be Frank Sinatra. I have a greenhouse to build, we have Compy's Howlathon playlist, p(nmi)t's Lady Killer, GREGORY's Piano Recital of Doom, I'll have to take a trip for minion food and pirate juice before we imbibe White Zombie's La Sexorcisto: Devil Music Vol. 1 as tonight's album. Jam packed day of excitement if you ask me.

E: I suppose that technically qualifies as something for everyone.

S: So, how do we proceed?

B: 3, 2, 1, blast off! Space cadets ahoy!

B: There it is, the Greenhouse of Doom!

S: That was quick.

B: I know. Only like 10 hours of actual work. Everything fit together, nothing broke, I'm suitably terrified.

S: The garden gnomes will be thrilled.

B: Good for them. Now I'm off on the grocery run of doom. Minions gotta eat, am I right? Until the rumming hour.

S: Ok. Toodles, then.

It's weird noticing what is or isn't in stock, what's fresh and what's molding on the shelf, which "stand in front of the thing I want" people are shopping this time/day. Two things are for certain, though. 1) I won't get something on the list, and 2) I will overhear a private phone conversation that I wish I could manage to not remember. Thankfully, this trip is over and we're a step closer to album time. One can only hope the brain cells that now archive Mark's embarrassingly itchy personal problem will be permanently destroyed in the near future....

Ah, welcome to the e'en of the hall of OW! Turns out I forgot to eat actual food in there somewhere, so I'm feeling rather more curmudgeonly than normal. I'm sure this sugar coated in sugar with a 3rd type of sugar drizzled on top, washed down with sugar water will help. I'm joking, real food was ingested, on with the festivities. 3 albums for this night of mystery and mayhem.

On with the ennui; let's glide into the gloam with the gloom of GREGORY's Piano Recital of Doom. This was, as you might say, a team effort. Compy Compilerson assembled an assortment of artworks featuring skeletons playing the piano. Mz. Sandra D. did what she does best and produced some mighty fine cover art. Yours truly, the Bottlemeister at large just placed as much sheet music as possible in front of GREGORY's adventures in keyboard land, and we concocted this little 3-act ode to Autumn in its multitude of metaphorical machinations. Old boney himself even surprised us with a dour tribute to our favorite month that starts with the letter O, a bit of a textural palindrome above a delicious i-bVII-#vi-V ostinato. Delightfully dour, even though I do say so myself.

https://bottleofbeef.bandcamp.com/album/piano-recital-of-doom

What next? Ah, I know, how about a blast from the ghost of Halloween's past? p(nmi)t's Lady Killer. It's the deliciously wordless soundtrack to the story of the Mistress Marauder Margaret. Bit of a bizarro Pied Piper she is, commanding a fearsome army of psychotically murderous ducks on a quest to cripple the corporate fashion industry.

https://paultompkins.bandcamp.com/album/lady-killer

Lovely, now on to the main event. You want Devil Music, I've got Devil Music, it's White Zombie's ode to plowing through crowds of zombies and spiders and space monsters in your Mustang while trying to find a good radio station to listen to. I personally don't think it needs much explanation. You got b-movie and Star Trek samples, Iggy Pop using a typewriter, as much sleaze, exploitation, and grindhouse depravity as anyone could want or handle. It's weird to call it psychedelic groove metal, but that's exactly what it is, 'cause it sounds like everyone is wearing go-go boots and stabbing vampires with sharpened broom handles. Glorious.

https://youtube.com/playlist?list=OLAK5uy_m1NkMYNRiPnL7b5fLodB8nNuV8JhGOIbw

Well, that was quite a lovely last day of October. Things got done, albums got listened to, diabetes inducing levels of candy got ingested. I don't want to go back to work tomorrow, but it's hard to argue that isn't the punishment they'll give me when they track me down at dawn. Se la mort. From all of us here at Bottle of Beef, bob your head and cheers (but maybe not at the same time, you might chip a tooth).

Frank Sinatra – Watertown

I cannot even begin to tell you how many dozens of people have been not asking me how I plan to follow up yesterday's nougat filled binge of Halloween-flavored albumstrocities. Which is good, because I'd just reply "my favorite Dean Martin tracks from this unfindable Rat Pack album in Compy's music folder of doom."

Speaking of things that are not understandable, let's listen to the other nightmarish thing Gaudio, Valli, and Holmes did. Those sons of mothers made Frank Sinatra record an entire concept album without live orchestral backing. Yeah, Sinatra had to record isolated vocals for the only time in his life in 1969. Just like LA, nobody liked Watertown.

Yeah, no one was going to like anything Sinatra did in 1970, his popularity was virtually non-existent. Today everyone's all Best Sinatra Album Ever, but back then this was Genuine Life Gazette Part No Thanks, I'll Pass. It's a shame, 'cause this is fantastic. For starters, it wasn't a musical first, nor is it a Vegas booze-schmooze land cruise. It's Sinatra's Red Headed Stranger. He doesn't kill her; she just leaves him to forget all her troubles and go downtown. So now he's raising his kids in the little podunk Watertown while grappling with those sushi quality emotions generally reserved for a fictional version of Phil Collins's divorce.

Here's what I think is going on. Genuine Imitation Life and Watertown are intellectually challenging albums. I won't rehash the 4 Seasons album, but I think the part everyone missed is that these aren't actually stereotypical manbearpig misogyny like your digestive system reacts to them on the first swig. These are role reversal albums that imagine what the through the looking glass version of "modern" life would be in the midst of cultural revolution. But, they don't tell you how to feel about it, there is absolutely no moral to these Gaudio/Holmes stories. Instead, they ask the question "is the opposite better, or is it just the mirror image of exactly the same amount of terrible?"

He still loves her, he wouldn't change the past, he's still being the best he can be, he's waiting for her to change her mind and come back. Yeah, this is a big no from Bottle. Girlfriend, you got some serious codependency issues.

And there's the sucker punch right at the end of The Train. Yeah, he never actually communicated any of this to her, she's never coming back, this is a delusional episode in his imagination. Maybe try telling your wife you love and appreciate her once in a while, ya schmuck.

Damn good album. Glad everyone's finally come around to rave about it.

The Bag Devoid of Cats

A year ago, we started reading volume 1 of Capital. So, in the spirit of that nostalgic fondness for adventure we share, I thought it apropos to reshare my tongue in cheek materialist critique of the music industry based on a year+ of listening to my inherited record collection. Remember, as I often say, if this isn't funny then you're reading it wrong:

Chapter 4

Not many people understand the idea of an imaginary record label. They think there's like a rule book, or something. Like a bunch of rich guys are just sitting around discussing the best way to disseminate the real art form of popular music to the discerning consumer. Have you ever met anyone like that?

Think about it. You've just got your hands on a couple million dollars through (let's be generous) only slightly mean spirited, but completely legal, activities. No way in hell you're going to pay taxes on that hard earned money, so the plan is to invest it in some useless crap actual working people will buy for fun, and only pay taxes on a portion of the profits from that investment. Sure, you could just open a few savings accounts and live comfortably off the federally insured interest they generate while using that money to actually make the world around you slightly nicer, but that's boring as hell.

Now, we don't want to do any actual work, so we'll look for bands that are starting to make some money and generate a fan base all on their own, work up some truly confusing contract that gets them to pay for the whole thing themselves like they were already doing, and pay them whatever trivial amount they think is worth it. If we have to. If someone makes us.

Now, obviously things are going to randomly happen to mess that up, so we need some contingency plans. Little stuff. A few dollars to DJs to play our songs more often, a few dollars to certain clubs and whatnot. Maybe it's a bad year, why not invent an act that will definitely sell and worry about the trivial problem of finding actual musicians later?

Oh crap, oh crap, oh crap, this all got way out of hand real quick, and now we have to buy any band that shows even a hint of possible success before those other guys snag them and we have to start using our own money. UMG wants to buy us? Why didn't you sell us to them yesterday? Thank goodness for our corporate overlords, or I'd have to sell my 15th mansion just to pay the electric bill for the other 14. Dodged a bullet on that one.

Can somebody tell me where in the hell all these speed freaks and heroin addicts came from? Oh, these are our bands? Sane people figured out they really could just do it themselves for more profit? Crap. What if we just lean into it? I mean, really go after the most unstable people we can find. Who says they have to actually play on their own albums? Yeah, sure, let the good ones play or hire them as staff and use their overdubs. Just find out what the last thing people bought was, and make 20 more of it. The hits will pay for the rest, nothing to worry about. Easy, Breezy, Beautiful. That reminds me, find pretty guys who don't mind wearing makeup. No, I'm not a pervert, hire ugly guys too, I just have a hunch that people really are that shallow and I want to see if it's true. Call it "market research" or whatever nonsense lets you write it off next quarter.

It's interesting to consider the actual geometric/spatial metaphor at play in our understanding. We imagine (correctly or not) that Monarchic society is the norm, a rigid hierarchy of power and economy in a sense "owned" by an individual and protected by force from within the structure itself. Chess seems an apropos analogy.

We then, by complete coincidence, note that the most steadfast adherents to such a socio-political system group themselves on the right of the assembly. What other logical reaction than to assign the opposition to the left? Thus, we have our schism of socio-political philosophy, Left being the developing opposition to the supposed natural right of Kings.

In between, Marx finds the Bourgeoisie. Bourgeois, however, is merely the identity of this now logically named "middle class." The political term is actually Liberal. This seems odd at first consideration, but becomes completely logical when we consider that to be Centrist is to straddle the fence, so to speak: to consider or be subject to the opposition itself, i.e., to mediate between the desire of both Upper and Lower classes inside the normative Monarchist hierarchies. They simultaneously wish to conserve the power structure of hierarchy and exploit the increased productive power of a feeling of progress. Liberal in this sense very much coincides with the notion of openness to new ideas, processes, and cultural knowledge which advance the accumulation of personal wealth.

And so, we see the defining characteristics of Leftist thought emerge: first, the power structure of Monarchy itself is philosophically undesirable; second, the mythologies (to borrow Barthes's term) employed to simultaneously usurp this power and exploit the production of social capital for personal gain is exponentially worse. A king may be benevolent or malevolent, but the Liberal has no choice but to exploit the common man.

In America today, this entire structure has been garbled beyond recognition by actually living the hyper-reality of post-modernism for approaching half a century. Language itself is now the weapon, and our inability to decipher its constant manipulation produces an even more heightened sense of cultural apathy on one hand, antagonism on the other.

Hopefully some wacky records will arrive next week, but for now we'll just revisit Kids See Ghosts. I like it more and more every time I listen to it. A real gem of experimental hip-hop.

So, we move from Kanye and Cudi back to this confusing reality that Capitalism = Liberal. Liberal in the sense that the individual mediates between the labor of the peasantry in exchange for the wealth of the aristocracy, and divides this acquired wealth between the subsistence of labor and personal wealth as he sees fit. Yet, note the discrepancy between Left and Right views on this relationship. The Right, in favor of Monarchy for its social hierarchy and more or less economic mobility by privilege, the Left critical of the exploitation inherent in the system. The working class has no ownership of its own production, the aristocracy no guarantee that they will "get their money's worth."

This brings us to an important question. On the Right we have a well understood system of patronage, and an equally understood "trickle down" of money, but what is the looking glass version of that system? How does one "invert" patronage except by directly compensating the working class for an agreed value of labor?

Marx comes to the conclusion that there is no way to effect that inversion without violence, but says that the level of violence will be determined by the industrial status of a particular nation/country. A day's labor is a day's labor, and it should thus be rewarded commensurate to the exchange. We can calculate the mandatory need, produce the additional surplus necessary for redistribution, and return the final surplus back to the workers themselves based on merit, i.e., the hardest/best/most loyal/most diligent workers receive a larger share of surplus to consume or further share as they will.

Now we see the true source of friction; this is the mythology of Capitalism itself, but the tangible opposite of its materialization. In reality, the acquisition of wealth is accompanied by a decrease in production. The ideal manager does nothing because the system "works" on its own inertia.

This is the "rats fleeing the ship" Marx describes. As the machine falls apart from its own internal friction, the middle class either clamors for a seat at the king's table, or else returns to the working class in whatever capacity is available.

This is the context in which we need to understand Hitler's rise to power. When viewed from the Left (and I do not mean to imply that it is a privileged or truthful vantage point), the Weimar Republic, Hitler's rise to power, Fascism itself, is one possible and demonstrably plausible reaction to the so called "tyranny of the proletariat."

Remember, socialism in its original form refers only to the distribution of the final surplus of production. Marx of course believed that control of "the State" was a necessary mechanism for creating this inversion, but his most vocal opponent, Bakunin, believed this a prime example of the corruption that comes from the quest for political power itself.

And so, thank you for sticking with me, here's the humorous (to me) conclusion: Capitalism only works when we all generally agree to act like ignorant Communists, and Communism only works if we act like intelligently compassionate Capitalists. Either way, it looks a whole lot like favoritism.

The Books!

This concludes our test of the Bottle Broadcast System. In the event of an actual emergency, your stewardess will administer refreshments on a first come first served basis. In the meantime, we offer this fine collection of literature for your amusement. Thank you for flying Bottle of Beef, may all your adventures eventually lead to somewhere.

Edgar Winter's L. Ron Hubbard's Mission Earth

B: How do you guys feel about being real?

E: How real we talking?

S: More importantly, what do you actually mean by "real." If we're talking about the trilogy of books that starts off with you listening to your record collection but ends up you rick-rolling us into the argument that most Americans don't realize they are already Communists, then we need to consider 1) that's a tough sell even if we're all in on the joke, and 2) holy hell what would happen if random people took you for serious?!

B: I'm a fictional character intentionally being a jackass. I said so every 50 pages or so. I'm the crazy guy at the bar gibbering to himself, who nevertheless produces the occasional epiphany. I'm cynical about my own cynicism, for crying out loud.

E: But, correct me if I'm wrong, you aren't those things, and you aren't actually lying.

B: That's the rub, isn't it? It's a logical conclusion derived from actual research. I intentionally cross-checked every obvious instance of confirmation bias. The American version of historical political terminology is completely bonkers.

Speaking of completely bonkers, did you know Edgar Winter made an L. Ron Hubbard album? I didn't until I saw Todd in the Shadows review it, and I said to myself "self, I don't care what it turns out to be, I must buy a copy of it, and some other random insanity to make it worth shipping from San Francisco to Iowa." All 4 albums arrived today. We might have to do a 4th book called "Oh crap, oh crap, oh crap, I guess I have to write a 4th book now!"

What I mean by real, Mz. Sandra D., is that now that we all know I'm not joking, what if we offered to help our friends self-publish their own insane ideas? We'll be like our own private little racket. I haven't fleshed out all the details, mostly 'cause I'm too busy being excited about listening to this mind melting terribleness Edgar Winter made for his former cult leader, but file it away for future consideration. Now, excuse me while I infringe on L. Ron Hubbard's copyright by telling you the name of the album, it's time to dive into the empty swimming pool of madness, here's Edgard Winter "arranging" L. Ron Hubbard's sure to be musical masterpiece, [Redacted]!

...

B: OH.   MY.   MARZIPAN. That was amazing!

E: What in the hell did we just listen to?

S: I'm with Skip, what? And where is that clapping coming from? *Is that you, Gladys?!*

G: Encore! Encore! Deary me, how exuberating. I haven't felt goosebumps like that since, well maybe we won't reminisce about that in earshot of the impressionables...

B: See, Gladys loved it. I laughed, I cried, I laughed even harder, possibly peed my pants when I read about a feat so astonishing as writing a 10-book epic sci-fi saga that everyone unanimously agreed was complete crap needing both the neologism "dekology" and an Edgar Winter album as the soundtrack, what's not to love?

S: But it's terrible!

B: Sure. No argues from me.

S: What the hell is it about?

B: Space losers saving the planet from radioactive sludge and buying us season passes to the amusement park. I thought that was fairly obvious.

S: Are any of those characters important to the actual plot?

B: I doubt it. I haven't read it, but my copy does have the original no postage necessary card. Think they'll still send me a copy of the first book if I include a check for $3.95?

E&S: What the hell is wrong with you?!

B: Jinx. Now you have to-

S: BUTTERCUP!!!

B: Damn, I should have countered that. Oh well. Nothing is wrong with me, this is fantastic.

E&S: Shut up, Bo-

B: Jinx, no buttercups, hum or a croak buys the next rum & coke.

E&S: ....!

A few moments of silence and at least three eyebrows of doom began to crackle. No, I take that back, it sounds more like someone running down the hallway. Ah, yes, Compy rounds the corner slightly out of breath.

C: Skip, Sandra, everything okay?! I heard you guys yelling but then it just stopped all of a sudden.

B: Damnit, Compy! I had them. I had them totally jinxed with a free adult beverage on the horizon and your concern for others had to go and blow it.

C: What did you make them listen to?

B: Edgar Winter.

C: He's not so bad, Frankenstein, Free Ride, classic stu... wait a minute. I see that stack over there. Which Edgar Winter Album?

B: Why should that matter?

C: Because you clearly just made them listen to Mission Earth.

B: Damnit again! Now the scientologists are gonna sue us because it clearly says the words "mission earth" are the intellectual property of L. Ron Hubbard.

C: What, is Tom Cruise going to Mission Impossible us in the night and suck out our midichlorians with a straw while Seinfeld and Doug E. Fresh take turns punching us in the kidneys?

B: It's thetans, but good use of sarcasm. Still, Xenu will be most displeased by the screaming of the tomatoes.

C: Is he from planet Kolob too?

B: No, that's Mormons. Look, pick on the Omicronions all you want, but go easy on the right here right now kind of alien worship.

E: Van Hagar!

B: Great News! Suddenly Last Summer Skip is here! Alright, maybe Mission Earth was a little too mind blowing for a Monday night. What's done is donOW! What was that for?!

S: For not letting me see how you were ending the 3rd book. It's a PR nightmare, and I still had the other Mr. Bungle shoe in my purse.

B: At least it wasn't the straight razor. Alright, look. You guys are clearly taking this way too serious. So, let's back up and calmly let me ask some questions. Hands on cans. Ready?

    ES&C: hhhhhhh, fine.

    B: Jinx no buttercups no saved by strangers Compy don't dawdle rummed coke for the Bottle. We'll do this next part rhetorical style.

    Is this good? No, this is absolutely terrible. It's exactly like Christmas at Singer, with special guest Donna Reed. But do I like it? Oh, how I love it. It's amazing. It's absolutely batshit insane and yet deliriously delicious. It's like the Astromusical House of Pisces, but with the added twist that Psychiatry was invented by satanic leprechauns. But, it's also just an over-the-top Edgar Winter album. He is hamming this thing like you forgot John Ratzenberger did the voice acting. I've heard the books are truly terrible, but there's no way they couldn't be a complete let down after hearing this. This is Arthur Brown level fire.

    Unreviewable. You have to have to have to sit in a chair with headphones on and try not to be giddy with delight listening to this insanity. I said Intergalactic Touring Band was the cream of the crop, but I was wrong. This is one of the greatest things ever produced by someone who just clearly didn't give a crap about whether anyone would like it or not. It's like a 9-year-old wrote it. Except for Teach Me. We'll have to defer to the fact that "Voltarian years aren't Earth years," otherwise this sounds suuuuuper creepy.

    So, you kind of have to approach this album like Edgar Winter was kind of bored but needed to use the studio time he was paying for, so he pulled out that shoebox dead L. Ron Hubbard sent him a few years earlier and just went ahead and saxophoned all over the campy space-fraud musical mess that waste of human energy dreamed would be the soundtrack.

The content is crap, but the execution is 10/10. No one other than Edgar Winter could ever make something like this, and I can truly appreciate it. Scientology is garbage, and I don't care who hears me say it, but this album is just a joy to listen to. I guarantee you'll laugh and/or pee your pants if you go honestly listen to it. Surreptitiously put it on in the background for unsuspecting company. It's worth it.

Bottle Talks Publishing

Part 1

So, you want to write a book, huh? Well, congratulations, it costs exactly zero, zilch, nada, nothing to do that. Think up an idea, actually write it, save it, and tada you're done. I'm proud of you, that was a lot of work.

Now that that's over, who's going to read it? I don't want to make you sad, but at this first stage the answer is nobody. Nobody cares. Unless you already have people texting or calling or emailing you to find out when that book they want is going to materialize, there is no market for your book.

I'm not a guru, and I'm not selling you anything, you create an audience by telling a person you wrote a book and asking them if they want to read it. Wash, rinse, repeat. Paying people to read it is totally your call, I personally say no to that one.

I publish with Ingram Spark; it costs $49 to have them make your book ready to print and you can order 0 or many for yourself. Only you can order them unless you buy an actual ISBN and allow Ingram to distribute it.

Hypothetically, you could buy a crate full and sell them out of the trunk of your car as your full-time job. It's your book.

That's all for this first post. In the future we'll get down to some of the nitty gritty details and frustrations you should be prepared to encounter. Nobody wants to open a door and stare into GREGORY's gaping maw on accident, now do they?

Part 2 - actual cost

Ok, Bottle. How much does it really cost?

49+85=134

It costs $134 to publish a book with Ingram. You can certainly find all sorts of ways to spend infinitely more money, but as far as the required infrastructure for selling your book all over the world for the rest of time, the price is one easy payment of $134 per book.

Ok, what do I actually get for that money?

The setup fee is $49, the ISBN is $85. We can break that down and say 24 goes to setting up your book PDF, 25 goes to setting up your cover art PDF, and 85 goes to buying the unique bar code on the back. Your book also gets listed online at Barnes & Noble and Amazon for no additional cost. Just so we're clear, no books exist yet. This is what it costs to publish your book through Ingram. Same price for me, you, the indie bookstore that has its own imprint, a major publishing house, anyone. You are buying lifetime access to Ingram's corporate services for that book that you own. They take care of the printing, accounting, shipping, etc., and send you, the publisher, the royalties. You are now a publishing company with a dedicated revenue stream. It costs you nothing to "sell" your book. Granted, you currently aren't making any money, but that just means you need to start telling people where they can buy it (there is no market until you create one, by talking to people).

Part 3

Believe it or not, I've just created a thousand branching hallways in B-space. They're weaving around like tree roots on steroids and could lead us anywhere. So, with that in mind, let's stop and smell a few of the philosophical flowers in the form of a Q&A.

Q: Isn't self-publishing bad?

A: Who told you that? Was it other competing publishers who want part of your revenue stream off the top for nothing in return? You're a big people now. You are a publishing company, same as them.

Q: But I'm just an author, how can I get anywhere without the help of a big publishing house? It's not real if I publish it myself.

A: So many problems with that, I'm not sure where to start. Ok, first of all, you are all the functions. You're Bottle, Skip, Sandra, Gladys, Bridbrad, Milton, you've got all those skeletons wasting valuable closet space, all your minions are imaginary, you have to figure out which of the 4 dozen helmets you're supposed to be wearing.

Second, you own your book, the only thing you can do is sell bits and pieces of its existence. We haven't looked at pricing, but all you can do is trade some of the profit from every book you sell for some of the profit from every book someone else sells. That can work or that can fail, but it's an entire book in its own right and I have more important things to think about at the moment.

Q: Ok, if I really am every woman like you say, then what do I do?

A: Every person you can talk to is a potential customer. Sell them your book. There is no help, there are no answers, start dealing. Ingram gives you two markets for free. Share the links, tell everyone where they can buy it. Friends and family, then acquaintances, then random strangers, if you know the owner of a bookstore, ask them to read it. Maybe budget some money to order a few copies knowing that you will hand them out for free to people who might be able to help you. Again, this is a completely different hallway than I plan to travel at the moment.

Q: What if I don't sell any books?

A: Welcome to capitalism! I warned you that nobody cares. You have to give them a reason to care. Sometimes that reason is completely unrelated to anything about the fact that you wrote a book. A conversation today can lead to a sale 3 years from now, that's why it's important to keep it alive without wasting any money now. Only pay for what will actually benefit the Bridbrad who sells your book. That Bridbrad is you, and you're 134 in the hole. Get past that 134 and then we'll talk.

Part 4

Let's talk about the weird major publishing formula you didn't know you already knew. First, they release a hardcover, then a paperback, then they farm it out on that crummy trade paperback pulp. See? That's what you've been brainwashed to expect from a "real" author. It's total nonsense. The reason they do that is to give first editions and collectors a higher level of prestige and/or resale value, then naturally lower the price for what most people find a more reasonable comparative price, then once they aren't using their own money anymore, they farm it out in mass media format to the now established market for that particular book. That's not Capitalism, it's market manipulation. It's not how *you* sell a book; it's how *they* sell publication to authors while simultaneously delegitimizing your entrepreneurship. The hardback pays for the paperback that pays for the copy us dirt wranglers actually buy. I actually like pulp, but that seemed weird for the actual content of my particular books. By all means consider going direct to the pulp rout for a novel or romance or smut or whatever it is you write. You have no market, remember?

The point is that you the random person in a bookstore are not the actual consumer, that's a complete illusion. Yes, you determine the end profit/loss for the retail store, but your impulse book buy represents pure profit for an already successful venture. That expensive first hardcover is not the original investment either, it's the product of several stages of getting past that magic "and then we'll talk" number. Again, this hallway is much too long for us to follow, we have to talk about a serious looming pitfall.

Selling a book is only half of the sale. Is your customer allowed to return that book? If so, then there is about a 3-month purgatory before you actually collect that royalty. Having your book on a bookstore shelf is absolutely pointless if that bookstore is going to send it back to you for a refund. Refund policy has to be part of your sales pitch. Ingram lets you have them sent back to your own physical address, or literally burn them. Throwing them in the incinerator is definitely cheaper, but either way you pay the cost from your publisher's share. 90 days with receipt is a pretty standard refund policy, right? I mean they hang signs that say that in the store. I specifically talked about it when I published the first book, if you remember that far back. Refund policy isn't arbitrary, it hurts actual people you didn't know exist when you try to return stuff 6 months later like a jackass. Never return anything, ever. Exchanging things is generally ok, but refunds are complete economy murdering mayhem.

Time for a break before delving into some technical aspects of actually preparing your book for Ingram. Not secrets, just stuff that looks insanely complicated if you don't know how to decide what you want. Thanks for reading, by the way. Toodles.

Spandau Ballet – True

    B: How am I doing, Sandra?

    S: Actually, I have to admit you're doing good on those first 4 parts. There's a fair bit of curmudgeon in there, but you aren't being overly pedantic or unfair. Really, everything you've said is true.

    B: Funny you should say that.

    S: Funny how?

    B: Calm down. Obviously, I'm gonna slice it in some insane direction in the future, but can we all agree I'm making a real effort here? This is relevant industry stuff that corroborates my crazy hypothesis that most Americans only ever experience the illusionary facade.

    E: That's a fair description. It's not heavy handed, just very salt-of-the-earth.

    B: Ok, good. I yam what I yam. Last night's album was a bit much for any day, let alone Monday. Let's go back to

Sandra's "true." I have Spandau Ballet's 3rd album called that, shall we?

S: Are they the "ha haha hai-hi" guys?

B: Excellent, yes that's the title track. It's the sample for PM Dawn's Set Adrift On Memory Bliss. This album should be the easy listening side of early 80s English New Wave. Let's adrift then, shall we?

...

B: Well? Thoughts?

E: You're noticeably deadpan, Bottle. I can't read you at all.

B: Yep.

S: Ok, ok, this is like right on the edge. There's New Wave in there, but there's also a fair bit of Wham! I can't read you either. Compy, what's really going on here?

C: Fffffffffffiii dunno. Well, clearly the saxophone solos are delightful. It's a tad kitsch, but in the Duran Duran rather than Boy George way. I'm gonna say the confusion is the point.

B: Hmm, interesting. Sandra? Care to elaborate on Compy's hypothesis?

S: Ok, you liked a lot of the Smooth Jazz stuff and that confused me. You're definitely presenting it as the other side of the Edgar Winter coin, but I'm not convinced that's the actual intent. That would mean this is the great content that you don't like version, or possibly the point is that this is their big mainstream breakthrough and they clearly care too much, but I'm not happy with that assessment. Skip, is this wackadoodle?

E: No, not really. This is normal 1983 as far as I can hear. I think this is one of those "lovely" albums. He likes it just as much as yesterday's album, but there's nothing to get hyped about. It a silent pleasure.

B: Compy, further considerations?

C: Ok ok, you clearly love this, but Sandra's onto something. The comparison is wrong. Lemme think... ok, I've got it! Yeah, it's the lead Saxophone that connects them, but it's an over/under because yesterday he was exuberant but now he's basically catatonic.

S: Oh! Oh! Edgar Winter was wackadoodle on top of Mother Hubbard's boring generic rock musical, but this is wackadoodle underneath the veneer of borderline fake sentimental balladry so you barely even notice.

B: Oh stop. Making an old man feel appreciated and understood. Called him Mother Hubbard and everything. Bunch of lily-livered ninnies you guys are. I can't lie though, those Sax solos are pretty freakin' sweet. Feel better? I told you I'm not a complete monster.

S: Apology accepted.

Part 5

One of the first choices you'll face is size. Size and page count are highly maneuverable, and yes 1/4 inch can have a noticeable effect on print cost for your specific book. Ingram has a publicly available cost calculator you can plug random numbers into to get an idea. We are being fiddly here. My 3 books are 6x9.

Little secret, I absolutely don't care. As long as it isn't awkward to hold and you don't actually have OCD, it absolutely doesn't matter. My books are 6x9 because they are fairly enormous. They'd be 1,000+ page monstrosities that fall apart from their own weight if I sized them like Vonnegut's Deadeye Dick. Roland Barthes's books are practically pamphlets by comparison.

Play around with your book in your word processor and see what you like, then plug those numbers into the calculator and see the price. The only trick is that you add 1/4 (.25) inch to the dimension. My word processor version is 6.25x9.25.

The second tricky thing is that odd pages go on the right, and that's the opposite of how it looks on your computer screen. I've paid for that mistake so you don't have to.

Now some good news, that's it. That's all the actual formatting you have to worry about. Believe me, try properly collating those pages for double-sided printing in sheafs one time and you'll be ecstatic that that's Ingram's problem now, not yours.

That's enough for one day. I need my beauty sleep, such as it is. Hopefully I can remain on this train of thought tomorrow, but you know we never know. Cheers.

Part 6

Ok, just so we're all clear here, there is no market, only an entire earth full of potential customers. You're going to be tempted to think that people who buy books are "the market," but that's not true at all. "The Market" exists in the past of a future you who has already successfully sold some number of books. I know that sounds a lot like the future, but it's not. You are stuck living chronological while future realities buzz around like a swarm of gnats near the lake. The Market is the measurement of done deals, and the photograph you take of it is a bifurcating reality where you guess about the future actions of all the people who lived inside that photograph, and end up somewhere along *that* future with the relevant photograph from *its* past.

The only data you have is the observable fact that nobody cares that you wrote a book, and they don't want to give you any money in the first place. The market is your interpretation of past sales as the basis for your guess as to how that picture will look in the future. In your brain, that fact contorts into the illusion of future people who might buy your book if you imagineer the conditions into just the right configuration of coincidences. That hallway leads to some heavy duty psychological feng shui, so we'll mosey off in a different direction. Plenty of familiar dirt to explore without inventing imaginary future dirt.

Instead, we'll take some time to consider why that extradimensional fold in perceived reality takes place.

Part 7

What the hell just happened in part 6? The answer is that I unfolded reality into its component parts as they really are, not as we psychologically experience them. This is the order of ideas, not the order in which we find out if those ideas are true or false. I am Bottle, welcome to my nightmare.

What you've really done is created the architecture of your own future confirmation bias. At some point you will forget you did that and believe a fictional version of reality that bears no resemblance to the actual experiential process of getting there. You might never notice, you might smash into yourself running the other direction and explode, that one's a coin flip.

You can see what's happening in my previous posts; we're thinking in two opposite directions at the same time. On one hand you have every human on earth as a potential customer and your brain tries to narrow that infinity down to some comprehendible demographic. On the other hand, you have the reality of 0 customers and you're trying to bootstrap your way to creating that previously mentioned imaginary reality. Somewhere looming in the middle is the potential metaphorical car crash.

The Motors – Tenement Steps

Great news everybody, today was so brain-meltingly terrible in terms of constructed reality being completely not actual reality that I totally lost my train of thought.

You might think I could just take some time and rethink it and eventually pick back up again, but nope! Trash can that idea, we'll just listen to what The Motors did after Bram Tchaikovsky and the other guy quit but before the two remaining members quit too. I don't know what to expect from Tenement Steps, and I don't care enough to try to find out. I'll either like it or I won't and then we'll listen to an incredibly obscure Metal album that some metalheads love and some metalheads hate. Then it'll be actual winter and I'll be totally at a loss as to what to do next. Maybe I'll just sell all my stuff on marketplace and go full hermit (relax, it's just cold November raining and I'm exaggerating the SAD).

This album has annoyingly cut corners on purpose. Someone thought that was a great way to stand out and be unique and they were wrong. Imma flip the insert around and stick the red inner sleeve through the missing corners because I need the mental stability of squares today.

Ok, I'm not crazy, am I? This is a bizarre New Wave-ish musical? Ok, I am crazy, but so is this. This is definitely a critique of the whole Urban/Suburban middle-class myth, complete with full chorus choruses and wacky orchestral accompaniment to a weird mash of New Wave of old-school Rock and Roll. It's weird for an actual album, but I gotta say it's pretty fun. Maybe I should have the whole crew create the actual libretto. Pointless, but intellectually adventurous. Nah, I'll just wait for the execution guaranteed by the skeleton gangster on tomorrow's album cover. Happy gloomy, rain-soaked Wednesday everybody.

Rage – Execution Guaranteed

I rock rough and stuff with my Afro Puffs... oh, wait, wrong Rage. Regardless, rock, excuse me, Metal on with your bad selves.

Now people who absolutely hate this album generally fall into two camps. A) people who love their first album and feel like this gives up speed for silliness and the vocals are subpar at times. B) people who think the synths are ridiculously counterproductive. I dunno, I think it's fine. I don't hate this at all. Yes, it's a little clumsy in places, and some of the solo work is vapid noodling, but if you're making the obvious comparison to Megadeth meets Skid Row at a Candlemass concert, this has a definite stamp of originality. It's completely normal silly for late 80s non-mainstream indie metal. Not embarrassing at all, in my opinion. I'd throw this on in the background for almost any occasion, it's approachably enjoyable and surprisingly creative. I can see how the "atmospherics" might turn off the real hard-core speed/thrash crowd.

Now, are the synths good? Absolutely not, but it's a (pardon the pun) execution problem, not a conceptually functional problem. So is the Allman Brothers-esque guitar solo interlude on Deadly Error. Right idea, terrible choice of actual sounds. The riffage is pretty stellar across the board. This is a highly experimental Thrashfest of Horror, but it manages to steer clear of some of the worst Hair Metal cliches. Rudy and Jochen don't need "Peavey" to actually cue their solo time in the lyrics.

I suppose I should mention this is a German band. You have to think in terms of Kreator, Accept, or Halloween rather than holding them accountable to Bay Area standards. They really are Speed Metal rather than Thrash. Still, this isn't cheesy or cringeworthy at all. Quite lovely.

Well, this certainly has been a strange week in the Bunker of Beefitude. Nothing turned out as expected, I blame diving face first into Mission Earth rather than building up to it, but I certainly didn't do it on purpose. Oh well, any suggestions for tomorrow's album? My brain is totally tapped out and Fridays are the worst. I need all the help I can get.

Andy Taylor – Thunder

One big problem we have is that the "American" definition of the word "socialism" makes no sense to the majority of the world. Rightfully so, those things a stereotypical American labels "socialist" are not by any historical or philosophical definition "socialist." Most of the programs, projects, the concept of "the Welfare State" as a whole, are in fact Capitalist devised compensations for the known structural flaws inherent to the division of labor itself. They are "remedies," or "medicine," to borrow a more accurate metaphor. Like medicine, many of these actions do not solve an actual problem. Instead, they simply postpone, reverse, or ease the consequences of the fundamental problems of monetary systems (universal equivalence) as a whole. A tangible example is the Infrastructure Bill, and we ask the question:

Which is larger? A) the amount of spending (aka the amount of new money created), or B) the savings of the Capitalist class who will remove the actual cost of producing the total product from general circulation?

The government does not give money to the poor. Instead, the government creates new money to fund "commercial social work" and attempts to collect that money back through taxation, cuts to other budgetary expenses, and other incentives for directionally destructive spending (destructive meaning money spent to specifically deflate the money supply itself, rather than acquisition of capital, aka "taxes" in the most general abstract form). This is conceptually much different than the more familiar metaphor of "repayment of debt." You can take over the cost of running those businesses any time you feel like writing a check.

From a psychological perspective, America at large has internalized and normalized the Red Scare propaganda version of reality. Not surprising considering the well documented and observable revisionism of public education curricula from the 1940s to the mid-2000s.

The fundamental problem of all capitalist structures, the inherent "unevenness," is that the value of labor, no matter how you define that labor, is always less than the market value of the product of that labor, and that "surplus value" is redistributed to the analogical Capitalist who watches the worker work, the Straw Boss if you will. That fact is a fundamental component of Capitalism itself, not what most Americans mistakenly call "Marxism."

Socialism, in all of its historical meanings represents the inversion of that relationship such that as much of that surplus value as possible is returned to the working class as a whole.

No social experiment or implementation has succeeded in accomplishing this inversion, and it may very well be that it is philosophically impossible, the same way that it might be impossible to reconcile the metaphysical Telos with its simultaneous rejection in Marx's own philosophy.

Taxation is the cost of having a Capitalist economic system, as it represents the theoretical surplus value itself. Again, that is entirely a feature of Capitalism as a functional system: all labor is by definition undervalued. The Economic Right argues that that surplus value is a reward for the speculative investment in the production of commodities, the Economic Left argues that that surplus value is an exploitation of the system over and above the fairly calculated profit of a reasonably competitive market. The Left argument is very compelling, and all things considered the side I associate with, because it's a powerful explanation for the seemingly natural tendency toward monopolization (which we observe as rising prices). We call it greed: the defense and legitimization of any social hierarchy one inherits upon birth and from which one receives tangible privilege.

What do we mean by surplus value? Ok, we need 3 people at a minimum. A laborer, a capitalist/owner, and a consumer. The capitalist pays for the material and wage that the laborer uses, and sells the product to the consumer for the total price plus his own wage. We'll use arbitrary percentages. Say 30% goes to the laborer, 30% goes to the "owner." The actual sale price is the maximum clearing price. Just for ease we'll say that price is 100% markup. If a doodad sells at the maximum clearing price of $50, we know that $25 represents the total cost of production: materials must cost 40% ($10), wages cost 60% (7.50 for the laborer, 7.50 for the owner). The remaining $25 represents surplus value, and we need to decide how to distribute it. Again, just to make the numbers easy, let's say 20% gets taxed for future instability, that $5 is saved/reserved for future changes in one of those costs. How does the remaining $20 get allocated? In a completely unregulated Capitalist system that $20 goes to the owner and he can do whatever he wants with it, we don't get to know. In a fully regulated socialist system that $20 gets divided between the laborer and the owner according to an explicitly agreed and legally binding contract between them. This contract can of course be renegotiated all the time, but that negotiation takes place only in relation to the surplus value generated from the sale. Socialism ceases to exist when the surplus value drops to zero or lower.

There is nothing stopping a Capitalist from running a Socialist business, and that is in fact the normal way most companies manage their internal structure. Bonuses, raises, parties, extra paid days off, all of these things are standard Socialist distributions of surplus value, but they are not regulated by any contractual agreement, and thus looked upon as "generosity" on the part of the owner. He doesn't have to do that; he can pocket all the money and go play golf 7 days a week if you let him.

It might seem silly on the level of 3 people, but it's not so silly at all when you scale it up to 30 people in a mid-sized private firm, 100 people in a multi-branch company, 2-million people all over the world in the case of Wal-Mart.

I said taxation itself is the cost of a Capitalist economy, but you could make the argument that the refund schedule is a Socialist program in its own right; your refund represents money the government didn't have to create based on your actual spending, and thus it is an egalitarian redistribution of surplus wealth based on merit.

Some people will obviously argue the other way around, but that requires pretending that money is real and the comparative value of labor is imaginary, the way a corporation thinks about its employees. You know, Sandra's 40 words per minute are somehow worth less money than Martin's because Sandra has a vagina. Julio can't possibly expect to earn the same salary as Kevin for doing identical work because he pronounces his Js wrong.

All of which of course in no way begs the question "what would happen if the guitarists from Duran Duran and the Sex Pistols made an album together?" The answer somehow involves copying the pen and ink style of Rockwell Kent, so your guess is as good/bad as mine.

Huey Lewis and the News

"Watch out for these golf balls!"

I think we should talk about how everybody completely misunderstands Huey Lewis in general, so it's no wonder they completely miss the sarcasm of their 4th album, Fore!. Stuck With You is a good example, but Hip To Be Square is the most egregiously misinterpreted. You forget that he's up there fist pumping the punchline, 'cause these are the jokes, son. "Bourgeois Hippies" is hilarious.

Huey Lewis and the News is pure hustle, they're hamming up the night club act and mocking all the false sentiments. The problem is that they sound invitingly sincere, they sound serious so you take it serious. It's confirmation bias, you hear the mythologies you tell yourself and feel validated. Then they get back to the bus after the set and say "what a pack o' maroons." Huey Lewis the person thinks the songs are funny in the same way his cameo in Back to the Future where he says Marty's band is "just too darn loud" is funny. It's one of those 14 flavors of irony, you figure it out. Did you catch that? That's the kind of humor I'm talking about.

Let's take the Back to the Future song, Power of Love. What's the real context of that song? He's saying "hey, bozo, this ain't rocket science. You think love is complicated and makes you dumb, but you don't have to pay to play and it might just be as awesome as Steve Miller says it is.

How about Bad is Bad from Sports? Oh, you thought when I said your kid's band is bad, I meant they're awesome? No, I meant they are objectively terrible.

Do you believe in love? Do you, 'cause that's the kind of desperate I'm out on the prowl to find.

Stuck with You is probably the most obvious, but even that gets mansplained away as "out of touch tedium."

I want a new drug that makes me feel like I'm in a meaningful relationship with another human being, wink wink.

Believe me, I hate defending Fred Durst, but that's exactly what's going on here. You're not on the same page, possibly reading a different book, and confusing any of this for sincerity is a serious problem for everyone. It's not the mean-spirited kind of sarcasm you might be more accustomed to, but it's sarcasm all the same.

Runt

Runt. It's so many things. Todd Rundgren's first solo album, the self-titled debut of a fake band, a studio version of McCartney drawing from Laura Nyro's Eli and the Thirteenth Confession, a do-it-yourself cornucopia of ballads and psychedelia, an amateurish adventure in learning how to produce an album with someone else's money. Mostly it's just sadness in the form of fun.

Broke Down & Busted leads off as a straight up 60s Psych-Rock relationship lament. Very "I Hear You Knockin'" at times.

Believe In Me is definitely a Laura Nyro style ballad, with the added fun of strumming inside the piano and an accordion, I think.

Then the big hit We Gotta Get You a Woman. It's an obvious radio single, but plenty of interesting stuff happening in the background.

Then the straight 70s Hard-Rock Boogie of Who's That Man?. Another radio friendly single, possible a few years ahead of its time. It's only 1970/71 after all. Power Pop.

Once Burned gives us an R&B cool down. Short, but effective.

Then the final up-tempo 70s Boogie Rock of Devil's Bite.

Side A, for all its stylistic borrowings, twists and turns, is a pretty solid EP. Hello Cleveland, we are Runt. Adventurish, but totally believable. I'd go see this band in concert, if they were real.

Then Side B. Now it gets weird. I'm In the Clique is basically a free jam around the chorus, bass and drum solos, weird sirens and percussion everywhere.

There Are No Words. Haunting, almost howl like vocal experimentation, like a Brian Wilson pastiche of Ligeti, a strange midnight barbershop choir of wolves and druids in the forest. Delightful.

1,2,3,5! The last two tracks of Side B are a kind of meandering suite of 60s Pop/70s Rock fragments, sorrowful string quartet, raunchy guitar solo, piano-man ballad ode to the sadness of growing old, with big-band Hard Blues Rock coda and string quartet/trumpet/flute postlude. Audio collage, I'd call it.

Runt is actually a really good concept, the scrawny kid with the hand-me-down life, the lovable loser. It's incredibly sad, but happily so, even though that makes no sense at all.

So, yeah, fantastic album. You might want to actually wind up in a real downer of a melancholic mood before slapping it on the table, just so it doesn't come as a shock when it happens, but it is definitely an affecting listen. Less SQUIRREL!, more box of mementos in the attic. Not too shabby for the first attempt at being an incredibly prolific producer who desperately doesn't want to play live anymore. Good stuff.

The Escape Club – White Fields

One of my greatest joys in life is picking up a decades old album that someone bought from a discount bin, never even bothered to open, then sold for certainly less than even that discounted price. Even better when it's awesome.

You know Escape Club from their one hit Wild Wild West. Well, before they were heading for the 90s as a crap radio pop band, they made an alternative rock album. This thing is The Cure meets R E.M. at a Bauhaus concert. Holy hell, this is amazing. Who cares what I have to say? This is awesome, go listen to White Fields by The Escape Club. No grains of salt, this is fantastic.

Less 4 Seasons, More Being Mad at Facebook

I had the whole thing done, but we're back to the garbage facebook app just closing the post I'm writing because it took too long, of course without saving a draft. Points: the 4 seasons never sold their master recordings, tie in to the long gone OKC restaurant Molly Murphy's, Valli and Gaudio are awesome. That's the gist, totally awesome end to my vinyl therapy session ruined by stupid feta, or whatever they renamed the company, who gives a crap? 6 years of opening this garbage prison diary was a good run. I'm not sure I made much of a difference, but 50 or 60 of you might hate me now, so that's fun.

Who am I kidding, I'll open this thing back up tomorrow like I always do. This aneurysm isn't gonna burst itself, you know? Cheers.

The art of the self-titled debut

Perhaps since the dawn of humanity, woman, man, child, possibly even door-to-door salesmen have sat with their chins in their palms thinking delicate thoughts of a complex nature. How do I collect a bunch of stuff together and present that collection as a coherent idea, a gestalt that can simultaneously bridge the gulf between strangers and forge a common revelry in telling those guys over there they suck? We'll tell the awesome guys they are awesome, of course, but it's the "you suck" part I'm trying to get a firm grasp upon.

Ok, maybe that's a bit of an exaggeration, maybe it's just "how do I present a full synopsis of an idea in the form of a few small pieces of detritus I picked up and crammed in my pocket like a magpie or squirrel or something?" Anyway, long and fruitlessly the two-legged brain monster poked and prodded at his cerebral electrical fire, until one day it flashed into existence:

AHA! I shall take it upon myself to codify the entirety of human existence in song, and collect these fragments of mouth-music into a metaphorical photo album of audio collage. I shall call it: Album. And the townsfolk rejoiced, for though they knew not what the crazy bearded man was talking about, they nevertheless understood the unease they felt at the thought of arguing with this clearly insane madman.

Upon seeing the fear and awe in their faces, the creature, as if to prove that fear a wise reaction, raised his fists and proclaimed:

I AM BOTTLE, hear me talk about the interesting phenomenon of a band making their debut album. The thunder rolled, the lightening striked, they cancelled the rodeo scheduled for that evening and instead huddled around the communal record player to hear the lunatic Bottle pontificate upon the naming of the album after the naming of the band.

B: Hey, Bridbrad as narrator dude, shut it. I got some 'splainin' to do....

Chapter 1

A self-aggrandizing wise man once said not all debut albums should be self-titled, but all self-titled albums should be a band's first. Something like that, I'm too lazy to look at what I wrote two years ago.

Is there any more coherent concept? I doubt it, "We are [band name], hear us act like lunatics for the next 40 minutes!" Maybe equally obvious, but certainly less interesting is the Greatest Hits album: "We are [band name], here are the songs you already like!" See? Much less interesting.

It's not foolproof, though. What if you just realized it's your 4th album? Surely that means something different than your first. What if you changed your name because some slightly more famous Swedish guys threatened to kick your ass? Do you get a mulligan? Can you use it as an actual gimmick, or like a pre-quel in the middle of your career? There are some important structural considerations before you just dive head first into the empty swimming pool of your studio recording career. Gimme some time to think about it, then give me some more time to write down those thoughts. Meet back here in chapter 2 after I write it.

Chapter 2

Runt, Van Halen, Weezer, Black Sabbath, The Doors, and those are just the top of everybody's list, even terrible bands do it. Sure, it's totally possible to interpret it as formulaic and passé, but that's an accumulative interpretation; it's your own fault for thinking "I've seen this a thousand times, you suck." You don't have to be that guy; that thought is as trite as the thing you think is trite.

Instead, what we need is some codification. Real self-titled debuts, fake self-titled debuts, debuts that are only debuts because no one would publish the first 927 songs the band has been playing live for the last 12 years. Does it count if you use your real name? What if the band isn't actually real? What if you pulled a Baz Luhrmann and made a complete cover called Our Band's Their Band's Self-Titled Debut? Deep stuff we're dealing with here.

Post-modern Jedi mind tricks aside, the point is not to answer those questions and pronounce sentence in your bug-infested powdered wig as the Magistrate of Culture, the point is to let the album create those questions and ask its own as we endlessly trek through Mirkwood on our way to see the treasure hoard below Mt. Doom.

If nothing else, it gives me a new reason to relisten to my own collection and an easy way for you to participate right along. C'mon, let's see what we see in the chapter of 3.

Seriously, suggest a self-titled album and I'll queue it up to write about some night. Make sure I can actually go listen to it though, I still haven't found a way to get paid for doing this yet. Aw man, I just waded into the ask for money swamp all willy-nilly. Oh well, when you're roaming in Rome.... If you're a kind-hearted soul who likes reading, maybe send a number to paypal.me/pnmit. I guarantee we'll appreciate it.

Chapter 3

Fun story about The Doors, they were the house band of the Whiskey a Go Go until Jim spoke those word things near the end of The End. That was the end of that. Strong first impression, as first impressions a go go.

That's our starting point, isn't it? If nothing else, the self-titled debut says "hi, we're the name we just called ourselves, you deal with figuring it out." Ok, but no guarantees, you know?

Obviously, populating a jury with people who've never heard The Doors is a monumental task, but me pretending to be Drew Barrymore and wake up every morning with total reset amnesia is just as ridiculous. I can pretend it's our 900th first date, but I've seen Sandra's pick for first impression boots and skirt. Still makes a powerful statement, but my appreciation has inevitably changed over time. No getting around the fact I know I like it very much. While we're on the subject of objectifying albums, let's try being objectively subjective. All the possible interpretations are by definition possible, so at least one of mine should be probable. That cover photo isn't any form of question, now is it? This so called "Jim" guy appears to know exactly what he's thinking, and his wing men do not appear to be surprised either.

I'm trying to imagine sitting in a bar and this is what starts blasting from the stage where Johnny Rivers, a couple go-go dancers and a DJ in a cage were standard nightclub entertainers only a few years earlier. I like pretty ladies and all, but these guys just jamming is way more mesmerizing.

This is also one of the practically no other albums where fully left panned drums don't bother me at all. Back Door Man is a fairly risqué song to begin with, it's the Southern term for an adulterer, but my goodness is Morrison more than a little uncomfortably believable. And that reverb. Just wowzers.

Now, I'm not a space-cadet, but this has to be as close to an LSD trip as it's possible to recreate in audio form. I can't even imagine the walls bulging and carpet patterns crawling up your legs while this happens into your brain. The flashing lights on the back of my eyelids are overpowering completely sober.

I guess the final verdict is that for a blind date first impression, you'll be lucky if her dad doesn't greet you in his boxers and white tank top holding a shotgun. You gotta have some serious not giving a damn about waking up tomorrow to hop on public transportation in Santa Monica with these crazies.

Contender for best debut album, no contextualization needed. So, as far as self-titling goes, this is the standard. We are The Doors, are you sure you're ready to find out what's on the other side?

Chapter 4 - Buffalo Nichols

Tonight, we get the real deal, my first listen to the self-titled debut of Buffalo Nichols. The vinyl I bought won't get here until December, but my bearded visage down there under the cover photo is just begging everyone to join me over at his bandcamp page:

https://buffalonichols.bandcamp.com/album/buffalo-nichols-2

I'm told we're in for some proper 21st-century Blues (I even managed to work an oblique Doors reference in here, how cool is that?) guitar from a world traveling man connecting to his heritage. It's "the soundtrack to a wandering soul."

Before we get there, though, I did an interestingly serendipitous thing. See, this was a staff pick from Plaid Room Records over in Ohio, and I instead went straight to his bandcamp page to buy it. I feel conflicted. I don't feel bad for choosing to support a musician in a way I think lets them keep more of the money I paid for it, I feel bad for not rewarding that lovely group of fellow record lovers. So, in the off chance that one or both read this review after I tag them, Plaid Room Records send an invoice for any record of your choosing to bottleofbeefmusic.gmail.com and I will buy it blindfolded, Buffalo Nichols (I can't seem to find a way to properly tag your facebook page so I'll put it in the comments) that's how I found your album and I hope you enjoy my honest to goodness first listen that accounts for at least one of however many complete listens to every track shows up in your bandcamp stats.

First, the drool started flowing for the first track. Second, that chord progression from Sick Bed Blues is the most haunting thing I've ever heard, and I'm the gúy who published a skeleton's piano recital. Third, if you listen to half as much Blues from the 30s and 40s as I have, you will definitely know that variety has degraded to trash can fodder in this day and age. Mr. Nichols is like my memories of pulling the stamens out of honeysuckle flowers and tasting that sweet floral nectar in the Summers of my childhood. 21st century don't mean anything to me either, my friend I've never met.

By pure coincidence, the Governor of Oklahoma chose to commute the death sentence today. Every journey back from the depths of hell has to have a first step, so here's hoping my birth state keeps walking forward and gets back to some quantitative proximity to "reasonable doubt."

Now back to the point. This is chapter 4 of my facebook book dedicated to self-titled debut albums. Hold on, gotta start this amazing album again, it's that good.

Ok, variety. There's way more to the Blues than that tired old 12-bar AAB big-business textbook form. Oh man, those chromatic fills and harmonic twists of Living Hell make my brain tingle. Dude, this is fantastic. I was trying to point out that he pushes it back to track 3 and basically reinvents the formula. Oh, that swooping top line of These Things is so melancholy, and the strings, Screw it, I can't write while this masterpiece is playing. This is phenomenal. Seriously, I beg you all to go check out this album. So good. So so good. Can't wait for the actual record to get here, but wait I shall.

Chapter 5 - Self-Titled Sophomore?

The Sandpipers debuted with Guantanamera, and then followed up with The Sandpipers. That's weird. It's like saying

SP: Check out our debut album, Bottle.

B: Who the hell are you guys?

SP: Oh, sorry. Check out our second album, we're The Sandpipers.

Or, like "welp, that first album was sort of ok, time to do it for real." It's awkward. Even more awkward, their first album got great reviews, this one not so much. I don't know why, it's lovely. It seems bizarre to apply the standard I invented for this book from a future century, but I never said I wasn't awkward either. Maybe it felt weird back then too.

Unlike The Doors or Buffalo Nichols however, we have a couple problems with the cover art. Note the similarity between The Doors and The Sandpipers. Disembodied photo-studio superimposed head with band in background. Note the difference though. For The Doors it's Jim Morrison's head, for The Sandpipers it's an unknown lady. Doors 2-4 are participating in this photo shoot by looking at the camera, the Sandpipers themselves are mopily wandering around on the beach in preppy sweaters. The Doors is intriguing, possibly even intimidating, The Sandpipers looks like they all got rejected by the same imaginary pretty lady.

Here's the interesting bit, we all understand that these covers influence our perception of the music. They give the album a context, but how you react to that message is something unique to you. Other people might have opinions that turn out to be as similar as these two album covers, but they don't have to be. You can sever that connection just as easily as tie its shoelaces together. One doesn't have to be good, or the other bad. I like both. I might not be in the mood for one or the other, but that is fully dependent on my own mood, my own state of mind, not an integral part of the album itself.

Interpretation is not a quiz or a contest, it's simply a mirror of acculturation. You hold up an album and see not an object itself in its own truth, but a reflection of your truth, your own acculturation. The stronger your reaction in any direction, the more shackled your synapses to the prison wall of inherited dogma. My pronouncement of "mopiness" onto The Sandpipers is the result of direct comparison to The Doors, not some objective truth embedded in the images.

We got real philosophical there, huh? That just shows you what frame of mind I'm in; the lack of attempted humor just means there isn't some humorous component tied to the process of interpretation. I'm not looking for a laugh, I'm not wink wink nudge nudging like I just did by saying "wink wink nudge nudge."

And that brings us to the coincidental unfolding of the albums themselves. The Doors as subject, the literal separation of the man from the music by an interpolated door, and the Sandpipers not as subject, but as signifier of their own psychological context. To watch it unfold with no conscious intention on my part is to watch the creation of meaning itself. It may be much harder for you the reader because you are left to imagine the covers and the sequence of assembly for yourself. I can only describe what I see in my mind as I experience it. We are, after all is said and done, alone in our own minds. Perhaps give it a try for yourself with your own albums or interests. As for me, I shall enjoy the soft-pop croonery of this frat-boy like serenade to the imaginary pretty lady in the sky of our mind's eye, and contemplate what I might say about tomorrow's even weirder boundary probing relisten to a Judy Collins album I half-liked the first time around.

Chapter 6 - The Curious Case of Judith

Back in a former life with fluorescent-lit hallways and eldritch doors to rooms with pianos and chalkboards I would often ponder seminars I wanted to give. One of my favorites was titled The Art of the Cover and we'd look at what happens to a song when you turn it into disco, or grunge up a Wham! song, or turn Neil Diamond into Reggae. Judy Collins did a cover of Salt of the Earth, and that would surely be on the list somewhere. Alas, this book is about self-titled albums, so we have 12th album and the quagmire of legal vs familiar names. The coal miner's daughter is Judith Marjorie Collins, but we've all been calling her Judy. That means it's much less "hello, Denver, I'm Judy," more "will the real Jude Shady please stand up and sing some eclectic selections from her vast repository of brain songs?"

First time around we talked about the split personality and I said the real Judy Collins has to deal with being multiple people. She has to please everybody. Some of those everybody's are worth 20 bucks, some have an "exponentially multiply that number" button.

Let's just do a quick thumbs up/down of every song.
1 - Up
2 - borderline
3 - nice save thumbs up, Houses is phenomenal.
4 - down. Nosir, I don't like it. Mostly 'cause I don't love the game.
5 - up up up, no Phil Collins jokes, this is a wonderful eulogy for Duke Ellington.
6 - hard to mess up Sondheim, and she doesn't, great Side A ender.

7 - tough song, she changes the lyrics but it still works because this is an ironic song. I think she nails that irony whether that was her intention or not.
8 - thumbs way up, half Sinatra half Girl from Ipanema, so bizarre and interesting.
9 - baaarf. Again, that's all my own prejudice against schlock Country. The song is fine, I just don't like rhinestone studded showtune Country.
10 - all the thumbs up, I'll cut off your thumbs so I can raise them too. I'll Be Seeing You is fantastic. Haunting, delirious, terrifying, luscious, you get the idea.
11 - another one of those really interesting covers. We could compare her version with The Cure's version. That would be interesting.
12 - meh. Kind of wimpy for the album closer, but not particularly terrible.

So, to sum up, put Judy in front of a real orchestra and give her emotionally complex songs to sing and I'm totally on board and clapping like a crazy guy after every song. Her voice is so clear and steady, her pitch is immaculate, and you can understand every syllable, not just a wah-wah of vowels like she's an adult in an episode of Peanuts. Sorry opera singers and Broadway belters, I just prefer vernacular vocals to bel canto.

Put it all together, and this isn't a Hello album at all. This is a self-eulogy. "Who was Judith Marjorie Collins? Here, I'll show you."

Now we can see what's really happening with that Jagger/Richards opening to Side B. That is not an honest song in the sense of taking the lyrics at face value, and you can see it when you read the original lyrics. The verses are that drinking song ode to the plight of the common man, but the chorus is the self-reflective recognition that it's feel-good lip-service (I the singer don't actually connect with the crowd as real human beings, I'm an elitist POS and coming from me this is actually demeaning). Judy is the girl up there on stage pandering to that crowd, but secretly criticizing herself for not going out and doing anything to change that. She's reminding herself she needs to do more. It's a subtle little change, but it makes a gigantic conceptual difference.

So, whether she truly succeeds or not in your own mind, here's what this album really does in mine. The first 11 Judy Collins albums are "Girl, you'll be a woman soon," and this 12th one is "I'm a woman now, time to reconsider and really do something." Now I don't hate those couple songs at all, at least not in their function for the album as a whole.

It's a great album except for the last song. Conceptually it works, sonically not so much. I have to try to hear it as not a conclusion, but as the artificial stopping point from which the real story continues. That's tough, and it doesn't feel right. Probably still my own fault, but the song itself as recorded isn't giving me any assistance in that regard.

Is it really a self-titled album in the same way as the previous 3? No, I think not. One, it contains its own enigma by differentiating the subject itself: stage Judy vs person Judith. It's a goodbye not hello album.

Interesting stuff.

Chapter 7 - What if we add an exclamation point?

After I finished chapter 6 it dawned on me that a year ago on this very day, I talked about the self-titled albums of Joe Cocker and Jose Feliciano, both of which have exclamation points. Crazy coincidence that one. Are there more like that? Excuse me while I wander the wild web yonder for a bit....

... well, waddya know? We've got Gracious! and their first two albums Gracious!, and This is...Gracious! Then there are the guys who left Kraftwerk to form Neu! and debut with Neu! Ornette Coleman's 7th album is Ornette! On!Air!Library!

Gives us the double whammy: self-titled EP becomes self-titled album. Andrew Hill's 6th album has 3 of the things, Andrew!!!.

I could keep going, but you get the idea. What a bizarre goldmine we've coincidentally chosen to dig in. Maybe we don't need to hammer each and every one into the ground like I tend to do, the point is that there is a whole subset of self-titled albums from anywhere in an artist's career that have exclamation points. It's an actual thing.

Chapter 8

Upon this night that's not that dreary, Bottle pondered weak and weary, over many a forgotten self-titled album from yesteryears.

While he pondered, nearly napping, suddenly there came a snapping, upon his conscious mind a tapping, some minion of subconscious trappings suggesting albums self-entitled for the feasting of his ears.

Suddenly awoke the Bottle, and combing through the crates full throttle, a scene we've grown accustomed to these desperate descending years.

A look of wild and fervent madness, a cackle filled the hallway's sadness, as Bottle scarce concealed his gladness, and bellowed at the evening's invisible engineers:

Quoth the raven, I am Bottle, watch your step but do not dawdle, as we assemble ourselves for the listening to the Blood and Sweat & Tears!

Before we get there though, I feel like I should map out how we got to BS&T, it's a crazy contorted hallway, indeed. I liked On!Air!Library! so much I found a copy for sale and sent money to Canada. Had to make it worthwhile though, so I bought some other random crap. We'll see if Canada still lets us buy stuff from them or not, but self-titled debuts seem perfect for Random Crap albums.

First, we have to unpack Random Crap, 'cause it sounds insulting. It's really not, Random Crap albums can of course be terrible if they aren't supposed to be random crap, but they can also be phenomenal. Gerard Smith's Lullabies in an Ancient Tongue is a fantastic Random Crap album. The Cars' Heartbeat City makes me want to intentionally hit a tree. Plus, he had to put a "2" at the end of his bandcamp page just like Buffalo Nichols, so Madam Coincidence is calling all the shots.

It's a problem with language, there's only so many words to go around. If we all just kept inventing neologisms for hard to pin down ideas, we'd all be totally lost at sea and spend all our time arguing about what words mean instead of doing anything productive. The entry in Bottle's Taxonomy is "Random Crap," we just have to deal with it. It's not good or bad until we decide it's good or bad, that's my point. Self-titled albums, random crap to make the shipping cost worthwhile, we looked at a punctuation gimmick, there's a Yahtzee for that called BS&T. Their 4 albums are all random crap, 3/4 are self-titled with a chronological index, unlike Led Zeppelin I actually have them on vinyl, totally not as non-sequitur as my poor parody of Poe prompted by ending yesterday evening with Weird Al videos (totally logical in my reality, presumably insane from yours). I am a scholar of imagining the invisible machinery that makes us all appear simultaneously chaotic and predictable at the same time, after all.

Can you do that? Name all your albums after yourself, add a number, then call it quits? Really? Whether you can or not, BS&T did, so we're really just asking is that cool or bad drool (as opposed to the good drool that flows when I really like what I'm hearing). See, I'm getting freakin' nowhere!

It works because BS&T was a performing ensemble like the Pointer Sisters. Their albums could just as easily have never been recorded. The world of royalties and residuals, in case you didn't know, has basically disappeared because everyone intentionally adjusts their prices as high as they possibly can. The harder you "capitalist," the faster the inflation. They don't teach that one very often, but I assure you it's true.

I'm gonna have to Sandra myself, shut up Bottle. Blood, Sweat & Tears. It works because, yeah, of course you can number your albums. It's hilarious when you do it wrong like Steppenwolf, annoying when you half-ass it like the Beatles, absolutely a horrible idea if you're Van Halen and only do it when you get a new lead singer.

For BS&T, it totally comes across as "here's the new stuff we've been playing or will play live." These really are set-list albums like Van Halen (retroactively implied 1 like non-lunatics would do). Makes total sense to me. They ruin it by starting with their second album, so Blood, Sweat & Tears is actually number 2. Child is Father to the shut up and invent a time machine to go back and title your albums properly, Man.

That sounded harsh. I'm not actually angry about anything, it's just nobody put much thought into any of this so it's tough going for a guy like me, you know? Oh well, we'll just chase butterflies and pee our pants every time David Clayton Thomas belts out SQUIRREL! Not literally, I'd have to check but I don't think he says the word "squirrel" ever in their entire discography; merely a metaphor. He can be startling if you're not paying attention, I tend to laugh out loud when it happens.

And with that meandering load of brain manure, we all know it's time to desperately wrap up this project before anyone loses an appendage. Sadly, it just dawned on me exactly which album we're inevitably going to listen to in Chapter 9, surely you can suss out tomorrow's revolver as well (wink, wink). Still 2 days until Thanksgiving pickles at Arlo's house, so at least I'll have Wednesday night to scrub my brain out afterward. Quoth the Bottle, toodles.

Chapter 9

Number 9...number 9... number 9... There it is, my dingy copy of the end of The Beatles, The BEATLES. Technically I'm supposed to take the "amazing mental kaleidoscope" hallway and talk about their TM retreat with everybody and their girlfriend's dog, and how everybody took a turn quitting during these final sessions before McCartney finally announced it. Meh. At heart it's a self-titled "we were The Beatles."

It is a kaleidoscope; I'll give you that. It's 4 dudes going back to being 4 separate dudes doing their own thing. Glass Onion pretty much sums up how they feel about that first half of their lives. As an album I hate it. It smells like cabbage farts in my brain. But, there's a light at the end of the tunnel that I'm positive isn't a freight train coming our way. You know what's good about it? It's a ridiculous behemoth double album and half the songs don't even contain a majority of The Beatles playing on them. There's more studio improvisation than Pop-Rock. You know what this album really says? Don't get mad at me, but it literally says "we were The Beatles, jesus christ we sucked. We're just 4 space cadets who happen to be great musicians and worked hard to write silly songs and make a lot of money for other people."

You might think I'm crazy, but in that context, this is a phenomenal achievement of recorded music. Look, I'm serious, this was 1968. Two months after this was released it was 1969 and we all know Bryan Adams found the only part of that year that wasn't 2020 to fondly remember.

The first time around I called it bad random crap. I think I'm wrong. I was looking at it from the wrong direction, let's try taking it literal. "We're the biggest band in the world, and we're pointless [jazz hands]." It's true. That's why it's a double album of random crap. It's good random crap.

Everybody points to the fact that all they had was 1 acoustic guitar in India, and that's why many of the songs feel stripped back and they plundered the studio sound effects library. Kay, sure, but let's really think about this. I've made albums that sound better than this. Not that my albums or my playing are better, I just mean I have better sound production with my cheap gear and computer than all of the equipment in Abbey Road Studios put together. This album sounds great for 1968, but I have actual bedroom recorded albums of equal/better audio quality for about 1/10,000th the price. Meanwhile, George no Rs Martin is saying "Paul, this raccoon song sucks, can we please record anything else?"

So much sloppy and out of tune playing, so many fragments stitched into abstract nothingness. Why don't we do it in the road? You're telling me that's better than McCartney? Yeah, now I love this album. It's inconsistent and trivial on purpose. I certainly like that context a whole lot better. It's giving it too much credit, but I like it. I like it a lot. 4 people picked to live as an internationally renowned pop phenomenon, go crazy and get mad at each other, then go 4 different directions afterward.

It's so weird, I truly love The Beatles. What I don't like is that this self-titled monstrosity feels like a retrospective mixtape from 3 different better projects. This sounds like they broke up halfway through the process and just handed a box of random mixes to The Compiler for final consolidation to fulfill contractual obligations. Listening to The BEATLES is exactly like listening to EL&P's Love Beach. I have to want it to be a trainwreck so I can appreciate that it isn't.

Crazily enough, that feels good. That's the context in which this album is fantastic. No before, no after, this is all The Beatles that exists; a brilliant bedroom collage album with no larger context than the fact that it now exists. Plus, it ends with Good Night, so I don't have to. I do have to finish this little exposé (not that it's particularly scandalous) with some sort of conclusion, but that is definitely tomorrow's problem. Cheers.

Chapter 10

This is the end... of this relatively quick survey of self-titled albums... the only end, my friend. Time to close the door and meander in another direction. Skipped His Medication, Editor con Carne, is giving me that "was there a point?" look. Careful man, you keep making that face it'll stick that way. I keep telling you there ain't no morals to these stories at all, I just find it refreshing to wander the hallways and see how they are intersecting at the moment. It had a clear trajectory, right? Best to worst, least effort to most effort in terms of liking them, debuts to squiggly middle-ground to a definite ending. If absolutely nothing else, Speed City Records in Ontario confirmed my order and shipped 3 records for future us-es to enjoy on their own obscure terms. Never would have happened if it weren't for that little picnic at Punctuation Pavilion.

A whole week of albums. I had fun. What more could you possibly want? And so, back to humming. This is the end... my only friend, the end. If that crystal ship doesn't get here soon, I guess I'll just have to hop on the blue bus....

Bottle's Unexpected Adventure Time

And I said to myself "self, we listened to Alice's Restaurant like the princess commands, and thanked our friends for not being mindless robots, wouldn't it be fun to have some discomfort chewing and reach in to feel that half of my top back molar is missing and schedule an appointment to probably end up having it extracted Saturday morning?"

I replied "goodness me, that sounds delightful, make it so."

Wisdom tooth gone; I wasn't even in the building for a full hour.

B: Gnn nuush. Bonnuln bagn.

C: What?

B: Oh, sorry, forgot about the cotton balls. I'm back.

E: How was Minion City?

B: It's still there, haven't been there in nearly 3 years, so lots of new stuff I'm not interested in. Old stuff is still where I left it, so that's nice. Interesting batch of records to torture you guys with.

S: Joy. How do you feel?

B: For a while there I was comfortably numb, but now I mostly feel like Steve Martin ripped a tooth out of my head with a freshly sanitized pair of vice grips. I'll have a Sportsman's Cocktail if you please.

C: Not familiar with that one, did you make it up?

B: Yes indeed, it's 2 parts ibuprofen, one part acetaminophen. Better make it a double. Administer every 6 hours. Better, not to mention cheaper, than opioids. Now, if you'll excuse me, I'm gonna go sit in a chair and wait for the right side of my face to stop hurting. Gonna let the self-titled debut from Odyssey do whatever it does.

Odyssey

E: What do they do?

C: Disco/Soul.

B: The Disco side of funky Soul.

S: New York City Soul, not Southern Soul.

B: Sure, that's a useful distinction. Think nightclub Soul, not Otis Redding. The group is a Linzer, Calello, and Randall vehicle post their 4 Seasons collaborations. Really good though. Much less flashy or dance-focused than 5th Dimension, but a totally enjoyable listen with flashes of Jackson 5, and a lot of Caribbean influence. Plus, that Ted Coconis watercolor is spectacular in its own right; there aren't many album covers that function as an actual visual overture like this. What a delightful album, I'm feeling better already.

Feargal Sharkey

Have you ever wondered what Michael Stipe's Jello Biafra impression might sound like? Me neither, but that's Feargal Sharkey. He was apparently the lead singer of Irish Punk band The Undertones. I'm reminded of Johnny Rotten's Public Image Limited. This doesn't sound like that at all, but that's the kind of 180 turn the 80s seemed to do to everybody. I'm also reminded of Bob Dylan's Empire Burlesque.
This isn't in any way bad, but it is definitely weird. Hello Michael Kamen's string arrangements. I have nothing to draw on for comparison. This is just freakin' weird, big sweeping 80s pop ballads, but he's screaming them. Not like Sam Kinison screaming, but like that Patti Smith level of unhinged and slightly crazy. It really is like Johnny Rotten

doing power ballads, or Rod Stewart on the down side of a cocaine/helium bender. It's manic when it shouldn't be. It's really growing on me. That's an impressive harmonica solo on Don't Leave It To Nature.

I can't really do this album justice. It's weird, and definitely unique. Disturbingly charming. You'll just have to hear it for yourself.

The Rascals

I think today we try to get a real grasp on The Rascals. I found two more of their albums yesterday, that should be enough to really dig into their shift from popular singles band to album-oriented space cadets. Groovin', Once Upon a Dream, Freedom Suite, and Search and Nearness. I don't have a copy of See, but we could probably youtube it if it becomes necessary. That's not their full discography, but it is the official name change through the last album for Atlantic.

The Young Rascals got their start competing with The Beatles and Rolling Stones for American attention. The 4 Seasons and The Supremes are in there as well, so it's a real big business agent/promoter/label free-for-all. What made The Young Rascals stand out was that they were very much an R&B band. They were the first white act ever signed to Atlantic, they refused to perform at segregated concerts, they were in fact the copilots to the Righteous Brothers under the moniker Blue-Eyed Soul. They had a ton of high-charting singles, and their first 3 albums are simply collections of those singles. The official genre label is Garage Rock/Blue-Eyed Soul. Enticing as that sounds, I only have the last of those, Groovin'. I don't think we necessarily need to hear the first 2, we're listening to the end of that band before a new band rises from its ashes to conceive of the album for which they will write songs, as opposed to designing a box to carry all the ala carte takeout food we ordered.

What do we get on Groovin'? A big orchestra opener followed by just about the nastiest garage rock guitar tone and truly terrible reverb and abysmal stereo experimentation. I adore Find Somebody, so you know it's objectively annoying and you'll hate it. Then the horns and sunshine harmonies are back because they're so happy now. Really, think of all the things that were popular in the early/mid 60s, The Rascals are good at all of it, but they do something interestingly weird on every track. They are psychedelic from the get-go, but it's subtle; only one component of their wildly eclectic style. They really really are fantastic. If you enjoy listening to Oldies radio, this album is a pretty stellar block of boundary pushing Pop-Rock.

Now, I've ragged on Sgt. Pepper a lot, but that's only because of its context in the Beatles discography. It undeniably blew everybody's mind. Everyone made their own version, and The (newly name-shortened) Rascals are no exception. Once Upon A Dream is definitely a better album than the Stones's Their Satanic Majesties Request, but it is quite possibly even more bizarre.

What did Sgt. Pepper really do? It showed everyone how to really give a concept the reins of the album. It's literally about the experience of a random Lonely Hearts Club Band concert. They have a backstory, there's all sorts of incidental stuff happening around you, you're high as balls, it's a real happening and that concept unifies all the experiments and styles and sound effects.

A lot of people say Once Upon a Dream is an overlooked gem that really should sit next to Pepper and Pet Sounds on your toppest of shelves. I don't have either, let's just listen to the first proper Rascals concept album...

... well, that definitely qualifies as bizarre. But, this isn't in any way a u-turn or a crazy out of nowhere shock-fest. They do torture a Sitar and everyone in earshot at the end, I don't want that to surprise you the way it did me (it's bad, I laughed out loud), but all the weirdness was totally there on Groovin'. Now it's what connects all the songs in this intentionally preconceived dream. I need another listen to really understand the larger statement.

Oh, ok, it really is a dream of peace and love. Disparate scenes of life being an interesting and enjoyable adventure, joined together by strange psych-noise transitions. Like the objects on the cover, these are all symbolic statements that speak to a collective rather than individually coherent experience. Side One ends up using the metaphor of a rainy day as an experience that makes the eventual vacation that much more enjoyable. Or, and this is the fun part, choosing to see the stormy rainy day as an opportunity is the dream vacation itself.

Side Two says "c'mon, join me, my delusional world is pretty awesome."

Maybe it's a reverse metaphor, love is a metaphor for society itself. Stop wondering how to solve all these insomnia-inducing problems and go out and love as big as possible. Walk the walk, it gets better every time you try.
That makes sense, we know Freedom Suite is next. This is the subtle, artistic, free your mind version, the next album tackles it head on to much less critical appreciation. Oh god, I just made it to the Sitar mangling of "do-wa diddy ditty dum ditty do" on this second listen. Truly atrocious, love it.

Then the proper finale; the dream is that everyone chooses to love and we make the world a happy place to live. Then they do it, and we're up to Freedom Suite.

Sure, it's a decadent double-album, but it's also not. Freedom Suite is really just the first record, complimented by a second fully instrumental jam album. We just want the first disk.

There's so much hatred and confusion, and heads are filled with disillusion. Yeah, you nailed that one, guys.

Here's the thing, this is an overtly political album. Everybody hates that because it forces you to worry that people might find out your opinions are secretly terrible. Also, there's a sample of a sheep bleating in the background of Of Course.

> Bigotry, hate and fear
> Got ten million votes this year.

Yeah, that's a direct reference to George Wallace. In hindsight, calling Nixon's subsequent election "law and order won" is some serious irony, but Wallace's campaign was the Southern Right arguing that segregation was the pillar of the American economy. King and Kennedy had just been assassinated, and Johnson quickly realized he wasn't going to win the nomination and dropped out.

Being mad that this album is political is extremely head in the sand, all things considered. Looking around at all the hate and violence and thinking "oh no, I'm in danger of losing all my profits," is pretty terrible. Really that's what this album is about; hate and fear and pulling people apart is bad, m'kay?

So, we'll skip over See and go straight to the end, Search and Nearness. We can always come back to it if we need to. What's this thing about?

Ok, I can see where some of the "meh" comes from. I disagree, this is a fantastic album. The whisps of psychedelia are still there, but mostly this is just a solid early 70s Jazz Rock album. It is incredibly consistent and potentially not that exciting. However, it's freakin' good. Still though, this is not The Young Rascals, and not even really The Rascals. Set against the backdrop of mainstream Rock/Soul, it feels very much like a one and done album from a great band that doesn't have an obvious future.

Is it a fair description of their trajectory? Highly enjoyable and often wackadoodle singles band turns to album shaped rock and fizzles out. I mean, sure you can hear it that way, but why? Plus, their entire career was spent in comparison to the Beatles, so I'm doing a fair bit of unfair projecting. I do need to hear See. Gimme a moment...

... no, see, See is great. The Sitar on Stop and Think is much better than the first time they tried that. I think the real problem is that The Rascals are so widely eclectic that it's really tough to pigeon hole them into a singular specific mood or vibe. If you're a really picky listener, it could be really hard to get into more than one or two tracks on any particular album. If you just accept that The Rascals are 3 different bands all the time, though, it's really rewarding.

Freedom Suite is definitely the least adventurous of their albums, but as albums go, I think each one gets better. Search and Nearness is a fitting culmination in my mind.

I wasn't overly fond of Freedom Suite the first time around, but now that I have the whole thing in my head, these guys are fantastic. You have to keep their whole history in your head, and that can be quite a bit more work than most people are willing to do, but definitely worth it. An acquired taste for sure, but The Rascals have definitely grown on me.

Interesting use of a Sunday morning. I still have two more albums to tide us over until the next batch arrives. Time for a break, though. Cheers.

Nektar – Remember The Future

S: How are you feeling, Bottle?

B: I'm fine.

S: Really?

B: Yeah. Sure. I mean, there's the normal not wanting to go back to work tomorrow, and I'm in total hypochondriac mode over the tooth I had pulled yesterday. I'm sleeping upright in an easy chair, my tongue is playing hockey goalie with everything I eat, I'm totally terrified the clot will fall out and I'll bleed to death, then I'll get a dry socket and half my face will fall off, plus I listened to 5 Rascals albums this morning and made 2 pounds of experimental chicken sausage. But more important, is Nektar's Remember The Future as good as I think it's going to be? The concept reads like a Mastodon album, but everybody says "wish there wasn't so much Funk on this one."

S: It's truly a mess in there, isn't it?

B: Yeah, for sure. But, imagine being a winged alien named Bluebird and every time you come to Earth half the people scream "ahhh! It's a blue winged alien, run away!" and the other half scream "catch that flying blue monster so I can shoot and or anally probe it!" My problems are trivial.

S: I'm not entirely sure how to respond to that.

B: How do you think his blind psychic pen pal feels? That kid's like "I don't even know how to imagine a winged blue alien because my eyes don't work." So, Bluebird's like "oh, why didn't you say so in the first place? I can totally fix that trivial problem." Then the kid is like " yay I can see! You're not nearly as hideous and frightening as I expected," and Bluebird's like "thank you formerly blind child, my work here is done."

S: [humorously elongated bong gurgle and exhale]

B: Was that really necessary?

S: Yes, Bottle. Yes, it was. That's not a synopsis anyone can process without copious amounts of THC in their bloodstream.

B: I'm not high, why should that matter?

S: You are also not normal. Any other human would have dangerously high blood pressure and a visible eye twitch if they tried to process all that sober.

B: Yeah, I guess so. That sounds like people. Ok, fine, wanna listen to an English band in Germany famous for listing people who contributed absolutely no musical material whatsoever as band members play a 2-act concept album about space birds with me?

S: No, no I don't. I'm barely high enough to get through this conversation with you. I'd need to use up all my Carl karma and have a Gladys brownie to get high enough to actually listen to it.

B: Am I really that difficult?

S: Sometimes. Only sometimes.

B: Time's like now?

S: Yes, exactly like now.

B: Sorry?

S: Not your fault, you aren't actually *being* difficult, it's just that the psychic radiation is metaphorically melting the neighbor's dog.

B: We don't have any neighbors.

S: [more bong gurgling] ... yes, that right there. That's what I'm talking about.

B: Now your eye is twitching. I know what will help, Nektar's 4th album. It's a concept album about an alien who-

S: I know what it's about!

B: Geez, you seem tense, Sandra. I'll be fine, you go relax.

S: Yes, thank you, I shall. [Exit, stage left]

B: Wowzers, I wonder what got old snagglepus's bikini twisted. Oh well, I'm sure she'll be better tomorrow. Time to check out Remember the Future... oh yeah. That's the good stuff. I'm not gonna feel much of anything after this....

Deerhunter – Why Hasn't Everything Already Disappeared?

Baudrillard. He coined the term "hyperreality." It essentially means that we cannot tell the difference between reality and simulated reality. I don't mean, and he didn't mean, a VR so realistic you live there like The Matrix, that's a naive surface interpretation. What he was really trying to get at was the facade of globalization becoming the only Truth we understand; the illusion that knowledge itself can reach completion. In short, we believe the propagandized version of reality and forget the agenda that propaganda advances.

His final posthumous book is titled Why Hasn't Everything Already Disappeared? That's also the title of Deerhunter's 2019 album. The book itself isn't the concept, the historical situation is the concept that envelopes the songs on the album. A philosopher predicting the disappearance of culture itself, but realizing that it has not happened during his lifetime. A prediction of the future in which we now live, sort of. "A sci-fi album about the present." The fight for the survival of culture is happening all around us, we see it every waking moment of the day. Baudrillard's argument was that this hyperreality leaves us vulnerable to complete psychological meltdown whenever events like 9/11, or a pandemic, or the sudden withdrawal of armed forces from another country disturb the illusion of a perfectly functioning universe, and each successive fallout will be worse. OK Computer comes to mind. I have no idea if any of that kind of mental fragility speaks for this Deerhunter album or not, I haven't listened to it yet. Let's change that.

But first, this probably unnecessary philosophical tangent. Baudrillard's ideas were accompanied by a logically increasing refutation and ultimate rejection of Smith/Marx, specifically with regard to the labor theory of value. Value, for Baudrillard, is not a quality derived from production. Rather, value itself is a semiosis dependent entirely upon the comparative value of consumption. Need and scarcity are fabricated constructs, mythologies, defined not by an abstract/inherent universal need, but by the significance of consumption inside a semiotic system. Thus, innovation and progress can never fulfill a supposed need, only exaggerate or heighten the hyperreal, and likewise the collateral damage of its disruption. This is of course the clash of ideologies themselves, and eventually culture itself will be nothing more than a commodity, in short, a delusion. Now Deerhunter.

Ho-o-o-o-oly crap, that's bleak. Ben Gibbard's a horse and buggy ride through Central Park on a sunny day compared to this. If the cutting out of a bad connection on the last track, Nocturne, doesn't leave you weeping on the floor in the fetal position, then your soul is already beyond repair. This is brutal.

Better yet, all that tangential background is totally relevant. That's the difference between hearing this as a brutal statement about how miserable these last couple years have been and "Deerhunter made a shimmery crap-pop album and I hate it." The latter being a shining example of the agonizingly vacant consumer culture itself; liking or hating this album is nothing more than a status symbol.

It's not a constructed album, though. It is very much a coincidentally well-designed take-out box, but magically enough it's a superb one. Bits of the anger and desperation shine through, but the presentation mutes all but the sharpest of fangs, and even those lack most of their real venom. It must feel like agony on the inside. It must because it does.

Reading through the descending rankings at anydecentmusic.com/review/9671/Deerhunter-Why-Hasnt-Everything-Already-Disappeared.aspx is like watching the spectrum unfold in front of your eyes. If I did "/10," this one's an 8.

Then again, I have that wider philosophical context this album references, but I don't have any preconceived perception of Deerhunter beyond their status as Indie Darlings. I've heard about them, but this is my first experience of them. Any attempt to change that now has me working backward and remembering the future.

Is the hypothetical 9 I'd give that Nektar album a valid assessment of their respective consumptive values? I dunno. I do know pitting this against SPK's Machine Age Voodoo and BTBAM's Automata I&II would be a much more fruitful compare/contrast. They all have a lot more in common than you might at first expect.

Instead, I did some more digging and Bradford Cox has an interesting approach to songwriting. It's a zone out and end up creating 5 or 6 songs all in one train of thought, and that actually goes a long way to explaining the serendipitous feel about this album. For all the production face paint, this is not a scripted, meticulous sounding album. He's just as surprised as you are at what the band produces from his ideas, and this very much sounds like a lonely miserable tirade through a surprisingly soundproof 4th wall.

    I love it, your milage may vary.

The Bird And The Bee

    Philosophy will phuck you up, my friend. How about we do a complete 180 and peruse a Bottle's Bootlegs or several while the postal service (chemtrail Ben Gibbard reference, drink 'em up) does its continental traversing with my internationally acquired analog audio. Surely The Bird and the Bee will help us forget how terrible now is.

    Nope, this is at least as worse. For starters, 2007 is the year both Baudrillard died and The Bird and the Bee's self-titled debut now existed. All I was going for is the ridiculous notion that WHEAD was Deerhunter's "pop" album. Madam Coincidence has her testicle-kicking boots laced up apparently. This is 12 years earlier and 27 decibels louder. Inara, sister, I might be dying too. I try as well. Supposedly this is a 7, but we've long since established those people who get paid to do this are morons. This album is a 10. For restarters, it's subtle, not Edward Scissor Hands. For continues, it's 2007 and they are intentionally doing the retro 60s mod veneer. Coup de gras, are you prepared for the atom bomb?

    This is one of the best albums in the entire universe. Nothing against Deerhunter, Baudrillard is quite right, but remember how I said The Specials lived 2020 for their entire career? Yeah, we'll just drop the mic on that one.

On! Air! Library!

I thought I had way more time to kill, so I was halfway through writing the next installment of Bottle's Bootlegs. Screw that, Canada sent me records! Let's listen to On! Air! Library!'s only album I liked so much back when I liked it so much the first time a week or so ago.

They formed in 1998, got enough local buzz to put out a split with The Album Leaf, made their debut LP, toured with Interpol and The Secret Machines, broke up in 2005. Easiest discography I've ever reviewed.

Ha! Inner sleeve bent to hell straight from the manufacturer. Hilarious.

Experimental Ambient Post-Rock? Sure, that's about the best you can do for this total downer collage of lethargic harmonies, fragile melodic duets, and musica concrete soundscapes. This sounds like what The Bird and the Bee implies it feels like on the inside. Not gonna lie, this is an incredibly accurate aural depiction of what those days I tell you were a struggle feel like. They feel like this. I wanted to say there is a real Industrial quality to the more experimental noise work, you really can hear traces of Throbbing Gristle, like Genesis P. Orrige is gonna take the next verse rather than p!.

This is not subtle, nor is it grotesque. This is just super-heavy, all encompassing, like the universe is made of molasses but you still have to get to work on time.

Oh wow, the "I need a bambulance" sample is hiding in here, but I'll let you find that Waldo on your own.

Ok, if you're going to go listen to it you need to realize the swings are extreme. Chilling at the bottom of the swimming pool level reverby post rock, to mind crushing noise cacophony, recorded phone conversations, doors opening and closing, out of tune instruments, you name it. This album might be the most depressing thing I've heard since Neutral Milk Hotel's On Avery Island. It's gorgeously disturbing. This album sounds like if Napoleon Dynamite was not in any way a comedy. I am of course making this up, but I imagine this is like that brief moment right before you never wake up from a fentanyl overdose because nobody wants to waste their Narcan on you.

Remember, these are just tasting notes. You know, like hints of cherry blossom in a tire fire, or an earthy bitterness that slowly morphs into overripe bananas. Faint whiffs of chlorine and sadness. A bizarrely unenergetic Mazzy Star/Butthole Surfers collaboration. It's really good, but you aren't going to want to do much of anything afterward except sleep.

Very interesting thing, this album is way better on vinyl. I wouldn't normally say that, and I can't really put a proper description to it. I could also be imagining it. Regardless, the next two albums are going to be even more interesting. I picked a fun batch this time around. Fun for me, at least.

Animal Slaves – Dog Eat Dog

The Dog Eat Dog LP from Animal Slaves is not going to be everyone's cup of tea. This is mid-80s, New Wave-ish, bass forward, post-punky cult-rock from the Vancouver underground. Elizabeth Fischer said her singing was terrible on this album. She does sound very reminiscent of post barrel-bottom Marianne Faithfull, and this is not happy, date-night music; I'm not complaining, but you know how you like your tea, I don't.

Interesting morbid fact, when she was diagnosed with terminal lung cancer in 2015, she raised enough money from friends and fans to visit Iceland on the way to her assisted suicide in Sweden. She tried some regular treatments first, but it became clear that she wasn't going to survive and she wanted her death to be as calm, painless, and legally/psychologically uncomplicated as possible for everyone. Reading interviews and her website you get the sense that she had a genuinely wicked sense of humor tempered by a hardcore dose of rationalism. Total Gladys in my mind. I bet she was a hoot, and that's why she had so much love and support from her whole scene.

More than anything this little trio of albums makes me wish I could be a real label. There's something a little bit magic about holding an obscure little document of real humans doing the impossible, reaching out and connecting with complete strangers across time and space. Vinyl, the archaic, horrible, laboriously wasteful medium that it is, reminds me of just how insane that accomplishment really is in a way that CDs and our digital landfill of an internet don't.

Listen to me, being a nostalgia bum. Enough of that mopey junk, we've got Animal Slaves' mopey junk to listen to. If you're a fan of hauntingly gloomy and morose 80s Post-Punk, but never heard of Animal Slaves, I think you'll enjoy this at least 3/4 as much as I do.

The Reactionaries – Ingenuity

Last but not least, it's Ingenuity from Belgian Punk Band The Reactionaries. Not to be confused with the 70s/80s American Punk band who morphed into The Minutemen. I should do a whole series called Names Are Hard, Let's Use That Discontinued One, Surely No One Will Notice.

Belgian politics is really fun because Liberal equals Right Wing. It's a Monarchy, and a Federation, it has a constitution, and its government is a Representative Democracy with a bicameral Parliament. Language is a major political issue because French and Dutch essentially represent the Upper class and the Proletariat respectively.

Many people consider Belgium a "flawed Democracy," but I am Bottle, hear me say "nope, they're using all those words properly. How refreshing." What's this album about, then?

The answer is half an hour of the most gloriously disheveled, dive-bar, stoner-tinged trashy rock and roll this side of Danzig era Misfits. Calling this fantastic is a tragic understatement. My head hasn't banged this hard in months, possibly years. Winner of the Bottle of Beef Proves My Theory That The Best Music Already Happened 10 Years Ago In A Different Country award. 2009 would have been a hell of a lot more enjoyable with this pumping into my earballs, I can tell you that.

But are their lyrics any good? Let's see, sarcastic swipe at consumer culture, wish someone would have told me I was making the same mistakes over and over again, now's a good time to look at the world and actually empower ourselves, peace out I quit, I'm done with your garbage so you try to make me the bad guy, some people are afraid of the discomfort of change, consumer culture is the real enemy, stealing your health, individuality, and human wealth. Yep, superbly coherent lyrical concept that circles back around and reiterates its point in a straightforwardly emphatic conclusion. Call this the second 10/10 I've ever awarded. 1) it rocks, 2) it's intelligent, 3) not a single swear word or derogatory sentiment on the whole album in spite of its critical perspective... I don't actually have 10 points to make, but you get the idea. Awesome album, definitely carve out some time to crank it up as loud as possible. I guarantee you won't be sorry.

Pissing In Action

Well, we wandered into the murky swamp of Bottle's Bootlegs a few days ago, might as well keep going. I have the 2nd run copy of Pissing in Action, a compilation of 3 concert bootlegs (including their headliner set from the 1992 Reading Festival) from Italian label Little Capone. The first batch was cooked up in March of 1994, this batch in July. It's one of several items in my collection specifically banned from sale on Discogs. None of that matters, when we pull the cork out of this particular bottle, we get the entire ant colony of intricately woven hallways that is my experience of visiting Moscow when I was 14 or 15. I'm fuzzy on when that trip actually took place, but the images in my mind are spectacularly vivid.

Your old friend Bottle has literally bartered with packs of cigarettes, ordered "water without gas," sat quietly through a police search of our chartered bus for stowaway Chechnyans, been showed the price of things I ordered on a calculator because communicating thousands of Rubles to tourists who speak broken child-like Russian is a massive waste of time and energy, seen a field being scythed, seen Lenin, been to the Bolshoi Theater.

Buying this particular album was really interesting. Pick it out from photos, wait in line to pay for it, take the receipt from paying for it to the next window and wait for them to get it, then leave. I bought some other CDs from a flea market as well.

Thousand other memories, but we're here to hear crappy back of room recordings from the early 90s. That Reading set did eventually get a properly mastered release, but I'm not sitting here with my pirate juice for anything less that the real deal.

That 1990 Michigan concert is basically Bleach and a couple other tracks. It's a great performance and the audience really doesn't detract even though you can hear them the whole time.

The Delmare concert is much less enjoyable. The performance is still great, and the mix gets better as the set progresses, but it's so much farther away and out in the open and it just sounds faded.

The Reading set is a bit like that too, far away and fuzzy, but you can hear how much bigger and louder the whole thing really is. Plus, you can hear how much fun they are having after the very not good rehearsal Krist mentions they had the night before.

This bootleg, and the two previous bootlegs it was stolen from is really unnecessary for casual listening, mostly because you can go find the properly mixed and mastered official Reading release, but for a long time this was all that existed as far as live mostly full concerts. It's not as rare as the original two bootlegs or the 3rd run. I personally think the terrible cover is part of the charm.

But you know what's really important? No, Bottle, what?

What's really important is that I twist the whole thing around and remind you how I'm so happy because my friends (that's all of you guys) are actually in my head, and Sunday morning is every day for all I care. Are you scared? I'm not, I excited. I can't wait to meet you there every time I pop in an album and put on the headphones. That all sounds like this is my last review and I won't wake up tomorrow. You know me, I'm just getting ending this 4th book out of the way somewhere in the middle so I don't have to worry about it later. We'll find a new adventure, or an old adventure, or actually produce some albums or something. I never know until I do it. Tomorrow, though. Now it's beddy-night time for Bottle, catch you on the flip side.

Rest Repose – The Sleep City EP

B: Told you I'd wake back up. Ok, Skiperninator, what's in your bottle?

E: You can't just lump Marx and Smith together. They are opposite.

B: No, they are qualitatively inverse. Economics is a two-headed beast, a sine wave, the actual breathing of humanity, inhale/exhale, the coin flipping. They exist at the same time. You're smashing completely different aspects of Marx's Philosophical project into a garbled mess of unintelligible nonsense, and you are mistaking what people do in response to Marx for Marx. This conversation right now is the clash of reality with your hyperreality.

Marx's description of Capitalism is completely different from Marx's feelings about the system he is describing. He expands upon Smith's explanations of Classical Economics and connects that system in all its historical forms to the effects that system has upon society at large. What he finds is that it contains the essential oils of its own decomposition. In other words, when left unchecked, Capitalism itself condenses wealth to a small number of elite and leads to social upheaval in the form of civil war. Capitalism is the Economics of slavery, and its participants generally behave according to the benefit/punishment that system forces upon them as individuals.

We in America have a very skewed perception of what "slavery" means in the philosophical sense because our definition artificially narrows the broader concept down to the European conquest of "the New World" and subsequent enslavement of Africans as private capital property. It might be tempered by some recognition of the biblical Israelites, or that kooky Egyptian pyramids thing, but it's a very small understanding. Slavery in the broader philosophical sense is ownership of the life and livelihood of people as private (capital) property. Now, we are people and we defend what we think is most beneficial to ourselves. Some people defend slavery because they think it is better than some alternative way of life, some people want to eliminate any form of slavery.

Marx says Capitalism originates by necessity from the division of labor into production and distribution. He explains this division with a description of the relationship between Weaver, Merchant, and the Market as it exists in the Merchant's imagination. Skip to the conclusion, they disagree in their qualitative assessment of the system as a whole, i.e., the effect that system has on human society. Smith says it's fantastic, Marx says look around you it's objectively horrible for the vast majority of the population. No relevant rebuttal of Marx's description of the results of living under a system of Classical Economics has ever been produced because it is demonstrably accurate.

We need some more relevant biographical information. Smith was by and large a public lecturer on moral philosophy. Marx was educated as a Lawyer, but became much more interested in philosophy, Hegel in particular. No hidden agenda in that description, but an important difference in terms of social origins. Both men were largely self-educated via lots of library time.

The point of all that information is that one cannot reject Marx's corroboration and elaboration upon Smith's description of Capitalism while defending Smith's Political Economy. Marx is describing the same abstract economic system in more detail with a better understanding of the larger implications of that system gained by observing a century's worth of watching that philosophical system operate. Capitalism, as manifested through living and learning it (according to Marx) has both a growth and a decline; it is a literal cycle. However, rather than happening successively (boom, bust, boom, bust), the two classes involved (Bourgeoisie and Proletariat) stand in an inverse relationship. As owners get rich, workers get poor, higher wages equals lower profits. This is the system of the card game War: eventually one side will win and the other will lose. What will we do when that happens?

We're about to enter 2022, and there is still no answer for that question. The answer is always [shoulder shrug] "I'm on the winning side, not my problem."

Marx, regardless of your own thoughts or opinions, says "I think what will happen is that we will abandon the whole stupid game and go back to a much more agreeable state of self-sufficiency and mutually beneficial exchange because it is psychologically and spiritually much more fulfilling."

At this point there are two completely different arguments you could make. First, you could disagree with Marx's prediction for human social evolution. Most people agree that it's nonsense. Second, you could point out that our today world has largely abandoned classical economics in favor of the comparative consumptive theory of value (that's Baudrillard in a nutshell) for exactly that reason. It is a proven doomed ideology. The problem is that these are not mutually exclusive hallways, they branch off from every step and there are wormholes that morph the logic from one argument to another without you noticing.

Remember, Marx is not arguing that Classical Economics is wrong; he is arguing that the surplus value generated by the inner logic of Capitalism can be distributed in two different directions: wealth can gradually accumulate to an ever-decreasing number of economic winners until there is only one Highlander, or it can be redistributed as agreeably as possible to gradually reduce the suffering of the collapse of the monetary system itself. Either way, Capitalism as an ideology in practice will always collapse, the value of money as a universal equivalent will always converge on zero. This raises the question "which is better for the majority of people?" Is it better to fail by letting all the money collect into a single garbage heap, or is it better to let the total money supply reach its ultimate per capita equilibrium? Marx the person says the latter is better for humanity at large. Remember, he believes both paths lead to the same end result: both money and the governments who legislate the direction it flows having no functional value at all. Imagine we all wake up tomorrow with all debts null and void and a complete reallocation of the American economy, say every person with a valid SSN has $35,000; that's the end result of Marxian inverse Capitalism. The non-inverse is of course some guy named Steve or Ted now owns 100% of all US dollars. Either way, there is no money actually being used, complete monetary stagnation.

Now that we understand that, we can rephrase the question. From this position, is it better to have King of the World Steve decide how that money begins to be divided/withheld, or is it better to go hands free and let every individual person choose how to start trading with each other again?

I'm not really interested in answering that question, I'm interested in how people got the whole thing twisted around so that they end up arguing for the opposite of what they actually want.

E: How is it twisted up?

B: Ok, here I can give you a great example. Mainstream 24-hr news-tainment. Everyone gets all up in arms that the news is highly politicized and every station has a definite bias. Everybody hates that, right?

E: Yes, I can completely agree with that statement.

B: Ok, can you also agree that identifiably Right-Wing media outlets call themselves "fair and balanced" while calling things like NPR and PBS "Marxist garbage."

E: Ok, yes. I have observed that. That does actually happen.

B: That is the opposite of true. So, either they are outright lying because it generates more profit from targeted advertising for the owners of those networks, or they actually believe that to be true which makes them delusional. There is no Leftist view being presented on mainstream media, only a representation of the Left from within a Right-Wing framework. That's a conversation for a different day. Right now, we have to go back to my passing mention of property. Luckily, I have an album for that. It's the Sleep City EP from Rest Repose.

This is not a Bottle's Bootleg, and we need to unpack it. First, I paid for the audio files, downloaded them, burned them to CD, printed the cover art and stuck it in the jewel case. This is my personal property; I can pop it into any CD player I want and listen to it whenever I feel like it. The music I hear when I do that, however, is the private property of the band published for public consumption. My purchase represents an agreement between me and the band that acknowledges my ownership of this physical disc that I made. I don't own the music or the lyrics, I don't own the band, I don't have the right to capitalize on the product of their labor by broadcasting/performing it for my own profit, I simply own this physical copy. Furthermore, there is no market for this EP. There is a market for recorded music in general, but there is no correlation between the entire output of a corporation like Sony and the band Rest Repose. The only economic relationship between the two would come from measuring the impact of Sony's actions on the band's sales and vice versa. If Sony wanted to invest in publishing this EP, then and only then would questions of Capitalism enter the discussion.

Now, the band itself doesn't actually exist anymore. It started out as a collaboration between two youtube personalities who live near each other, Ryan "Fluff" Bruce and Jared Dines plus a couple other people. They went through a lot of lineup changes, tour drama, real life complications, and have morphed into a new band called Dragged Under. I lost interest in the midst of all that, and though Dragged Under is quite enjoyable and I follow their facebook page, it's a very different band and not as exciting for me as this EP was at the time. Not fair, but totally honest. The point for this essay is that nowhere in that entire chain of events has any form of Capitalism taken place. No one paid Rest Repose to make this album so they could sell it to me for profit. Capitalism probably did take place on the part of the studio owner selling the product of the labor of his employees to the band for profit, but that has no bearing on my copy, or any tangible influence on the price I paid to obtain/create it. No one is measuring my owning this CD in their sales figures or deciding whether or not to publish some other album I'll never hear about based on this one. The recording of the album was a thing that band did and I happened to trade dollars for it. From my perspective this CD has a commodity value of basically zero, but a positive comparative consumption value because I enjoy listening to it. I would not willingly give away that consumptive value, nor would I give more value to something I know I won't enjoy listening to as much. Dolly Parton singing Christmas songs springs to mind.

    What I just described goes completely against Classical Economics. Brand loyalty does not factor into my purchasing decisions, and with a few specific personal luxuries my spending is based on a minimum desired level of comfort. I will probably never buy a new car during my life on this planet. I don't need a phone in addition to a computer, but I have one and I exploit that luxury to the fullest extent. I won't be sad if you take it away. I think we can all agree that if the labor theory of value were universally true, my observable dedication to reviewing albums would garner a decent wage from those seeking to buy an impartial review. My reviews have very miniscule commodity and consumptive values. People read my posts, so the consumptive value is positive, but no one shares them or sends me money, so commodity value is 0. If that mattered to me, I would have quit long ago. So, Classical Economics is pretty much irrelevant to me, I do not live inside that ideological universe.

The one exception is of course the commodity form of money. It is obvious that the supply of available money is very far below the corresponding amount of goods and services to be had. I should by all accounts quit my job right now and find anywhere else that pays more because the market is ridiculous. Why don't I? That's not my problem, that's Right-Wing Liberal Capitalism's problem. Now please excuse me while I Rest and/or Repose.

Helmet – Meantime

S: Bottle, can we wrap up this Marx thing soon?

B: Yeah, it's probably time. I'm dangerously close to sticking my finger in the socket and becoming real again. Nip me in the bud. Here we go.

I believe it was Beavis and/or Butthead who said of tonight's 10/10 sophomore album "that drummer looks like a regular guy... If you, like, saw these guys on the street, you wouldn't even know they were cool." Said that then drummer is none other than now Battles drummer John Stanier. The band is of course Helmet, jazz guitarist Page Hamilton's Alternative Metal meets Noise Rock masterclass in harmonically and metrically complex dropped-d riffage. He really does have a hard time playing and singing this stuff at the same time.

I believe it was a much younger version of me who upon seeing the movie Jerky Boys said "that band really sounds like Helmet. Oh, it is Helmet? Ok, I guess I do know what I'm talking about." They have a very distinct sound. I imagine it is not likable for a large number of humans or wildlife. I personally love it and so did most every rock/metal kid in the late 90s. People make a strong case for Nu-metal being the result of emulating Helmet. Obviously, the extended jazz harmonies and metrical variety got lost in distortion, sorry I meant translation, so only the dropped-d riffs and anger survived.

Lyrically, Page is obtuse. These aren't stories or diatribes or lectures, these things are inner monologue responses to experiences, situations, etc. It's completely possible to not understand any of it, and that's a big part of their idiosyncratic charm. What does come through is the very clear sarcasm, skepticism, frustration, and even awe we might logically connect to a kid from Oregon moving to New York City to study Jazz guitar and living right down at the bottom of the barrel. It's like the East Coast version of Axl goes to Hollywood, only much more metaphorically obscure.

It also owes a large debt to Nirvana in the sense that labels were much more willing to give bands creative, if not financial, control of their output. That quickly ended as the new millennium approached, but the mid-90s were pretty spectacular in terms of wildly eclectic new music actually reaching a national audience.

Why? Well, Mike Judge told us at the beginning of this review. This is a t-shirt and jeans band. I just straight up like this. No pretense, no image, no hidden agenda, no attempt to appeal to anything other than my brain cells via my ear drums. That is not a market that ever really existed before the post-modern apocalypse. A rapidly growing number of consumers rather than investors controlled the market by flat out not buying what the major corporations were pushing, we walked into stores and said "I don't want anything from your million plus inventory, I want this awesome thing I just heard, order it for me." Do that enough times and that inventory changes fairly quickly. MTV and commercial radio were the driving force behind that revolution because this was the pre-high-speed internet era.

All sorts of hallways branch off from that atrium, but my argument should be pretty obvious. Technological advancement led to the democratization of exposure and file sharing eliminated the need for the big business of creating a niche market in the first place. To put it in terms of Classical Economics, the internet eliminated scarcity, the supply of new music transcended all geographic and logistical limitations and eliminated any economic value from distribution itself.

Said another way, the industry shifted from a Capitalist system to a Communist system all on its own according to the internal logic of Capitalism itself. The surplus value used to physically move music from creator to consumer was absorbed back into the savings of creators and consumers, and the total economy shrank accordingly. Labels in the new millennium were by and large forced to produce only that which was absolutely necessary to survive, rather than exploit the bourgeois mythologies that birthed the recorded music economy in the first place. More and more middle-class independent labels crumbled and wealth consolidated into the hands of a few major corporations. As the cost of distributing the music itself fell due to this democratization, the cost of turning that digital information back into physical form consequently and equivalently rose creating the price inflation we observe over time: 8 to 10 1970s dollars equals 20 to 25 today dollars. The capitalist response is to legally and punitively reprivatize the digital distribution itself. We see it every day in the rise of Spotify, subscription media, the shift from buying software to leasing software, the fight surrounding Right to Repair and planned obsolescence, the pay-to-play structure of the music business itself. Every human on Earth is theoretically a record label, every person on earth a musician and a consumer at the same time, so we are conceptually trading the music we produce for the equivalent music we consume with no surplus economic value. I'll buy your album if you buy mine. Logically, the monetary flow evaporates and whatever government exists must switch from taxation to subsidization. If your elected representatives don't understand and try to prevent that like the Republican party right now, we're all in for a nasty surprise. Not saying Democrats are doing a good job at this exact moment, just saying they understand the situation slightly better.

From a psychological/sociological perspective, having Capitalism creates a desperate need for the stress-relief of Communism and having Communism creates a desperate need for obtaining the propulsive power of Capitalism. We want the opposite of what we have. That's why I say wear a helmet, because we're approaching the point where it doesn't matter which side you're on, the car is going off the side of the cliff regardless. In the meantime, I'll just keep enjoying as much of the enjoyable I can find and throwing as much garbage into the dumpster as possible.

We can't actually escape Marx because we're all just passengers in the self-driving car. There's no AI steering, by the way, all we have is a brake pedal and a wrench to retork whichever bolts we think need it at the moment. The only real choice is to keep going or get out of the car and walk. We might find a better car to steal down the road, but it's still the same gamble. The car behind us could just as easily hit a pothole and take us out even after we've been happily walking for miles.

S: Jeez, Bottle, that's depressing.

B: Is it? Why? I don't find that part depressing. I find it depressing that so few people accept it and end up making the whole experience miserable for everyone else. I keep throwing away the garbage in any dumpster I can find, but people keep bringing it back to me like I'm supposed to love receiving intellectual garbage as a present. I don't mind the extra weight of useful things, and I don't mind carrying your useful things for a while if you need me to, but I don't want to carry your industrial strength hairdryer if it isn't useful for either of us. I want to throw it in the dumpster to lighten our collective burden. I'm not forcing you to walk with or even near me, but I'm also not screaming at you to go away.

That's all metaphorical, by the way. I'm describing the entire socio-political apparatus using mundane terminology and real-world relationships. The Right says life is better if all the money pools and the rest of us fight over it, Marx says no matter how you look at it that fight leads to its own destruction so it's better to let material wealth go and make the best of what's available, Bottle says pay me and I'll try to do a good job but I can't make any promises.

Now, here's where it gets tough and you're going to argue. "Marxism" is nothing more than the recognition that Capitalism fails no matter which direction we take, and that we should take the direction that actually distributes the material wealth as equitably as possible, as opposed to legally because law always favors the lawmaker.

For Helmet everything was going fine (minus breaking up in 1998 and not reforming until 2003) until Interscope dropped them for low sales in 2005. He signed with Warcon but they broke contract by not actually paying their share of tour support among other things, so ownership of the album they made returned to Helmet and everything was as well as it could be. They put out 2 more albums since then and they were making a new album as of 2019 and that's as much as I know. Page makes his actual money through other projects like film music, royalties, jazz concerts, etc. Hell, I could offer to pay for the next Helmet album if I really wanted to, I'm sure he wouldn't say no right off the bat except for the fact that I can't afford to.

S: Shut up, Bottle, you're meandering.

B: No, I'm not, it's totally relevant. What part of any of that is Capitalism? The label hopping part. The part where a guy with millions of dollars pays Page to make a Helmet album and a pressing plant to make physical copies and record stores buy them to sell to me and 900,000 of my friends.

I don't have 900,000 friends, there aren't many record stores left, and there aren't any millionaires stimulating the economy by investing in a new Helmet album. I might not even buy it if they did. On the other hand, if there were some reasonable socialized system where I could submit an ongoing list of albums I wanted and they sent them to me accordingly as compensation for whatever I do, Helmet would certainly be on the list of bands I'd like my money to pay for. A Democratically Socialized music industry, it sounds ridiculous, but is the end result actually any different than walking into a record store once a paycheck and telling them exactly what you will and won't pay for? I submit that it is not, and am reasonably convinced that when properly administered the results are tangibly better than some guy in an office trying to figure out what I might buy from 3rd party internet search data. Feel free to debate.

The Lettermen – Let It Be Me

B: Alright, crew. Most ridiculous thing we could listen to after taking off our Helmets?

S: The Mississippi abortion case.

B: Oof, no. My position is already well documented. I can't do any more than I've already done.

C: The MLB lockout?

B: Double oof. No intelligent conversation to be found on either side of that one. Hard pass.

E: We could all pick a record we think you'll hate and you pick your poison?

B: Hmmmm. That has potential. Brain damage quotient is still astronomical, but at least I can educated guess in my own favor. Yeah, let's do it. On your marks, get set, scamper!

[The sounds of scampering with assorted comical banter and giggles]

S: Ok, I think we're all ready. We just grabbed whatever we found, here's 5 choices.

B: Whaddawe got? Barry Manilow? Not the worst. Anne Murray? Not great. The Statler Bothers? Might be hilarious, but very risky. Oliver Again? Tempting, but I didn't do Oliver the first time, so my standard joke won't make any sense. The Lettermen? 60s pop trio, actual hit pop songs choir style, yeah this won't hurt much at all. Go ahead and spin it.

Oh yeah. This is delightful. Granted, this is the background soundtrack to washing a sink full of dishes and occasionally petting the cat on the windowsill, but it goes down real smooth. Strong enough for a man, but Ph balanced for a woman. I could actually cheat and hear the entire record as the rearrangements of the Punk arrangements of all of these songs, but I won't. This is lovely. I don't think anyone could possibly argue that this is terrible, or annoying, or that these 3 guys are not great singers. We can just not walk down that hallway clearly labeled "Bourgeois Mythologies." Even if we did, I'd just end up asking who's being exploited here? Obviously, the law favors the lawmaker, but that doesn't affect the end result in any way I can hear. My earballs are good, but this is a retitled re-issue. Impossible to argue that effort wasn't being made in either direction. Nope, delightful. I win.

C: Well, that was underwhelming.

B: For you, maybe. I just narrowly avoided listening to a Statler Bros album. Don't let my cool, composed demeanor fool you, I'm high as a kite on a windy day right now.

Bottle and Sandra Talk for a While

We're gonna have to skip the album review tonight. I know, I know, you're all heartbroken, but 1) I'm working on a massive secret chapter about shipping insurance for the 4th book, and 2) my brain has been singing "dead butterflies" for several hours. Send your hate mail to Architects, it's their fault.

S: Bottle, I think you have a serious image problem. You're so angry about everything.

B: That's the real problem, I'm not angry. You, not you specifically Sandra, I mean the rhetorical you, think I'm angry, you think I hate everything, you think I'm a Communist, you think I'm out to destroy the world, you think I should do this or that. Where in there do I get to say anything? In fact, when have I ever done that to anyone? I say "I can do this, I can't do that, if I do that then this might happen and everyone will be unhappy so here's how I have to prevent that." I'm not sitting here waiting for someone to give me instructions, I just go do whatever the next thing is. I already know what that thing is because I think about it and plan for it.

S: But how do you know?

B: I don't. I plan for it to work, I plan for what I'll do if it doesn't work, I plan for how to prevent the next however dominoes from falling if it doesn't work, and so on. I worry about me and how it affects everyone else, not everyone else and how they affects me. You might think one or the other is selfish, but they are equally selfish in inverse proportion to each other.

I'm secretly a bleeding-heart liberal in the Capitalism sense of Liberal. I want the good parts of capitalism, I want to own the means of producing all the things people need, I want to work really hard at it and succeed, but I am deeply upset and remorseful about what I have to do to get it. I have to take advantage of good people so I can trick them into feeling like I'm one of the good guys when a real person in the real world actually said to me "you don't have a mean bone in your body" and I replied "guilty as charged." I have to push somebody out of the way to take their spot. That's a lie on top of a lie. I hate it, it makes me want to puke. So, I quit. I hand my money to people who do things that make my world more enjoyable to inhabit. Mrs. Bottle and the kidlets obviously, but musicians, artists, and writers are at the top of the list. I value music and ideas, even if not the particular noises you're making at the moment. I can't like or hate what you make unless you have the ability to make it. Either way, I'm happy you made it.

Things, machinery, toys, they're only as valuable as what you can do with them. I want to take some rich guy's money and spread it around to my friends so I can enjoy what they do. I don't need money to be happy, I need money to reward you for being awesome. The guys with all the money don't like that because it means they have to actually start spending their money for no return like I do. They want to keep it juggling for as long as possible because they don't like the way it feels to be the bad guy either. You end up forcing me to pretend to be the bad guy.

So, what I'm trying to show everybody is the actual tug of war. The money has to actually complete the figure 8. People with money have to spend it so someone else can have a turn, then they have to spend it, and on an on until the plane crashes and we have to eat our own soccer team. Best estimate is that that cycle takes about 30 years to crash. That wasn't much of a problem back when life expectancy was only 40 to 50 years, but that has grown to twice as many people living twice as long experiencing twice as many cataclysms.

Now, you're going to read that and say "that's pseudo-psychological jibber-jabber, Bottle. You're talking nonsense."

What do you think the "generation name calling is?" Baby boomers, gen x, millennials, gen z. We're rapidly approaching trying to support 5 generations of people on only two generations' worth of wealth and resources. It's not pleasant to walk down this hallway, but somewhere down at the bottom of the barrel comes this nasty little clique of Auditors whispering "just kill more people, that will solve that." Let 'em starve, make it a game, throw 'em in jail, pick an enemy and eliminate them. I've been down that hallway, I've sat in those offices, then one day I just walked away and built my own fortress of solitude. The only trouble with my design is that it's super easy to stumble in, but next to impossible to get back out. You're pretty much stuck here and I can either shove you in a bottle or let you freely wander the place.

I try not to bother the minions more than I need to; they have their own lives to live. GREGORY rampaged and ate more than his fair share, so I put a lid on him and that made things a lot nicer. Buuuut, Carl's dog isn't producing anything to shove in the tube, and I as you say have that PR problem: there's no public to relate to anymore. I'm a dying breed, the guy who wants to pay for it, the guy who will pay for it, who was paying for it. Now I have to collect it all back. The mob bosses who didn't tell me they were mob bosses are coming for my kneecaps. I having no real problem giving 'em back like Warcon gave Page back his album if that evens the score and we go our separate ways. I wanted to teach whole new generations of kids to appreciate it, after all. They aren't in the kneecap repossessing or the letting me do that business, though. They're in the die of natural causes so we can collect the insurance business; how many natural causes can we invent today?

Again, this is all metaphorical. They'd much rather my thing succeeded and I gladly paid them back. Doesn't work that way in practice. The reason it doesn't work is that nobody else is taking care of their own garbage first; they think I'm supposed to do that for them. That's a huge problem because now the titles we have on paper are opposite of how things actually work. Your piece of paper says "Boss," mine says "Minion." You don't have the foggiest idea how I do your job for you as an inconvenient interruption while I'm still doing my actual job, so reality is now the opposite.

S: Ok, ok, I think I see where this is going. We're circling back around the other side.

B: Exactly! Rhetorical You's turn is over, you cash in your chips and go back to paying for it. You can't balk halfway through the process or the car crashes start piling up behind you. You've climbed up the ladder, now you have to slide back down, not tell everyone to take a hike and go build their own playground.

S: Oh, oh! Then you go wait your turn for the swing set, then the monkey bars, then back to the slide.

B: Exactly. Obviously, we have to close down the equipment every once in a while, for repairs, and we have to be patient when it opens back up, and we have to be ok with some of our friends, or even ourselves, not wanting to wait any longer and running away to a shorter line, but we don't own the playground, and sometimes we have to share it with some other kids whose own playground burned down, and sometimes we just want to go lie down in the grass and not play at all. All that stuff is just normal stuff, and as long as the whole thing doesn't turn into everybody kicking each other in the teeth all the time then we should all just be glad that it's not raining and we get to have recess at all, 'cause some of those jerks on the school board want to tear it all down and build a strip mall or use it as a landfill for all their garbage. Now, how do you feel?

S: Good, actually. I feel like I understand you better.

B: Great! No throw it all in the garbage can because who cares? Or, we could try to use it to understand a real problem. How do you feel about mandatory insurance?

S: What? That's totally non-sequitur.

B: No, it's totally sequitur. The question of insuring your package is a microcosm of the entire global socio-economic problem. Planes crash, boats sink, frustrated Newman's chuck packages off cliffs, some jerks knowingly send broken stuff and try to blame other people for it. How do we deal with that?

S: I... I... don't know. I've never really thought about it.

B: Ok, well let's start at some starting place. Maybe not the question of whether we reserve international shipping for the cheapest cargo and manufacture the most valuable in our own country because stabilizing physical flow is super important, that's like a graduate seminar in its own right. How about a 3-pound box on delivery trucks? That's pretty easy.

S: Ok.

B: I box up a thing and hand it to a delivery driver, but it gets lost or damaged. We all do the refund/ship a new one thing like nice humans, but we always lose the cost of the replacement item and the cost of the driver's labor. Who pays that cost? I think most people would instinctively want to pinpoint blame and that person pays the additional cost. Most of the time that's actually impossible so we have to ask is it better to arbitrarily blame someone, or is it better to devise some built-in cushion for "accidents"? The answer of course depends on how big a problem it really is. A box with a coffee mug in it isn't much of a problem, but a freighter with millions of dollars worth of coffee mugs sure is.

Now, obviously, in a perfect world the guy who dropped the box says "oh crap, that was my fault, and he or his company pays the expense." That happens all the time, people are generally honest, all things considered. This leads to what should be our familiar 4-hallway atrium. 1) no plan everything is actually fine, 2) no plan, things are not fine at all, 3) yes plan, but everything is fine so we're wasting money, 4) yes plan, problems are solved by that plan and we're all as happy as possible. Make sense?

S: Sure, that makes sense.

B: Ok, well you can enter those hallways from either direction. There can be no plan and everyone knows that, or there can be no plan but everyone mistakenly thinks there is one. There can be a plan that should work but doesn't, and there can be a plan that nobody knows about, or we could just be jerks and not follow the plan 'cause it's "Grumpy Thursday." What if there is a plan that worked for a long time, but only like 1/10,000 packages gets damaged so we all decide to just not bother and buy another one?

S: Ok, now it's getting out of hand.

B: Welcome to Bottleville, population crazy old me. Let's say accidental loss or damage is frequent enough to need a plan, but nowhere near frequent enough to make buying insurance mandatory. You can choose, so you'll probably insure expensive packages and eat the cost of replacing cheap stuff.

S: Sure, that's realistic.

B: Ok, what happens to the money paid to insure packages that get there perfectly fine and don't have to be replaced?

S: Oh, *OH*! You mean is that a reward for the delivery company, or should it be returned to the person who paid for the now unneeded insurance?

B: Yes, that's exactly what I mean. That is "surplus value," and we have to redistribute it. If I don't need the insurance then I'm wasting money, but if you've intentionally tricked me into thinking I need that insurance then the referee throws the fraud flag. Hello doorway to the room where we argue about "socialism." Oh, I see they've installed a card reader to determine if I'm a consumer buying insurance as financial protection, or a business buying insurance to protect my business from disgruntled customers and/or employees. Wish real life had those, it would make things a whole lot easier. For now, though, we'll just pretend it doesn't matter and describe both sides.
Do we build this insurance into the cost of our service, or do we offer optional insurance for the consumer to decide? There's a further question about managing the insurance ourselves or outsourcing it to a 3rd party, but we're only

interested in the distribution of the surplus value. We could argue back and forth, but the real question is are we using the insurance from one customer to pay for another? Are we using the system in good faith, or are we using it as an impenetrable buffer between our business and the consumer's impression of our business? In other words, are we misappropriating unused package insurance to cover up other unrelated internal problems and artificially boost our overall profits and only paying out of pocket if we absolutely have to?

S: Holy crap, how deep is this rabbit hole?

B: Infinite. We could keep going, but I want to back up and think about the transition from one system to another. What happens when we go from no system at all to a built-in system where we keep the unused insurance as profit? The answer is exactly the same as transitioning from a competitive market to a monopoly. There is a deadweight loss to the total economy and we now have to ask how that affects the comparative value of our company in relation to all the other companies in our economic network. Our profits will go up, but the available money supply will go down and we will lose customers. Those customers may invest in our competitor who can now lower their own price across their total customer base and pull us back below prior profit levels or send us down the bankruptcy hallway. What if that happens and the loss of our entire fleet is larger than the absorption capacity of all of our competitors combined?

S: Well, I mean, you can just calculate that, right?

B: You're trying to figure out if this obvious good thing is secretly a bad thing. How confident in your own answer should you realistically be at this point? Furthermore, what's the financial impact of paying someone smarter than you to give you their educated guess? You're a moron now, so you end up electing anyone who even hints that it's way better to just have no plan at all in the first place, and we all get a little bit dumber and/or angrier.

I think you know my answer. My answer is we all learn to accept a little bit of cushion in the up-front price, return as much unused surplus value as possible, and stop treating each other like garbage.

The faster we collectively pay off my student loan debt, the faster I can go back to just handing people money I don't need because they're awesome just the way they are. You're watching me do everything I want to do within the confines of my perfectly reasonable paycheck, my refrigerator always has food in it, my cars go forward and backward, I'm not wasting money on disposable razors that end up in a landfill (I really did use hair clippers that time I shaved last Summer), and everything beyond that is a waste of good brain power. Like I said, rhetorical you needs literal me to trick you into paying me to be awesome when I'm already being as awesome as I possibly can be for free and it ends up leaving your wallet hungry, not mine. Extremely immodest, totally honest because I am perfectly happy if my level of awesome isn't good enough for you. It's more than good enough for me, so who's actually winning?

UB40 – Labour of Love

Good lord, seriously? "Unvaccination" remedies? I just can't even. All I wanted to do after last night of no power in an ice storm during potentially our last weekend inventory was enjoy a random stack of new old records. I've tried to end the Marx thing like a thousand times, but here I am holding UB40s 4th album, and it's an album of covers called Labour of Love. Why can't I stop waking up every morning?

Now, this might come as a real shock, but UB40 has been known to express a leftist opinion or two. They wanted this to be their first album, but the label said no. Now here they are with the label demanding another album like they're a hot commodity or something. UB40 has had a stable lineup and tangible success for close to 30 years, but I need to go check something, be right back... yep, their 8th album is self-titled. Ridiculous.

Also ridiculous, Communism only exists in the future. Saying The Soviet Union was a Communist Nation is absolute nonsense. What you mean is that Lenin successfully led the Bolshevik Revolution that violently seized control of the government and forcibly attempted to convert the still tangibly peasant subsistence-farming majority of the Russian population into a Capitalist society, which then passed to a State Monopoly under Stalin's unified Communist Party and politically crumbled under Gorbachev's gradual shift to Liberal political and economic policies that weakened the one-party regime. The Soviet Union was in every sense of the word a Corporation of Republics that operated under a very strict model of Socialism (which as I've pointed out is still Capitalism, but with an inversion of the distribution of surplus). We also have to remember that we abandoned Smith/Marx Classical Economics during our own Revolutionary War and France's Revolution where they executed Louis the XVI. So, you have to keep in mind that the Bolsheviks in 1917 are looking around thinking "it's like we're living in the 1700s here, c'mon people!" Lenin very much believed in Communism, but notice that he isn't calling himself that because Communism is what happens *after* we get through this Capitalism thing.

He *is* waging a truly horrible war on any peasant population he can find by forcibly taking all the food and goods they produce to feed and clothe his armies and only returning their allotted surplus which forced them to increasingly move to industrial centers exactly like every other country including us did. Gotta cram a couple hundred years of civil unrest and technological innovation into a few decades, after all; we just can't let oligarchs do it to make themselves the economic elite at the expense of the workers (which is exactly what happened when the Soviet Union fell and those business leaders with ties to former Communist officials made a fortune buying unsecured government resources whose prices hadn't yet adjusted to the wider market). The peasants fought back by growing less food and being openly hostile. Lenin and Stalin sent them to the Gulag like any other enemy of the Proletariat. If you actually go read personal accounts of people who lived there, you'll find quite a lot of people much preferred their lives under Soviet Socialism as opposed to their parents' lives as peasants or the shock of having to pay for medicine on top of rising food costs afterward, particularly the availability and freedom of choice they had in where they worked and what they actually did to earn money. A lot of people didn't like it though, and I'm not picking sides; I'm arguing about the too many contradictory meanings for the words we vomit into the ether.

    Would you look at that, we managed to actually get back to unemployment benefits. There's lots of propagandized versions of arguments about the purpose and effectiveness of unemployment benefits from all sides, but what there isn't is any argument about the actual structure of the American version. It is a corporate managed insurance system audited as part of the State budget, a completely capitalist alternative to taxation, so there's 51 of the darned things. You see, when you fire people for no reason other than you're tired of paying them they lose their source of income and often have to accept lower pay to find a new job if they are desperate. That makes lots of things worse for everyone except the guy who gets to keep that money and yell at everyone else to work harder.

Labour of Love is much like David Bowie's Pin Ups (which I totally skipped when doing his entire discography), these were songs that meant something to them as Reggae when they were kids. Colin Irwin says it's beautiful and comparing these versions to the originals misses the point, Christgau says it really does grow on you after repeated listens, Bottle points out that they had just obtained the means of production in the form of their own studio so they felt happy, relaxed, and free to experiment while also feeling pressured to churn out albums for their label/owners (that's Socialism inside a Capitalism bubble if you're trying to keep track of it all like their labels certainly are). You see, "the economy" is just the data collected from business deals, not the actual business, and whoever it is who actually interprets that data is "the government." Actually, an Auditor goes through it first and the government makes decisions based on the filtered version of the results from it, but that's a bit fussy. The point is that there are governments who tell you what they are doing and governments who don't; I much prefer the former.

The UBs are telling me to shut up. These were Reggae songs some kids loved back before using Reggae as a political statement was even a thing, just pure love of the music. They honestly had no idea Neil Diamond wrote Red Red Wine. The artwork has some shrapnel in its eye, but we'll accept the naivete for the wink they say it is. These are mostly all love songs of one form or another, it's street party dance music, and it's fun. It is. I like it a lot.

Architects – For Those that Wish To Exist

Welp, I tried. I really did. But arguing is the least productive human activity and I'm a lean into it kind of guy, so guess we're going to listen to the entire For Those That Wish To Exist album by Architects while synopsizing the conceptual problem we're having living in the middle of the story Marx used to explain the entire history, present, and future of humans. You see, you can't actually argue for or against Marxism without accidentally folding through the 4th dimension and becoming Marxist. The harder you argue the more Marxist you become. We all fall in parallel.

Why did this coincidence happen? I dunno, Madam Coincidence does what she does. Dan Searle says "this album was me looking at our inability to change to a way of life that would sustain the human race and save the planet...." Looking in the mirror, personal responsibility, the culture of "wanting someone else to deal with it." See? Creepy, isn't it? I'm putting no effort into it at all. It's not really surprising, though. No matter how much architecture you try to build on top of it, it's all just an elaborate attempt to run away from death.

DS: I just want to live and die in peace.

Me too, Dan. Not a fan of p(nmi)t's dead butterfly album either. Washed my hands of it in the 3rd book, even.

So, if you've been really reading, you'll know that I've raised 3 objections to Marx. 1) you don't logically have to believe his story, 2) he did a bad job of explaining that you can't make it happen on an arbitrary timetable, and 3) Marxist thought is itself essentially a religion with a preconditional origin mythology. Lenin and Stalin truly believed they could accelerate their country through the whole crappy Capitalism part as quickly as possible. He also didn't really explain that none of his ideas had anything to do with the accumulation of wealth itself beyond recognizing that you can't create material wealth without exploiting the labor that creates it. "The means of production" is technologically assisted human labor. There is a grain of truth to the argument that "nobody gets rich," but that's only because there isn't any money or even a need for money anymore. It's a nonsense argument, is what I'm saying.

"The fiction that I'm living in says I should pull the pin." I don't for one millisecond believe that Dan Searle reads much Marx or Lenin for fun in his spare time, and he certainly wasn't reading my facebook posts in early 2020 while writing the album. Although, I did sell a few copies in England so that's a ridiculously hilarious conspiracy theory I just invented.

So, what is the mythology from which Marxist thought originates? It is simply this: there was a before Economics, there is now Economics, and there will be an after Economics. Economics, much like Pop, will eat itself.

Now, that's a pretty tough pill to swallow at first. It sounds wackadoodle because it is. Not irredeemable, but silly without the added notion that systems create their own Truth rather than emulating an objective one. We just have to accept that it's impossible to imagine a world without some underlying mythology to justify its own existence, because you can't unthink it without a lot of collateral brain damage.

A common misconception is that Marxism equals poverty. That's ridiculous because Marxist economics is just Classical Economics with actual Christmas bonuses as opposed to Jelly of the Month clubs. Marxism proper equals ensuring the baseline of subsistence is met for the entire population before we start handing out bonuses at all. Remember that this baseline subsistence is predicated on showing up to work and actually doing something productive every day. You can choose to stay home and starve if you want to, but that seems pretty counterintuitive if you ask me. Also remember that the three pages of The Wealth of Nations I could stomach to read contained an explicit defense of the Welfare State. You can't argue out of that one, Smith says 50% unemployment with no access to book learnin' is still better than not living in Western Europe. A hundred years later watching people still dumping chamber pots out their windows, Marx called shenanigans.

Now don't get me wrong, being a successful Capitalist is tangibly more physically comfortable than being a homeless bum, at least I think that's the technical term for "unsuccessful capitalist." You could of course choose to be a rich homeless bum like Elon Musk, but that seems unnecessarily stupid. I only say that to point out that the opposite is even more ridiculous, a rich guy borrowing money to pay for some idiotic vacation. Capitalism gives two thumbs up to both those things: "I invented Clear Cola; everybody loves it so that definitely deserves an all-expenses paid trip to the Galapagos to shoot penguins. It's not like I can just hand all of my employees an extra $50 this week because I feel like it, it wouldn't be fair to the ship's crew or the penguins.

Man, this album is lovely. I was honestly expecting a lot more Metalcore from a Metalcore band, but traces of Industrial, Emo, EDM, and Arena Rock, this is complex and quite frankly refreshing.

Here's the thing about Marx, and yes I know I've hammer-and-sickled this to a pulpy mush, he says "look, there's normal life and that's normal, but as soon as you separate the labor from the product of that labor, the guy who made it is stuck with less money than it costs to buy a new one from himself. How many toasters do you need to make to earn enough money to buy the toaster you just made? This, by the way, is the point where Proudhon stands up and yells "property is theft!" He means private capital property, not personal property.

All well and good, but we don't have any actual numbers to evaluate the situation. All we have is a predetermined cost of manufacturing, a guesstimate of the final selling price, and no idea what actually happens to the surplus value. All we know is that two groups of people walk out of the same factory. One group is dirty, tired, and grumpy, the other is clean, expensively dressed, and pleased as punch. Follow them home and the shiny happy people live in huge mansions in gated communities while the dirty grumpy people live in rundown neighborhoods, apartment buildings, trailer parks. Seems a bit suspicious, if you ask me.

Anywho, we have to ask two important questions. Do you work in Richard Corey's factory and curse the life you're living? Or, do you own your own factory and try to put him out of business? What if the answer is neither?

Can you hear them? Just stomping and jittering and ruckusing about like squirrels in a place where you don't want squirrels. Auditors. All they do is count, and recount, but who's paying them, so now we can't even be sure they're doing a good job.

Then the temptation is just too much. One little aspiring painter gets madder and madder and that one nasty little Auditor in the corner whispers "pick a problem and kill it." All of a sudden, it's Marx vs Hitler with little old Liberal America sliced right in two.

Now, I know this is all confusing, and that's because everybody likes to use words that get people to think they agree with you and ignore what you're actually doing. Well, no secrets here, I'm doing a Marxist reading of the history of albums by listening to them.

Marxism is an analytical methodology that seeks to explain its subject in terms of the real-world forces and architecture that force people to act in a certain way. Marx's own primary subject was Capitalism: how it works, what it does, where it will lead, what we can or cannot control about it; mine is the recorded music industry. I personally think the music industry has already gone through its capitalist mode of production (music being produced for the sole purpose of selling it as a commodity), musicians collectively own the means of production, and we are once again producing and supporting music for its consumptive value. We are, in essence, back in the pre-capitalist state of complete musical freedom. There is no hierarchy of musical classes exploiting each other, no one type of music is better than another, and all that is lacking is a wider industrial willingness to make an equivalent trade for our efforts. Some amount of music must be equal to some amount of food, clothing, shelter, appreciation. It's not about competition, it's about value. Give music back its actual value, not merely use it to accumulate money at the expense of all our hard work.

Billy Joel – The Nylon Curtain

B: Hahahahaha! Wowzers, that's a title. I just love Billy Joel; I didn't think it would be relevant.

S: A strange and complicated man once told us "it's all relevant."

B: I'm not complicated, ideas are. But it is true that it depends on which hallway you're walking. We tripped over Gorbachev and now here's Billy Joel's critique of the Reagan Era, very pointedly titled The Nylon Curtain.
Did you know this is his favorite of his own albums? He put way more effort into this one than anything before it. A motorcycle crash was involved, but that's less important. The album itself is a collage of criticisms surrounding the death of the American Dream, summarized here as the assurance of a life as good or better than your parents had. You know, work hard and prosper. Even a poor scholar of Vulcan logic can tell you it sure doesn't look that way when the steel mills are closing, men and women can't seem to love each other, Vietnam Vets are just kind of swept under the rug and ignored, everybody's on hard drugs, and the only official response to all of it is "worship America, we're number 1."
Wanna talk about PR problems? How do you spin the blatant and obvious discrepancy between being told a story and watching reality not work that way at all?

I think Billy Joel is onto something here. Not about the Capitalism v Socialism crap, about the Baby Boomer generation as a whole. Kids born after WWII Kai Ryssdoled the numbers and said "yeah, this isn't gonna work for the vast majority of us because you aren't handing us enough money to pay for all the collateral damage. You're only handing us enough money to take care of one or the other, and just barely at that.

That's not an economic problem, that a social problem caused by economic manipulation. That problem is not caused by the government, that problem is caused by the Bourgeoisie desperately trying to not slide down the slide.

Before you get all angry and the spittle starts spraying, what am I really talking about? I'm talking about the logical contradiction between the idea that the wealthiest individuals should be privately making all the economic decisions that affect our lives and the reality that they aren't going to do anything that knowingly lowers their bank account balance.

So, the question morphs into is this album only good because Reaganism wasn't working for the vast majority of people? Some people are likely to say that Billy Joel made millions of dollars, but those millions are the spare change from someone else's billions and he spends them paying his employees to build boats and motorcycles while pointing out that he had his turn and he is not the vast majority of people. Marx would of course argue that that is the inherent conservative bias of Capitalism and Billy Joel would probably for the most part agree. His argument, after all, is where's the orchestra, and it musically circles right back around to Allentown.

And at this point you can say "ok, I misunderstood the situation. I get it, I realize that this is just one little piece of the larger puzzle, and I can appreciate that, but the question still stands, where's the orchestra? Those are the chairs they sit in, and they are empty."

The Cars – Candy-O

You know what doesn't have war or death or exploitation or economics? The Cars' sophomore album Candy-O. It doesn't have some important letter ems either, and that needs some explanation.

I'm absolutely convinced he meant "cadmium car" in Shoo Be Doo and "germanium lover" in The Dangerous Type because I don't think "cadium" is actually a word at all and she definitely doesn't seem like the kind of girl who waters the "geraniums" on her front porch. This album is about a pinup girl named Candy-O who loves cruising around looking for nighttime excitement in her futuristic and definitely made out of metal automobile, leaving Rik to desperately try to keep up.

They scrapped all the leftovers from the first album and said "maybe let's tone down the multi-tracked vocals and over production for this one." It's thin and quirky, youthful but not juvenile. A lot of people didn't like it, but more people did and I gotta say it's a fantastic sounding album for its obvious concept. The keyboards and sound effects are ridiculous, the guitars are totally raunchy, the beats are frantic, and Rik has the quintessential New Wave out of his depth vocal style. It sounds like my astigmatism exacerbating the flashing neon lights on a rainy night driving through the city, so that's fun.

It's way better than Heartbeat City, but I will cop to agreeing that it isn't as exciting as their first. Elektra wanted to shelve it for a while, but they said "hell no, why you trying to hold us back? It's what we made, publish the thing already!" It certainly doesn't sound like it needed more time in the incubator, it's not actually missing anything in terms of instrumentation or arranging, and if anything, it's actually a bit weirder than the first album. Not as weird as Panorama, but there's a lot of clearly improvised keyboards and futuristic (for the time) noises. You could probably be "meh" on a song or two, but as an overall album it's stellar. I love The Cars anyway, but Candy-O's album value would be pretty much inarguable even if I didn't. Delightful.

UB40 – Little Baggariddim

Little Baggariddim, not to be confused with the actual LP Baggariddim or the 2021 Bigga Baggariddim, is a UB40 EP featuring 2, count 'em 2, versions of the mortal Sonny Bono classic I Got You Babe. Sorry, that was uncouth. I'm dropping ems like Rik Ocasek now. See how I borrowed the "im-" for the next sentence. How droll of me.

People often say UB40 and The Specials are the same band, but other than being from the same place and time, both mixed race bands expressing Socialist views at a time when conservative racist policies were rising to political power, and not at all beating around the Thatch about it, I disagree. The Specials merged Punk and Ska to create Two-Tone while UB40 is straight Reggae/Dub. Image-wise similar, music-wise incredibly different.

I don't think any sane person is gonna run out onto the streets or the rooftops to loudly pretend that I Got You Babe is one of the greatest songs a human brain ever wrote, but I definitely like this version with Chrissie Hynde better than the original. It's syrupy and sweet as opposed to silly and ditzy, plus the pun works perfect.

You might say "Bottle, why are there so many albums that are just reworked versions of their own songs with various guest performers? That seems kinda lame."

What are you, some kinda jerk? It's not lame at all. Jamaican music culture is fascinating and I definitely recommend reading about it on your own, I'm just gonna skim the parts that are relevant for UB40. We're talking actual parties with actual DJs spinning records, toasting over the musical interludes, building their own sound systems, searching for rare and new records that other DJs don't have or know about, trying out potential singles to see how the crowd reacts before investing in thousands of copies, getting bands to make special and exclusive versions of songs to stand out, using their equipment to overdub and mess around with the recordings by cutting the vocals or adding reverb.

So, Dub as a genre is essentially the "riddim" of the song with prominent drum and bass and no vocals. The last track is their Dub version of I Got You Babe. The best song is by far One In Ten. I don't need to dissect it; it speaks for itself. If you only want to hear one real UB40 song, make it that one.

I do have to dissect the prominence of Reggae in popular music though. It's pretty common to raise an eyebrow at UB40, Shaggy, Snow, I was even on the fence about Fire From The Gods if you recall. There are large populations of Jamaicans in the US, the UK, and Canada because Jamaica's switch from slave plantations to subsistence farming to national independence from the British Empire happened rather quickly and lots of people left looking for better international opportunities. But, that means there's no shortage of non-Jamaicans puttin' on the patois. Most of them did have an honest appreciation for the music and the leafy greens and honestly wanted to popularize the music, but if you can name any names other than Bob Marley and Jimmy Cliff I'll be really surprised. UB40 is inarguably less cringeworthy than most because you can hear they mean it rather than trying to make it a surprise gimmick.

I think we all learned something in there somewhere, tomorrow's album should be a total non-sequitur, if I know me.

The 5th Dimension – The Magic Garden (gets some 70-degree December thunderstorms for some reason)

And just when you least expect it, I'll pull it out and you'll all knowingly wink because you're in on it. Did you forget? I specifically told you don't forget. What am I going to do with you guys? I give up.

As is often the case, I coincidentally ended up ending this batch of records acquired when I had to go have my tooth removed, no that's not right, oh yeah when I finally decided I couldn't expound upon Marx any more than I already have, on the night of a major storm. Uncanny. Even better, it's The Magic Garden, the sophomore concept album from the 5th Dimension. With the exception of one track left over from Up Up and Away, it's a semi-autobiographical tale about Jimmy Web and Susan Horton. Spoiler alert, they eventually break up.

The allmusic review is harsh. It basically says "Nick Drake loved this album, so a bunch of Nick Drake fans are gonna buy up all the used copies and return them a few days later." Oof, heartless. I'm still on the comedown from Reggae versions of a Sonny and Cher song, so this is downright sophisticated and romantic. Why in the world would anyone feel compelled to compare this to Brian Wilson's dad's least favorite Beach Boys album? It's probably because both albums have that annoying hit single that shouldn't be there, not because the entire animal population of Bottleville is currently inside the Bunker of Beef rather than outside: the covers of Ticket to Ride on this album and Sloop John B on Pet Sounds.

The sitar on this album is way better than either The Rascals, the Stones, or The Incredible String Band, I can tell you that much. And just like that the storm has passed, we're good. Now, please excuse me as I continue to enjoy this delightful album of psychedelic pop-soul and hope that everyone east of me has an equally uneventful/delightful experience. May your power stay on long enough to enjoy the whole thing as the staycation from going back to work tomorrow it really is. Cheers.

Pearl Jam – Gigaton

B: Hey guys, guess what? I started a group on facebook.

S: Chocoholics anonymous?

E: The non-ideologically aligned lefty anarchist's soup recipe club?

C: The John Candy appreciators club?

B: Canadian national treasure, if you ask me, but no. My epic imagination muscle had a cramp, so it's underwhelmingly titled Bottle's Album Club, but my real friends all joined, so raspberries to you guys. What should we listen to to kick it off?

S: Bottle, honey, we don't actually care.

C: I care a little, but not enough to pick an album.

B: Harsh. What is wrong with all of you? Fine, I've been meaning to check out Pearl Jam's latest album, Gigaton. Here we go.
Off to a great start. Op! I found Waldo. See, Eddie Vedder has this interesting habit of pronouncing random words wrong on every album. Right in the middle of Superblood Wolfmoon, the word is "danger" but he is clearly saying "deenger" with a hard G.

First 3 tracks are fantastic brain bashing rock'n'roll. Then we morph into some kind of electronic thing, but it's cool.

What the hell is Buckle Up? Then Comes and Goes. We turned into a sketchy alleyway all of a sudden. Actually, bed sores and vivisection are much more normal fare for Pearl Jam than the bizarre half Rock half electronica of the first half with werewolves and guys filing their dicks and running away from all the terrible stuff Trump did. Oh, hi Greta. Yeah, polar bears and stuff.

Don't get me wrong, I'm on Eddie's side on all of it, it's just what the hell kind of genre is River Cross? Doom organ and tom toms?

Ok, this is a 3-act thing. It's straight rock, then electronica sort of and some more rock, then track 9 just smacks you with a frying pan and he says "horm" instead of harm, and that's the least insane thing about the last four tracks.

I realize it's hard to bargle nawdle zous with all those marbles in your mouth, but what the hell is going on? The queen of collections? You mean Garbage Lady? I made her up just to have somebody to talk to about Warren Buffett. "It's gonna take much more than ordinary love...," ok you got me there, I made that a real point of interest along the tour; insulted Des'ree and everything. Yeah, the river of doom gets wider no matter where you cross. Clearly, we're connecting to the same zeitgeist, and I know I've skipped 2 decades of albums, but how is the last 66% of this Pearl Jam? Way to go 2020, even Eddie Vedder can't do a good job of describing how terrible you were.

I can't really call this a bad album, per se. It has structure, we're all noticeably different people by the end, it's all interesting, but it's freakin' weird. You know what it's like? It's like Pearl Jam started to make a Pearl Jam album, then wrote some demos for a Bjork collaboration that never happened, then just shrugged and said "meh, it's 2020, who cares?" I do find myself repeatedly listening to songs and wanting them to grow on me, but I lived it too so all I can really say is "yeah, that was 2020. Started out strong, frying pan to the noggin, wish we weren't caught in the toilet flush of history.

No, it won't hold us down, but we're still in the middle of it so share all the light you want, we still have to get past the next round of terrible candidates before the round after that. I'm done, I'm just rambling, man this is a downer of an album. Not bad, but underwhelming. I feel like it won't age very well at all, and that's a shame. Oh well, won't let it get us down. Just have to try something else tomorrow.

doubleVee

Today we're fully enjoying both kooky albums from doubleVee (Allan and Barb Vest). If Pop-cabre were a genre, that's what I'd call it. I'm a huge fan of Starlight Mints so it's pure delight to hear Allan's eclectic orchestration and downright catchy melodies in any context. Go give The Moonlit Fables of Jack the Rider and/or Songs for Birds and Bats a listen.

Doublevee.bandcamp.com

Oh Crap... a 4th Book

C: Hey Bottle, guess what.

B: Chi...cken...butt??

C: Nonono, we've officially recouped the expense of the first book.

B: So, you're saying my joke wasn't just a clairvoyant marketing gimmick?

C: No, I'm saying it only took 3 books worth of work to pay for the first book worth of work.

B: But correct me if I'm wrong, I'm still the expense of 2 books in the hole.

C: Well, yeah, I mean there is that, but you put less time, effort, and investment into each successive one, so the karma kind of works if you squint just right.

B: Fair rebuttal.

CSN&Y – So Far

I've been here many times before, and nope I have no idea just what to do. I'm not at all happy I experienced today. What's going on is that I'm just gonna listen to this ingeniously titled greatest hits of hippy Leftist Lumpenproletariat who don't care much about violent revolution, they mostly just want to be left alone to live their lives in peace, helplessly hoping to raise their children and not get shot by the National Guard for protesting expanding our engagement in a proxy war not officially called a war.
May I have some of those purple berries?

Bottle Has A Bit Of A Breakdown

It occurs to me that there is a significant difference between "individuals own the means of production" and "an individual owns the means of production."

The former would imply that each person has the means and knowledge to produce what is needed and exchange it with others for mutual benefit. This is, I think, what most Americans have in mind when they think of what America calls Capitalism.

The latter, however, appears to be the prevailing reality in which an individual controls not simply his own life and labor, but the entire economic life of a community. In short, a monopoly, a monarchy, a dictatorship. This is obviously what most people find unacceptable and oppressive.

I'm reminded of the story of Putin's car. Not that this has anything to do with Putin, I just recently came across it and it's just a good illustration of the dynamics at play. After he left the KGB and the Soviet Union collapsed, Putin owned a personal car. In addition to driving his friends and family around to where they needed to go (the obvious result of being the only person with a car) he also occasionally "bombed," aka illegally acted like a taxi for money.

You can look at that situation in many different ways. At face value it seems ludicrous for that to be a crime. On the other hand, if enough individuals start doing it then it will economically impact both "real" taxi drivers and any form of public transportation. What distinguishes those two situations? The answer is of course taxation.

Keep in mind, we are thinking about honest systems where supply and demand are inverse equivalents; the demand for the service is equal to the demand to provide that service. In reality, these inversions are often unequal, and that ever-changing inequivalence is what drives price fluctuations.

So, taxation both legitimizes the profession itself and stabilizes the economic exchange such that those who wish to drive a bus or taxi are less susceptible to varying demand; for example, a bus driver isn't paid according to the number of passengers, rather according the overall economic value of public transportation in relation to all of the alternative modes of transportation. Taxes in this sense being used to save and subsidize appropriately.

I mention all of that to underline the real dynamics at play when we consider the difference between a private individual owned business and a corporate government run business because that difference is not as straightforward as most people think.

Logically, not everyone can be a full-time bus driver; there would be no passengers to necessitate busses, or busses would be the only type of vehicle anyone could manufacture.

Equally logical, imagining a Governor running the public transportation system is no different than any other individual running it, except that a Governor has theoretically more power, influence, and resources to use and/or abuse at his or her discretion. Pardon the pun, that's not our bus stop. All it tells us is that structurally speaking a Governor and a Mob boss are pretty much the same. Can you really say that the people who loved Pablo Escobar loved him less than the people who loved Lenin or Reagan? Likewise, for those who loathed them.

No, what we're really thinking about is the distinction between an abstract system of rules vs individual discretion. Is a corrupt legislature any different than a malevolent tyrant? Are the rules if practiced in good faith an adequate regulator of the game, or is every meeting between heads of state merely an exercise in determining whether or not to send our respective armies out to kill each other tomorrow?

Well, we need to address this bizarre concept of a "free market" that has somehow blurred the distinction between a monarch and a squabbling group of wannabe monarchs; the idea of Liberalism being simultaneously championed by the would-be kings who then decry the process the moment one emerges victorious. There is no market, it exists only in the past as recorded and interpreted data and in the future as the hypothetically speculated change of that interpretation; more specifically how that interpretation will change with the accumulation of new data. What we are really contemplating is the nature of economic freedom. Who benefits from an enforced general ignorance of socio-economic activity and who benefits from a codified system of stable relationships? The answer, not surprisingly, is the same in both cases: he who owns the product of production.

Let's put that into a real-life situation. Insulin. Does the total production of insulin belong to the kings and queens who own its manufacture? Does it belong the people who need insulin to stay alive? Or, a third more difficult to grasp possibility, does the production/manufacture actually belong to the balance of the exchange itself? I think this is the real answer, though it is very hard to conceptualize. Actually, achieving the balance between need and fulfillment without unduly burdening either side should be our goal.

Capitalism, for all the good it *can* do, has the very real downside that only the most popular (not the best, not the most valuable in terms of money or equivalence) will survive until the next popular thing comes along.

This is just my personal opinion, but a government that refuses to take on that responsibility is just as bad as a government that misappropriates its resources. In other words, a government should not make the rules to suit some ulterior motive. Instead, it must hold itself accountable to the resources it manages and we must be completely uncompromising in "unelecting" any representative who misunderstands that responsibility as a personal success.

Which brings me to this non-sequitur, how did Republicanism morph from Left-wing to Right-wing? How did Thomas Paine, for example, morph from the reviled and ostracized Leftist defender of the French and American Revolutions, whom Teddy Roosevelt called a "filthy little atheist," the New York Times called a Socialist, whose complete works were published by the Communist Party in 1937, and cited by Eugene Debs in his sedition trial, praised by freakin' Marx who I've been talking about ad nauseam, and secretly but documentedly admired by Lincoln, turn into the go to guy for Reagan and Glenn Beck? Reagan was a union boss before becoming Governor then President and abandoning any sense of logical reality, by the way.

Come to think of it, how is Putin the former KGB agent who quit over how mad he was at the attempted coup of Gorbechev's liberalism a more understandable evil Capitalist than any of our billionaires?

Look, I'm fully willing to admit that I have no idea what's going on, but doesn't that really mean everyone out there is an actual lunatic? Am I the only weirdo left on earth with a dictionary in my house? Left is Right and up is down like that super annoying Marble Madness level I could never beat, and I'm supposed to give a crap?

In fact, the more I read that dictionary, the more I give up. I need a 1990s English to 2020s Gibberish translation manual. Sam Kinison impression on 3,2,1...

AHHHHHHHHHHHHHHHHHHHHHHHHHHHHH
HHHHHHHHHHHHHHHHHHHHHHHHHHHHHH
HHHHHHHHHHHHHHHHHHHHHHHHHHHHHH
HHHHHHHHHHHHHHHHHHHHHHHHHHHHHH
HHHHHHHHHHHHHHHHHHHHHHHHHHHHHH
HH!!!!!!!!!!!

Soundgarden – Down On The Upside

S: Gladys, I'm worried about Bottle.

G: Deary, dear. That's not true at all, now, is it? You're worried about the parts of you that depend on Bottle.

S: What?! How can you-

G: Missy, don't you start with me, I was old and mean before you were even a clump of spit and stardust. Like I've told you a thousand times, you can't predict the future if you don't even know which hallway you're following. Now, close your eyes and imagine everything is opposite. How did we get here and where has it led?

S: Deja vu. We've been here before. And he fell through the hole in his own pocket and oh... I think I know...

G: Flip that around...

S: oh, oh! I know, I know! I know what album we'll listen to tonight. Yes, I'm sure of it.

G: Good, now just you worry about you. Bottle takes care of himself, and you can't help by taking that away from him. You help by doing what you do....

[Meanwhile, in Bottle's office]

B: [thud] why do I keep waking up? [thud] I don't wanna be the highlander [thud] I don't like what you got me hanging from...

Inevitable, really. Yesterday made that clear, we're Down on the Upside.
It's just so dumb and pointless. I know you don't know what I'm talking about, I know you don't have any idea how it relates to a Soundgarden album. I mean, really this is the best depiction of inhabiting your own mind I can think of. It's one of my favorite albums in the universe.

If nothing else, we should all understand this album for what it is. Soundgarden spent a couple months self-producing their 5th album in their real-life friend Stone Gossard's recording studio. It is all over the place, but I can't think of a single thing that's missing or here when it shouldn't be. It definitely qualifies as a total work of art in my book.

It may not make me want to blow up the outside world any less, but as a momentary force field against the Auditors of Imagination you're gonna have a hard time getting me to take off the headphones for the full 66 minutes. Nigh on impossible, I'd say.

Post Updown Sideways

And just like that, I'm stage right as rain. Up on the downside? It's hard being the only practitioner of Bottleism, mostly because it's so hard to think while talking to myself.

I suppose you can blame Ozzy Osbourne's No More Tours Tour for that. Maybe it was No More Tours Tour 2, I dunno. I am of course referring to seeing the news that the student loan interest deferral has been pushed back to May instead of a couple weeks from now. Crazy considering I got the email that the transfer from Navient to whothehellever was finalized yesterday or the day before or whatever. It's like Gladys said, you have to know which hallway you're walking which direction. I'm sure I mentioned in writing that sound travels freely down here. Compy for the confirmation...

C: It just so happens I read that second book recently, and yes that's exactly what you said.

B: Ok, good, glad I'm not crazier than the crazy I fully admit to being.

Now, we're halfway through this 4th book and I'm out of records. That's a lie of course, I just don't feel like listening to a lot of them at the moment. Logically we should find an Ozzy or Black Sabbath album to listen to while I logorhate all over the ethersphere; roll your own.

Look, I didn't grow up in Soviet Russia or newly Republicanized Iceland like Björk (she says it rhymes with "jerk" in case you didn't know), and I don't have any firsthand experience with being in "government," but I do have a fair bit more than professional experience being me. I'm the leading world expert, you might say. Stoic Skepticism. I neither believe in absolute knowledge, nor care much about the whimsical oscillations of pleasure and pain. Que será será, except of course that it's not in any way mandatory. Nothing *has* to be the way it is, and you certainly don't have to believe it if you don't want to.

I choose to view life as an endless series of smashing your face against the wall because that's what people seem to want to build. What I've noticed is that other people seem to be very confused as they watch me just walk through them, or around them. None of that garbage actually affects me, it affects other people who then freak out and infiltrate my secret lair of minding my own business.

The saving grace at the moment is that most of the Republican legislation being drafted is deposited directly into a garbage can, but sadly the Democrats aren't making any headway because they aren't writing any legislation and when they do, they vote against it because it isn't mildly left of hard right enough.

This might sting a lot, but Biden isn't Left, Sanders isn't Left, Alexandria Ocasio-Cortez isn't Left. Same argument I've been making all along. How can you be a Capitalist if you don't own a factory and employ thousands of workers both in house and by proxy? You can't, that's the definition of Capitalism.

What's the real issue here? Well, us people can't pay our debts without money, and we can't get money without being taxed by the same people who handed it to us. If the government pays that debt, I owe the income tax on 200,000. I don't feel like actually doing math so let's go overboard and say 40% effective tax rate. That's 80,000 due the next time April rolls around. I currently have 10,000 of that. So yeah, not good. What's the opposite, no income tax and no payoff? How would that help? The answer is that both things have to happen simultaneously, or the whole thing really does have to crash into a pile of rubble. Is the outcome actually any different in either direction? Does it actually matter if you intentionally or negligently drive your car off the cliff?

If you've read this far, you're probably wondering where this hallway is going. I don't know. I do know the next room is all about how the roles get switched when you're actually out here living it.

Just to show a baseline let's say the money supply (aka national debt) averages 30,000 per person. How do you create one legitimate billionaire, a person who actually possesses a billion dollars? Well, you can take away 33,333.33 peoples' money. You could take 333.33 dollars from 3 million people and leave them with an average of 29,666.66 each. 10 billionaires? 20? 30?

I'm just a regular schmuck on the street, the only money I have access to is the money that trickled down from some billionaire. It doesn't matter what I think or feel or want or hope for, I have to wake up and put on pants and go do whatever it is that makes a person with more money than me more money than that so they'll hand me some of it. Does it matter if that person is nice or terrible? Sure, of course it matters, but only if you actually have the ability to choose, and again only if consistently choosing to associate with the nice people lowers the number of terrible people. I worry that it actually increases the number of terrible people.

At the end of the day, all decisions are made by the person who decided them based on the known and unknown consequences. I can't do anything about it, there's like 98 degrees of Kevin Bacons between me and the President, and I'd be willing to bet close to 94 of them don't want to be the person who decides anything. If I wanted to waste the time and energy to write them a letter it would really just say "do it or don't, you wanted to be in charge so you get the responsibility of being in charge. You're allowed to quit as far as I'm concerned. In the meantime, I have a building full of chicken poop to shovel."

My opinion has always been, and probably always will be, we don't need a centralized governmental authority making poorly informed laws that do nothing. Instead, we need people who will do what they say they are going to do and clean up the mess afterward. You don't need 47 pieces of paper and 12 initials after your name on a cheap plaque on an expensive door; the results should speak for themselves.

It's not a governor's or mayor's job to tell us how to live our lives, it their job to make sure that some jerk doesn't sell us a monorail we don't need then tear down our houses to build it.

The Mombums of Bottlemas

Ghost – Prequelle

B: Alright, look. I did the first Christmas in good faith. I made a valiant effort on the second one before intentionally picking a different hallway. This year we do Christmas my way.

E: What does that entail, exactly?

B: First I'm gonna brew up some prequels of this Venom from Mean Bean Coffee Company in Edmond, OK. Then I'm gonna pour it into this really nice insulated stainless-steel mug with a silicon lip that someone clearly misspelled "Bottle" all over, and then we're gonna do the Mombums of Bottlemas (the 3 random albums my mom bought me, she's pretty awesome).

Ooh, delightful. I haven't had good coffee in quite a while, so my palate is in very bad shape. I definitely get apple, though, it's unmistakable. Now we listen to them in the order they were opened, and first up is Ghost's Prequelle.
Not gonna lie, I've kinda always agreed with Kerry King in that I love everything about Ghost except the actual songs I've heard. Totally not fair, so we'll give it the old "oh god don't clean out your ears with cotton swabs" and appreciate it for the post-ironic satire I'm certain it is supposed to be. Do I need to do the whole image gimmick rundown?

S: No, I think everyone is as familiar with Ghost as they are ever going to be.

B: Thank goodness, 'cause I lost interest after the 3rd incarnation of Dead Pope they elected, so I don't much care that this is the first one where we know it's Swedish musician Tobias Forge. It's their 4th album, so we got that intellectual time space wormhole to wrestle with, not to mention the castle has wings and that guy on the horse in one of the 5 places you might find him on your copy doesn't seem to think anything is out of the ordinary here, so let it roll. Nope, first we'll restart this antiquated 20th-century circuit box.

Oh, creepy children singing some version of ring around the plague victim, and yep that sounds like Ghost, and blech yep that's Tobias. He is not a bad singer at all, it's the juxtaposition of metal with Paul Simon-esque vocals that melts my synapses. It's a case of just the wrong vocalist. I'm trying, but it's so jarring I can't get past it.

Just so we're clear, I'm wrong. This is great, I just don't enjoy hearing it. Will 37 listens over the next few years change that? Almost certainly, this is what we call an acquired taste. He's like a bizarro Disney tween villain going through that awkward phase of grappling with the confusing emotions of crushing on the ghoul next door, but knowing it will never work out because you have to grow up and inherit your dad's dumb satanic papacy when he retires, and you'd just have to feed them to the three-headed hell frog, so what's the point?

No, see, I love everything about ghost except the vocals, and that's not fair. Inverse of James Seals, whose voice I'm fine with but whose lyrics I hate.

Sax solo?

"I wanna bewitch you in the moonlight." I giggled at that one. I'm a sucker for terrible puns, and that's a great one.

K, it's growing on me. It is funny. If Pro Memoria doesn't leave you rotfl-ing, then I don't know what to tell you. I'm dying here, it's hysterical. Yeah, I'm hooked. I need to relisten to it a few times, but I'm laughing so hard my eyes are watering. You have to go cold-listen to Pro Memoria, at the very least.

It really does remind me of Type O Negative, or Alkaline Trio. Not that it sounds anything like either, it's the understated deadpan hilarity of it all.

And track 9, Helvetesfönster is musically hilarious. It translates as "hell window," but it refers to the side cleavage of medieval dresses.

So, you have to think of this album in the proper context. Take the abundance of celebrities (especially musicians) dying over the last 3 years, and compare that to the plague. Every morning you wake up and you're just stepping over dead rotting corpses all day, and you're keenly aware that everyone you talk to or know could just be dead tomorrow and ultimately you get to the question "would you really want to live forever?" No part of that on its own is funny at all, the humor comes from trying to hold it all in your mind at the same time as a conscious experience. I can't, I just end up laughing. Actual death is sad, it hurts, we all have the same gaping wounds but we keep walking around treating each other like garbage in a desperate attempt to avoid that sadness and hurt. Just don't.

I'm not saying it's fun all the time, and I'm not saying you won't do a miserable job of it, but I am saying that in my experience it's much better to treat everyone like they're making the best choice they can from an endless assortment of terrible options and the best thing you can do is to make the part of their day you inhabit as pleasant as possible. Memento mori; remember we must die.

Joe Bonamossa – Tour de Force

On the second day of Bottlemas the Momler sent to me, a Joe Bonamassa CD.

Tour de Force: Live in London at Royal Albert Hall, to be exact. He was a legit child prodigy and was gigging by the time he was 11, toured as the opening act for BB King when he was 12, and puts out all his music on his own label.

This series is mildly insane. It's 4 concerts at 4 venues with different personnel and slightly different set lists published as a complete 7-hour audiovisual boxed set and independently as videos and recordings and a book. If you thought MC5 was decadent back in the day, this is a ridonculous chronicle of his entire career from a small 3-piece band in a smoky club, to a full Blues band with horns, to a rock-star wankfest with opening acoustic set, to this acoustic/electric greatest hits extravaganza. Am I being unfair with my not subtle snidish dog-fart nose crinkle? Yes, of course, that's what I do. I'm probably going to love it if I ever shut up long enough to start listening to it. He's a great musician, I'm a dork. He's doing a week of concerts in London with more vintage gear than I could afford in 3 lifetimes, I'm out recapping an old hog waterer that starts leaking every winter because I don't have the time or money or energy to dig down below the frost line to properly remove it.

Do his $2,000 Alvarez Yairi's sound good? No. I mean, they sound good for piezos with several thousand more dollars' worth of sound conditioning hardware filtering out the worst of the percussive mid frequencies, but they still sound unmistakably like rubber bands played ponticello with a parking lot rock. The miced banjos and mandolins sound a thousand times better.

Does any of that make this unenjoyable? No, he's great, this is phenomenal. And, it has those genuine awkward little stumbles and clanks and fret buzzes of actually just playing. Oh yeah, Jockey Full of Bourbon is a fantastic song and it sounds absolutely atrocious. Love it. Still though, From the Valley starts up and my brain would rather turn it off and pull out Buffalo Nichols again.

That's all I can do at the moment. I just can't sit here not doing anything for a full hour without a proper plot line, let alone disc 2, so I'll have to come back to it later, I guess. I expect the rest will be every bit as enjoyable. It's dumb, but I seem to be living in 40-to-50-minute chunks at the moment.

Pause.

Happy Christmas Eve from Bottle of Beef

Hello, friends. Compy here. While Bottle's doing his Frank Sinatra impersonating the Burger King impression (having Christmas his way), the rest of us here at Bottle of Beef wanted to extend our best wishes this holiday season by assembling a few of our favorite Bottlisms. So, here's your Christmas Eve present in no particular order:

- Who says you're not allowed to suck, and why am I not allowed to enjoy it?

- What good is winning if you still have to sit in the same room with all the losers?

- This all sounds suspiciously like a group of people who aren't friends anymore.

And last but not least, the quintessential question resonating through the universe, asked in every possible way with every possible inflection and accompanied by the smirkiest of smirks, completely off-kilter on every occasion:

- What the hell am I listening to?

Don't tell him, but we got him a present with his name on it, properly spelled in all caps just the way he likes it:

Actual Christmas – Dare To Be Stupid

It's beginning to look a lot like Christmas again. The first time around we listened to my original concept album version of Jesus Christ Superstar. The second time around I chose to go down Marty Friedman's New Age hallway instead. This year, Awesomelady McBottlesmom threw down the gauntlet and dared us all to be stupid.
I'll accept that dare, and I'll let Madam Coincidence body slam all challengers by listening to my small but mighty Weird Al collection which begins with said 1985 album Dare To Be Stupid and ends up at the very last song of Bad Hair Day chronicling The Night Santa Went Crazy. Yeah, that's a real thing I noticed after I decided to do it. Am I good, or am I in the bizarre position of looking like I did it on purpose? The world may never know.
Here's the thing about Weird Al, he is literally the only person who can be Weird Al. We all sing funny lyrics to songs, people parody things all the time, but Weird Al is so good at it

and so funny that he won. That's incredible. Nobody's out there saying "Top 10 Weird Al songs whose humor hasn't aged well." You know why? Because if you're out there spotting famous musicians and yelling the Weird Al version of their own song at them from across the street then you're a grade a horrible person with no connection to reality.

Weird Al does 3 things. First, the straight up parodies of famous songs. Second, funny songs in the style of famous bands/musicians. Third, Polka medleys of bits and pieces from other famous songs that don't change the lyrics. It's simple and it's genius.

His only complaint about file sharing is all the horrible stuff that gets misattributed to him (and the legal hassles it causes). He started playing accordion when he was 7 and his parents believed you should do what you love for a living and that accordion would revolutionize Rock music. I for one am glad because the world just wouldn't be as much fun without him having made fun of it. Plus, UHF is a cinematic masterpiece.

Anywho, Merry Christmas from all of us here in Bottleville. Stay weird, stay warm, stay hydrated. Most of all, enjoy Weird Al while we have him, he's the only one we've got. Cheers

doubleVee – Songs for Birds and Bats

Oh, the left kind of people are the right kind of people with the right kind of people jumping through the loopholes...

EO: Merry day after Christmas, Bottle.

B: Merry day after Christmas to you too!

E: You sound suspiciously happy.

B: That's because you're suspicious. You should be, of course, but not to the point where you lose objectivity and argue for the opposite of what you actually want. What do you want, Skip?

E: I... uh... ummagumma, I don't know.

B: Great!

E: It doesn't feel great. It feels terrible. I hate it.

B: Then stop not knowing what you want, Skip. Here, I'll give you an example. I'm remembering the future when you give me a Boxing Day present and I'm super happy because it's music and I get to listen to it. It could be great, it could be terrible, but in my experience, nothing is as terrible as people say it is or think it will be. I want to move past that, not dwell on it. So, I do what I have to do and then enjoy it. I also want to finish this book, but it's tough because I don't have any control over how the plot unfolds. The Republicans might win and Aidvantage (who ever the hell they are) will jack up my 200k to whatever number suits them. The Democrats might win and stick me with the income tax on 200k which is still some ridiculous 5-digit number that I can't pay. Either way I lose my decade of hard work scrambling back to zero. Biden's administration extending the moratorium on collection and interest is the only possible logical choice given that the House and Senate won't compromise and do both. So yeah, he's doing a great job as far as I'm concerned.

As for the broader Left/Right thing, it's all still right-wing. All this junk on my facebook feed is total nonsense. Conservatives are trying to conserve who the hell knows what because they don't ever actually tell you what they are trying to conserve. Traditional institutions? Which ones are those?

Economic liberty? For whom? Competition? What are we competing for?

How do you expect to conserve the Leftist ideas this country was founded upon by championing the Rightist ideas that most everyone agrees corrode them into a pile of unusably rusty parts on the courthouse lawn?

The key to understanding this quite frankly terrible situation is to take a step back and remember that you are not a person. You are a number and a vector. If your number is getting bigger in the positive direction you get a lot of leeway and permissivity. That's it. That's Capitalism. But remember, it's a double-sided coin. Why is the death sentence called "capital punishment?"

That's morose, but we have to understand what we're really talking about. The concept of Capitalism only exists inside an industrialized society in relation to ownership of the means of production, aka the physical factory, equipment, and resources used in the process of the technologically assisted manufacturing of goods for mass consumption and monetary profit for the owner. If the owner hands us as little money as possible, and we hand back as much as they can possibly charge, then we are poor and the owner is doing a bad job of running the economy.

S: Then what is anybody supposed to do?

B: That's not my job. Do what you do. Remember when I suddenly stopped imagineering you last Summer? Well, it means we switched to a mutually beneficial relationship where I only drag you into my thing when I need your help. Remember when I had to go find Bridbrad 'cause we needed money to keep GREGORY occupied and he ended up being the narrator? Remember when Skip freaked out so I just let him get lost and in the end we both agreed he was happiest just fixing the typos? I keep running full steam into the quitting wall, but I still wake up tomorrow and keep trying. Why? Well, showing the actual struggle of being stuck in the middle is important to me, and I want people to see the actual system exert its annoying brain damage on me.

What is it that's really happening? What are the rules of the game I have no choice but to play? Here they are:

My next 200,000 is already spoken for. If I win the metaphorical lottery, I will pay it all now and be done. If I keep going status quo, that 200k turns into 400k by the end. There's an Auditor who very much wants that 400k to become reality, but there's this amazingly impervious force field that prevents that Auditor from succeeding. Inside that forcefield I have an entertainment budget of $50 per paycheck. I use it to buy records and entertain us all by listening to them and writing about it. But, every paycheck I decide whether or not to do that. Sometimes I don't spend the whole 50, sometimes I use it for something more important, sometimes I offer it up to help pay for things other people want to do. The point here is that either way it puts me farther behind. Helping you hurts me. I have to micromanage my brain and only consume what helps me keep doing it. If I beg for money, you all think I'm a greedy little weasel and point out there are people much worse off than I am. If I point out that there are people much worse off than I am then people with more money than me scold me for being a lazy loser trying to destroy their hard-earned wealth. That's a lose lose lose situation.

Normally there are only two loses in that idiom, but I'm a stickler for accuracy. If I give up, I lose, if I keep going, I lose, and if I lose then everybody loses. These aren't my rules, and this isn't my game.

Will they come up with a tolerable solution before that first payment is due in June? Will they do yet another 6-month extension? Dunno, I'm not in charge of anything and I'm not the one injecting the profits from cutting corners and filing fraudulent insurance claims into high-risk investments to avoid paying taxes. The government doesn't *do* anything, it manages the process of paying for it and tries to make sure we get what we paid for. Individuals hiding behind corporate loopholes are draining the money supply and convincing otherwise good people to cheer them on for doing it. Individuals are terrible at making economic choices for other people and a rich guy is about the worst possible choice.

Which brings me to the cream cheese shortage. Here's a great copy and pasted synopsis:

"What caused the cream cheese shortage?

The shortage started when Schreiber Foods, a major cream cheese producer in Green Bay, Wisconsin, shut down for several days in October after a cyber breach. Other companies stepped up production to fill the void, including Kraft-owned Philadelphia, but it wasn't enough. [6 days ago]."

Spin that however you want, I guess, the point is that competing corporations under private management aren't capable of meeting total demand in a crisis, and at the same time people care way more about being able to buy cheap industrially homogenized cream cheese than supporting local farmers and creameries or being able to produce their own cream cheese if they love it so much. It's lovely stuff, but it's not exactly the end of the world or the difference between a whole town staving or not. Tons of people don't eat cream cheese at all, ever.

I think the underlying issue is that specialization and monopolization of production exacerbates the catastrophes of completely normal everyday "shit happens." It's not like I can call 4 friends and get it loaded on a truck in Wisconsin any faster, now, can I? "Cyber Attack Destroys Big Dairy, Tucker Carlson Blames Nose Piercings." I need to go get chicken food because I forgot to last Friday. That's much more important to me.

What does any of this have to do with early 20th-century Soviet Socialism? As Sandra pointed out, I'm not the one bringing it up, I'm just weighing in on the subject because it's a philosophical topic I happen to know a lot about and I can tell when you're spouting nonsense you yourself don't understand. Misconstruing those arguments is a very lucrative business because most people don't understand the crucial distinction between bureaucracy itself as an exploitative economic class and the more honest but naive (dare I say stupid) anachronistic metaphor of a fast forward button. Insanely wealthy people would rather spend their money endorsing political candidates than paying regular people to do anything, so that must mean they get way more profit that way.

Now, what is my inflammatory polemic? I argue that if it looks like a fish and smells like a fish then it's a fish but probably well past its best if eaten by date. If you want to walk around spouting vomit inducing levels of propaganda while citing Leftist philosophers in the name of Rightist Capitalism and arguing that the modern working class is being exploited by big corporations who elected a government to give handouts to the displaced lazy masses, then you look indistinguishable from what you yourself call a Communist. Come to think of it, our privatized prison system of forced labor, with a dramatically large population of petty criminals and drug offenders as an economic instrument is pretty darned Communist, not to mention the Japanese internment camps. Is that one of those "traditional institutions" you guys keep mentioning? I can't justify any of that from either direction. Remember, my non-ideological ideology is founded on aphorisms and questions like "if you kill me, I'll be dead," and "why do you keep demanding I lie to you?" Of course forced labor is dramatically less productive than free labor. Of course "work or die" is a slogan we instinctively reject. It's the same amount of terrible from either direction.

And now we're right back to slavery and our own Civil War, with Marx firmly on the abolitionist side of that equation. That hums right along and we finally get to the early 20th century and what an amazing coincidence, Lenin is doing his thing at the same time the Southern Democrats are migrating to the Republican party. Did you know Strom Thurmond was a Democrat until 1964 when Civil Rights became a real political issue and he just couldn't support that so he switched to Republican?

I know, I know, this is getting to be too much. I'm trying to get there, just a little bit more.

What is a record label? A record label is a Capitalist. It invests in your already successful musician business (aka loans you money) so that you can make a ridiculously expensive recording that it can sell for its own profit. It owns the process of making and distributing records, divides it up into small tasks that any chump can do if they are a hard worker, and sells it to people who want to listen to it.

E: Hold on, I thought only factory owners were Capitalists.

B: True, we're well into the two volumes of Kapital assembled after Marx was dead as a doornail. Capitalists are like Jenga, they keep pulling a piece out from the bottom and delicately stacking it on top.

C: What about record store owners? Are they Capitalists?

B: Glad you asked. No. Those are what we call merchants. See how the component parts separate and become independent parts of the larger corporate structure?

Pretty soon it gets to the point where people are buying the entire corporate structure, then that gets too big and they sell bits and pieces of that massive investment back to the general public so that everyone owns your work and no one can profit from it.

S: That's terrible.

B: Yes. Everyone agrees that's terrible; no one can find any proof that Marx is wrong in his description of the illogic of Capitalism. Instead, what they do is intentionally sabotage the process at some point so that they get to keep the fairly calculated profit from their initial investment and hand off control to the newly separated subsidiary. Sometimes they fire people, close a small factory, buy another subsidiary to drain their surplus, give it to charity, buy New Zealand citizenship, take a rocket into space, wrap a Lamborghini around a tree, etc., but mostly they just collect their royalties and act important. Why? Because what possible reason do they have to care?

The answer is that they care very much about their own liberty and autonomy at the expense of everyone else. So, what do I want to do? I want to be real.

I want to publish stuff, read, listen, make music, have an audience, sell things, fund other peoples' albums, learn new things. I want to have a life, not just serve a mind-numbing function in somebody else's idea of greatness.

Was there a moral to this story? I doubt it, I'm not known for doing that at all. I am known for just letting my brain wander, so this time I think I delivered the goods. So, every thanks I can possibly muster to doubleVee for creating Songs for Birds and Bats and autographing my copy "for BOTTLE." I absolutely love it. Apologies for dragging you into this mess of a post-Christmas rantathon (winky face).

The Flaming Lips – Yoshimi Battles the Pink Robots

Today I think I'm going to be a very specific kind of annoying person, and pedantically dissect In The Morning of the Magicians.

The book Wayne is referencing is a favorite among conspiracy theorists, new age weirdos, and occult leaning axis aficionados. It is a somewhat intentional experiment in cognitive dissonance, what with its prehistoric astronauts and Lovecraftian similarities. That's not really important, we're interested in defeating the pink robots. As he describes it, the song is a deep consideration of love and hate: if you feel loved then you are loved, but where is the proof?

There are a couple really tricky ideas in the lyrics (and my wink wink nudge nudge friends will no doubt intuit that it's the same kind of nuance I think leads everyone to misunderstand Marx) that we need to put under the microscope. First thing's first, we have to unpack all the contractions.

"In the morning I'd awake, and I couldn't remember"

Couldn't is easy, it's "could not." "I'd" is trickier, we need a deep dive into the grammar pool. Could, would, had, should, did, I think that's all the possibilities. Then we need to decide if "calculations" needs an apostrophe, and if error is a verb or a noun, and the truly mind-bending rhetorical twist that tells us love and hate very much matter but we don't know why.

But back to "I'd." What happens when we put each one in there?

"I could awake" - grammatically lovely, but it puts the whole song in a conditional future context which we may or may not want to do.

"I would awake" - still conditional, but without a clear distinction of tense.

"I had awake" - no, that's just silly.

"I should awake" - another future conditional, but with the added implication of external expectation, i.e., he is compelled to awake in a state of not remembering. That's pretty iffy if you ask me.

"I did awake" - ooh, a rhetorical past tense. Past tense for the narrator. It's a fact, he awoke that one time.

I don't think it makes much difference if we unpack it as "I would" or "I did," neither skews the rest of the song in some weird direction. I suppose it should go without saying that "I" is a magician, whatever that might entail for you, but I warned you I was being pedantic, so of course I said it.

WC: And I could not remember.

B: Remember what?

WC: What is love and what is hate.

B: Ok, gotcha. You woke up and you couldn't remember what the difference between love and hate actually is.

WC: The calculations error.

B: Hold up. Are love and hate the resulting error of some calculation? Are you using "error" as a verb, saying "error" when you mean "err?" Or, is it like a hyphenated double predicate nominative; love and hate are the calculations-error?

WC: ....

B: Kay, thanks for clearing *that* up.

WC: What is love and what is hate, and why does it matter?

B: Ok, ok, I smell what you're saying. This is a really tough conceptual contraction.
We have to reach for our old friend "structural problem solving," and think backward. Love and hate very much do matter, but you can't remember why because you don't really understand the tangible difference between the two. Yeah, that's one of those weird communication failures where you totally hate somebody, but they think you love them, and all the rest of the permutations. If you feel loved, then you are loved, but you could be completely mistaken.

WC: Is to love just a waste?

B: That tastes like a rhetorical question.

WC: How can it matter?

B: Yeah, that's a tough one. How can the distinction between love and hate be important if we can totally misinterpret your hate as love and vice versa? Bad news, Wayne, there's no actual answer to that question. It's what we call an irreducible binary opposition. Collapse that puppy and we end up in an alternate universe with feet for ears and our internal organs in a suitcase we have to carry around with us everywhere.

WC: As the dawn began to break, I had to surrender....

B: Past tense for you, then. I had my suspicions.

WC: The universe will have its way, too powerful to master.

B: I've always said so. Some things just are the way they are. Can't live with 'em, can't send 'em to boarding school. Best you can do is take it one relationship at a time and be as honest as possible.

WC: Oh-oh-oh-what is love...

B: Stuck in the end loop there, huh? Ok, look, if one more robot is learning to be something more than a machine, then you have to build in some fuzzy logic. I call it binary flipping, and it's a doozy of confusionment. I find it helps if you explain that it feels like you want me to be horrible, and I just can't do that. Sometimes it doesn't help, and you just have to cry it all out until it passes.

I'm kind of the opposite of a motivational speaker, so if it's not going in a direction you think is "improving," you might want to talk to your doctor or see a professional therapist. Me, I'm the kind of guy who wakes up in the middle of the night with a leg cramp and starts kneading my calf until it relaxes. You're already in excruciating pain, it's not like you can make it actually hurt *more* at the moment. Maybe call off the evil robots, or reprogram them not to destroy us? I don't know, you're the one who can't remember the difference, remember? If failing is objectively less worse than succeeding, maybe that's the logical way to go. But again, I'm not the boss of anyone, so grains of salt and stuff. Buck up, buttercup. A wise Jane of the Siberry Janes once told me "it can't rain all the time."

Well, that was fun (for me because I'm weird). Look for the sequel, How To Read Marx Like A Human Not A Tool, wherever future things I write appear after I write them. Should be at least as fun as differentiating contractions, or my name isn't Whatis Wrongwithyou Jones (most people just accept it and call me Bottle).

How to Read Marx Like a Human Not a Tool.

Ok, we need to set some ground rules here. First, we aren't debating anything. I'm telling you my reading of the English translation of Marx's most famous works. All I care about is The Communist Manifesto and Volume 1 of Capital. 2) I think Lenin was wrong in his interpretation of a couple important aspects, and I think Stalin was a buffoon. I don't mean that in the common offhanded dismissal of mainstream Marxist Thought way, as in "ugh, those backtracking wusses, afraid of a little oppression and murder," I mean if Marx had lived to see Lenin's rise to despotism he would have said "no, dirtbags, you're doing it wrong. This is exactly what I said was the stupid part."

Again, we aren't debating my opinion, I'm allowed to be wrong (if I am) because I'm not telling you to do or not do anything other than form your own opinion and compare and contrast it with mine. That sounds antagonistic, I know, but it's the only accurate description of the scenario I can utter. You don't get to tell me that my opinion isn't my opinion, you just file it in the "Bottle's opinion as I understand it" folder until you have something to contribute to the conversation. I think we can both agree I would have been extra-special worked/starved to death in the gulags of 100 years ago Soviet Union because I'm a loud-mouthed jackass.

I have a limit test/rule. If you end up having to kill or torture people to get a road repaved, you are some flavor of wrong. Marx doesn't try to justify it; he very clearly says violence and rebellion and war are an inevitable reaction to exploitation and oppression and History tells us there's no obvious way to actually escape it. The more developed an industrial society the less violence actually takes place, but the end result is always some qualitative version of war. His actual suggestion is the democratic election of representatives who will politically advocate for the working class so that people can support themselves rather than depending on generosity and pity (nothing is fair until you agree it's fair). He advocated spreading people out, giving them land and technology to support themselves and freely trade the surplus with others, rather than forcing them to owe a debt to a landlord for the privilege of being allowed to live in poverty. It's still possible to choose to be lazy and starve under that plan, but you can't argue you didn't have access to the knowledge and technology necessary for a productive and fulfilling life. I used to tell my students "I'm telling you what to do to pass this course, the people who do it get As and Bs, the people who don't get Ds and Fs. I have no idea how hard or easy it will be for any particular one of you, so drive your struggle bus over to my office hours and I'll gladly give you extra help." I didn't actually say it in those exact words, but maybe it would have been more productive. Se la mort on that one.

  The first problem I have with Lenin is that he clearly took the "inevitability of exploitation" as a justification for oppressing and exploiting the predominantly peasant population of Eastern Asia. Some days I'd rather be a subsistence farmer, to be honest. I know which part Lenin misunderstood, it's the part where Marx talks about looking down on the farmer as lazy and inefficient. It's easy to misunderstand, Marx doesn't reiterate the context of that statement as a specifically Capitalist point of view inside the larger process of exploitation; he doesn't clarify his rhetorical approach, he shortsightedly assumes you understand it.

  Stalin's notion of single-nation Communism is equally problematic, because that is just about as opposite of a global proletariat as I can imagine. The story about the hand-picked bloody roses and apology to Konstantin Rokossovsky is pretty interesting though, as are the happy birthday exchanges between him and Churchill right up until that Iron Curtain diatribe. FDR's in there somewhere as well. I know I'm rambling; I just think people tend to not actually conceptualize all the things that were happening at the same time. How many people mistakenly think Stalin was Axis rather than Ally and ignore the fact that Pearl Harbor is what actually forced us to choose a side in WWII? It was Stalin's war against Hitler and Mussolini when you brass tack it, and we had so many fascism fanatics Vonnegut had to write a book about it. Killed an imaginary pregnant lady and everything.

Where was I? Oh yeah, it is certainly true that Marx envisioned a type of globalized society, but I think we have to look at that in its most honest and simple manifestation. A carpenter should be able to go anywhere on Earth and have a productive and comfortable life as a carpenter. A doctor is a doctor, a lawyer a lawyer, a mechanic a mechanic, and so on. Professions might have varying levels of importance in different places, but some amount of what you do is equal to some amount of what another person does; we should all be able to adapt to the changing needs of society as a whole and we should all have access to the technology and education that makes that possible.

The next problem is Communism itself. Communism is clearly a religion in Marx's brain (he compares them to all the really nasty drugs made from poppies like Marcy Playground did): it has an origin story, it has a teleological goal, and it has a detailed series of devout behaviors that assure you'll get to the promised reward. I skipped over that chapter of the manifesto, but I told you that's what it actually does, it criticizes the utopian aspects of broader Communist ideas, and says true revolution can only come from the people usurping the power of their handlers. You know me, I say there's no bowl of Lucky Charms at the end of the rainbow, but I completely and respectfully accept your right to disagree with me so long as you aren't using it to try to take advantage of me. Marx might scold me for that, but I ain't afraid of no ghost.

Back to the point. What are the real dynamics of Marx's evaluation of Capitalism? First of all, Capitalism very much works. The boss exploits his workers for profit, consumers get happy and demand more, it gets bigger and bigger, but before any one guy actually wins, the people being exploited chop off his head. That's not allegorical, by the way, that's literally the French Revolution and the umpteenth time it's happened in Marx's "History is Fun" library reading list. Marx very clearly implies that's stupid. The end result is a crash either way, so we should use the best tools we have to make the process as survivable as possible. Economically speaking, Marx says it would be better to approach the cataclysm by letting the global economy actually reach its equilibrium rather than waking up one morning to find that one guy actually won and the entire rest of the world has no money until he decides how to divide it all up again.

I'm reminded of the very peculiar and interesting distinction between a Republic and a Soviet Democracy. The term "Soviet," by the way is the actual name for the type of democratically elected representative and by extension the congress of elected representatives. Soviet isn't merely a synonym for "Russian" like most of us Americans naively think it is. If you are one of those Americans then you're really gonna hate the fact that our Electoral College is really difficult to intellectually differentiate from Soviet Democracy. By all means, go read the thousands of pages of text about it and pick my consolidated appraisal apart, I will very much respect your efforts.

I myself am a "do it or don't" kind of guy. I don't find much value in putting off what you're still not going to want to do tomorrow; if it's a coin flip, I'll flip an actual coin so I don't have to care anymore. If you have to waste time threatening me, you could have already killed me by now. James Spader would have (a Blacklist reference, where did that come from?). And that, believe it or not, winds us all the way around to a sentiment best expressed by Neil Gaiman's Mary Katherine Gallagher impression from American Gods. We all know the game is rigged, but it's the only game in town.

My question is, do you think he punned his own name on purpose, or was it just a happy little Bob Rossian coincidence?

The Penultimate Album of 2021 – Rolling Stones Biggest Hits Volume 2

Tomorrow has its own album, like every other holiday, so tonight is the last album of 2021. I think we can all agree that while not particularly great, it was a tangibly better year than 2020 (if you squint just right). So, even though I know I'm going to regret it, we're spinning the second volume of greatest hits by the Rolling Stones. Quick glance at the track list... yes, these are exactly all of my favorite Rolling Stones songs, what the hell did they publish for the first volume? But more important, will I hate the experience of actually listening to it as much as I hate every actual Rolling Stones album?

I don't know if I just have really fresh ears, or if it's a legitimate fluke, but Paint It Black sounds lovely; exactly as I expect it to sound. Oh good, pure misery ensues after that. First, left and right channels are not the same volume. Trust me, I flipped my headphones around at least 4 times across Side A, the stereo channels are definitely normalized to different levels.

As is always the case, this thing is pristine without any surface noise at all (because nobody enjoys repeatedly listening to Rolling Stones on vinyl). It's not just one thing though, it's a cornucopia of terrible things. It's like pouring chocolate milk on your Lucky Charms and washing it down with orange juice. One song will have drum and bass both panned hard left then the next will keep the drums there but pan the bass hard right. Mick Jagger might assault you from anywhere in the stereo field. Random acoustic instruments that couldn't possibly be run through a fuzz pedal sound like they were run through two daisy-chained fuzz pedals. Sometimes there's reverb, sometimes it disappears. Some tracks are super muddy, some tracks sound like there are brillo pads between the headphones and my ear drums.

But Bottle, you pointlessly opine, try listening through speakers instead. Har har har I retort, that's even worse. I wish I was making it up, I want so badly to be wrong, I want to enjoy the truly wonderful songs and wackadoodle arrangements, but what netherworld of grotesqueness still-birthed the audio circuitry that a guy in an ill-fitting tweed jacket sold to the Rolling Stones, and who let them produce their own music on it? Was there a board room meeting where everyone agreed to secretly steal the masters in the middle of the night and send any potential radio single to a professional?

As I've said before, the playing is incredible, I love their songs, I love *what* they created, but as for actually listening to it pressed into molten polyvinyl chloride, I'd rather just stick my head into the pressing machine. I can't have the only terrible copies on Earth, can I? Surely someone has experienced this specific phenomenon but felt afraid to say anything. Regardless, it's time for Side B.

Honky Tonk Women, now with vuvuzela choir! Dandelion don't tell no lies, this is lopsided agony; a perfectly lovely song in my right ear and absolute Muppet Show cacophony in my left ear. I adore 2000 Light Years From Home, but Jagger's panned full left again and I desperately want to turn around and punch him in the face. Oh gawd, Have You Seen Your Mother... is ghastly. You know how those old warped VHS uploads to youtube sound? It's like that but in a racquetball court with all the squeaking shoes and embarrassment. No, Street Fighting Man doesn't finish on a high note, it sounds like you're trying to listen to it on a cheap boom box while some inconsiderate jerk bangs on metal garbage cans down the alley.

I mean, it already had a couple strikes against it. Lopping off all 4 corners of the jacket and inner sleeve is suuuuper annoying, and it's not even an actual application for joining the fan club. Enjoy this collection of Rolling Stones songs, but we're not really even sure anyone would want to be in their fan club. We're not opposed to creating one, I guess, but we definitely aren't going to waste all that money on the off chance you don't think this sounds like it was recorded into an obsolete dictaphone.

Sayonara 2021, feel free to let the door hit you harder than necessary on the way out. See you tomorrow night for our annual Mastodon around the sun-athon. I think the space monster's gonna finally wake up and eat us next year.

Once More 'Round the Sun

3 o'clock is probably too early for my official new year's post, but I am a curmudgeon so sorry, not sorry (winky face). Alright Mastodon, usher in this next trip 'round the sun.

Some truly amazing things happened in 2021. First, we'll get me out of the way. I published 3 books this year, and many of you have physical copies of them. That's just a thing I decided to do back in 2020 and I made it happen so you could see the whole thing take place. I also massively expanded my record collection, bought an electric piano and made an EP with it, and had wonderful conversations with old and new friends who I can't physically go hang out with in the real world.

Speaking of friends, my friends made tons of new music this year. Dave published Architectronics, Steven put out tons of new music as Noonish Moon and started a really funny Tiktok series, I met Gerard because I randomly heard his songs and interview with Josh on the radio, Kris is out there busier than ever entertaining the masses. I'm willing to bet each and every one of you did something equally amazing just because you felt like it, and that's what's truly amazing! I want 2022 to be more of that.

I'm gonna finish this 4th book. You're gonna keep doing you and I'm gonna keep cheering you on because you don't have to take away anyone else's success to have some of your own, all you have to do is go do it.

There's your pep talk from your favorite old anti-motivational speaker. Even though I hate the chorus from Aunt Lisa, it's our anthem for the new year:

"...I don't see the fearsome fright, all I see is beauty shine... hey ho, let's fucking go, hey ho, let's get up and rock and roll."

As always, cheers!

Bottle's New Year's Resolution

N6 – V7 – I I I

Welcome to 2022, Brian Setzer Will Take Your Order Shortly

Welcome to 2022, everyone. This is not gonna help your hangover. At the risk of sounding sarcastic when I assure you I am not, Betty White heard we ran out of cream cheese and refused to join us for this adventure. I hear you cringing, but that's exactly the kind of dark humor she would have liked very much. I wanted to be a Golden Girl when I grew up, but I had to settle for being a self-appointed beardly princess. Such is life, I'm afraid.

To be fair, I liked her as Sue Ann Nivens on the Mary Tyler Moore show better. I might be two months shy of 42 on the outside, but I'm 13,000 years old on the inside, so I know a little bit about what I like. Now we have to pick our first album of 2022. Both potential possibilities are still sealed, never been opened things I tend to like less than other things of their respective ilks, so coin flip it is. Heads we hear today what we otherwise would have put off until tomorrow, tails we yesterday tomorrow and today it from the other direction. Call it in the air... oh crap I looked straight into the light and fumbled the catch [plop]. Damnit! Who imagineered a storm grate in the middle of my basement floor? If I had a Pennywise album, we'd listen to that instead of either of these. Oh well, guess we'll just eenie meenie miney monniff 'em, then intentionally thwart that rhyme scheme by listening to songs Brian Setzer wrote himself.

  Calling him Catpiss McPompadour was obviously just my 2020 sense of humor being overly aggressive, I like Brian Setzer just fine. Officially titling the album Rockabilly Riot! All Original, however, is testing my patience. To quote the man himself, Cock-a-doodle Don't frickin' do that. No one was gonna refuse to buy this album in 2014 because they were afraid it would be another batch of unnecessary covers. It's a bit like implying all your previous albums are subtitled "Crap You've Already Heard Me Play a Dozen Times!"

  Ugh, Surfdog's corporate schtick is even worse than a Kenny Chesney album, and that's saying a lot. I bet their coffee tastes horrible, and their artist royalty percentage is probably sub-35. 50/50 or just walk away people, you're literally paying them to publish your album. It's a business loan, not "an advance." I don't know Dave Kaplan and I doubt he's related to Gabe, so his feelings can shove rubber hoses up their own noses. There's nothing inherently wrong about that loan structure, by the way. It can and does work for artists with mass market appeal, but upwards of 93% of bands/artists will never have mass market appeal, so intentionally calling things cutesy reverse psychology names to trick people into thinking you can magically change that from your surfboard is a thing I don't like. I guess technically we do have to listen to it, so here goes nothin'.

First though, let's flip this over and see if the track titles give us any sense of potential coherence. Oh, ok, yeah that's promising: stuff about stuff, stuff about a girl, stuff about his inner dopiness, some kind of allegorical ending. Whether or not I like the end result, the architecture of the album seems pretty solid. 4 people isn't enough for a horn section, so one of those non-self-infringing stray cats plays keyboard or sax. Trepidations assuaged, commence with the rioting.

Opening it up we see that it's piano, this version of the band is called The Riot Squad, and this is very much a "this is real music, people!" album. I am not a fan of that schtick because you only get it after you bought the album and opened it up. It's almost like they are apologizing. "Sorry we suck and you hate it, we're just dudes trying to keep Rockabilly alive and commercially viable." Barf.

I've been known to compare him less favorably to Reverend Horton Heat at every possible opportunity, and this is definitely Brian's closest attempt at that raspy, campy personality. But, it's not campy or actually humorous, more nostalgic and awkward. The whole style is supposed to be a vehicle for innuendo, but there simply isn't any.

It's good though. There's nothing embarrassing about it, it's not Dad-Rock-abilly, but there is a feeling that you have to have an actual inner 1950s teenager to really appreciate it. Not so much nostalgia, more like you have to actually be a greaser to enjoy it on a semi-regular basis. It really does feel more like a themed birthday party, or taking your actual girlfriend to that restaurant from Pulp Fiction and there is zero chance of either her OD-ing or you getting machine gunned after coming out of the bathroom the next day. It's too clean and innocent is what I'm saying, the Disney trademarked, family friendly version of a riot.

And yet, you don't have to be underwhelmed by that at all. As albums go, it's really good. It does sound like real musicians playing real music they love. The smiles aren't fake, the sentimentality of The Girl With the Blues in Her Eyes is authentic, the playing is phenomenal across the board. I'm not sure I needed to know which actual hospital Brian was born in, and I've already expressed my skepticism about the "love and patience" of business surfer dude Dave Kaplan.

I am a little bit pleased by I Should'a Had a V-8, it's a pun on the tomato beverage about actual car motors. That's as intellectually stimulating as it gets, though, and Cock-a-doodle Don't is as close to the good Reverend's sense of humor as you can get.

I guess I'd have to say that even in spite of all the things I don't like about the package, this is a great album. I kinda feel like this whole thing was way more complicated and frustrating behind the scenes than it ever needed to be, like it was a hard sell to get it to happen at all. Not really surprising for 2014, but it has an impact because image is a delicate thing when it's your only thing. A net worth of $10 million should be more than enough to do it yourself, but if 95% of that is tied up in just getting your crew to the next gig, the other 5% goes to management no matter what you do, and there are only 2 or 3 actual retailers still in business to even consider buying it, I guess there isn't much choice. Kaplan can at least buoy your album against the other artists he's managing, whereas you'd probably have to actually sell some stuff to finance it yourself...

Are you on the edge of your seat anticipating the punch line? Ok, I guess I'll give it to you:

... Bit of a catch 22, that one.

Ray Conniff Will Make The Arrangements

Eenie meenie miney metzer, here are the 16 Most Requested Songs of Ray Conniff. Ray Conniff didn't write any of these songs, these are just things some random audience member yelled at him one time. You know, like FREEBIRD!, or DEVIL WENT DOWN TO GEORGIA!, or DICK IN A BOX! Who's the mystery lady in the yellow hat on the cover? No clue, maybe the liner notes will tell us.

Conniff's origin story is "random Trombonist lives through the decline of the Big Band era and goes on to be a fairly renowned arranger of Pop standards." We should just expect a fairly wide array of nightclub light jazz. Maybe not as flash as Count Basie, or as boozy as Jackie Gleason, certainly not as wackadoodle as my hero Marty Paich, but totally enjoyable in a Lawrence Welk, bubbles floating through the air kind of way.

And yeah, this is total mingle music. You and the boys are out on the town with the girls for a dance and a martini. Check your trench coat and fedora at the door, catch up on a little society gossip, secretly shuffle to the back room and join the illegal poker game for a few hands, then threaten to beat up Sammy Slick in the parking lot before storming out during the terrible disco/funk version of Lara's Theme from Doctor Zhivago. It's more like a bizarre noirish version of The Love Boat than a tale about a doctor's bizarre love life during WWI. Thought Bolero couldn't be turned into a campy Samba-esque vocalise? Hold Conniff's white wine spritzer and find out just how truly wrong you are. And we're only half way through it.

So, this is a compilation from 1986 of recordings from the 60s and 70s, and holy cow is this a total anachronism for 2022. It sounds fantastic, but the people who love this are weirdos like me and octogenarians. I was joking yesterday, but it really does conjure up memories of MTM and Welcome Back Kotter reruns. This is like the dressed up middle-class date-night facade for which Taxi was the gritty, urban dose of realism; the Felix half of the Odd Couple. The disco tracks are drenched in polyester, and it all has that kind of flat-line sappiness you expect from the only the mediocre-est of quickly dropped 70s/80s sitcom themes. No, it's not what you would normally expect me to quite enjoy, but I liked Mr. Belvedere and Mork and Mindy and Family Ties as a kid.

If you like this kind of unobtrusive background schmooze, then this is a great album to have around. Not an evening of art type of experience, but if constant noise is a necessity, you could do much, much worse. I mean, he himself says that rock and roll fad thing was barely a blip on his storied career of total middle of the road anonymity, and he seemed to keep finding plenty of work. It's not gonna knock your socks off, but there's an accordion hiding in there, so it's got that going for it. Still no idea who the lady is, it must just be that old standby marketing gimmick of putting a photo of the exact type of lady you'd be trying to impress by buying this album on the cover.

Well, this year is off to a strange start, might as well do some kind of Memo power ballad type stuff tomorrow. That's Metal plus Emo if you're portmanteau-ly challenged.

This Is (a) War

Here's something I don't normally do, but I was desperately trying to remember what the hell song whispers "this is a war" before the chorus; I was astonished to find out just how many damned songs there are called This Is (a) War. I had Compy make an entire playlist of nothing but that. Let's experience it together:

https://youtube.com/playlist?list=PLtKAqUuys5n3HIa6mhxDE0Zyg3apmBQCU

There are few honorable mentions, 'cause I think we can all agree, horseshoes and hand grenades (close enough). [Covers mic] Did you put any effort into the order, C-lector?

C: None whatsoever.

B: Ok good.

[Uncovers mic] Great news everybody, I'd highly encourage hitting that shuffle button, because this is an intentionally disorganized mess.

First, I don't know which is more hilarious, the parody of A Whole New World or normal every day Five Finger Death Punch. I know which one's better and more intellectually valuable, FFDP is just awful incarnate.

The real lesson here is that not a single one of these songs is meaningful in any way. This is your battle cry workout jam regardless of which side of any argument you happen to be on, and speaking as a guy who was just patiently waiting to pay for his fortnight worth of groceries, you're all obnoxious jerks. Except for Leonard Cohen and Looking For Group, you guys are awesome and that Aladdin spoof is très magnifique.

Jokes on me, it turns out I was thinking of the whisper "this is a war" from Bring Me The Horizon's Parasite Eve, so this whole thing was a total tangent of truly ridiculous proportions. And no, no Bring Me The Horizon albums on the horizon. No Black Veil Brides, no 12 Foot Ninja, definitely nothing Ronnie Radke was ever involved with. We might do We Came As Romans if they ever drop this new album (only because I like Darkbloom and Black Hole), and I'm morbidly curious how terrible the band Sumo Cyco actually is (not even remotely, I checked and they're actually amazing). Of course, now that I said it it'll be Metalcore until we all puke. Maybe I'll find a secret passageway away from there, we'll just have to see what we see. See how dangerous straying from full albums is? Oh well, what's done is done, can't take it back. Onward we go, raging against the dying of the light like Dylan Thomas implored us.

[Some amount of time later]

B: Well, whaddya think?

S: About what?

B: About the This is (a) War playlist. You guys all listened to it, right?

S: No, Bottle. Just, no.

E: Also no. And you're not going to get me to fall for it again.

B: Fall for what? Oh, you mean like that time I found that speech by that guy? This isn't like that at all.

S: What's it like, then?

B: It's like 2 hours of hyperbole to the point of hysteria. The first few tracks are mildly amusing, then you'll get mad about one of 'em, then you realize none of it actually connects to real reality, then the Clockwork Orange insanity kicks in and you'll gladly agree to anything to make it stop, then the K-pop track will come on and you'll get the giggles, then there's still like 11 tracks to go and you'll want to hit yourself in the head with a nice heavy metal stapler, and when it's all over you'll feel incredibly depressed that this is where we are, every boo boo, every bummed out, every I'll never get to buy a jet ski is the end of the world, and politicians are murdering pedophile lizard people saying don't drink that flavoraid, drink my flavoraid.

Is it wrong how much the whole thing makes me laugh? The videos are mostly terrible, the messages make no sense, what possible larger context were these songs shoved into?

Like I said, the two best tracks here are LFG and Leonard Cohen, they're the only ones making a statement about it: that statement is it's ridiculous. "There is a war between the ones who say there is a war and the ones who say there isn't."

Now, I've been known to say there is the very real possibility that it will turn into war, and what other purpose does this cornucopia of nonsense purport to encourage? Wake the unwoke and unwake the awoken, it's vitally important we kill each other to prevent each other from killing us! You can't tell me what I'm not allowed to tell you you can't tell me!

What does it all remind me of? It reminds me of the Cone of Silence from Get Smart. Or, you know how people think that their phone conversations are somehow magically private when they are walking through the grocery store or standing on their front porch? That conversation is never "oh crap, groceries be damned, I'll be there as quick as possible, keep pressure on it," or "they don't have that one, have you tried this brand?" No, that phone conversation is always significantly less important than the thing you are actually doing, and I can hear you having it when it could have easily waited 10 more minutes until you get back to your car, or finish your cigarette, or whatever. It's always the people who most inconvenience others championing fighting about stupid shit. I guarantee the cashier at this gas station doesn't care about the car wash at a different gas station, I just want to pay for my crummy gas station lunch and take a half-hour nap. That's selfish, I know, so I keep it inside and smile and don't hold up the person behind me. Don't get me wrong, I still chit-chat and banter like a normal person, I just don't feel like that conversation is more important than the lady behind me with a kid who probably should have waited in the car.

S: Shut up, Bottle.

B: What was I talking about? Oh yeah, I remember, *NONE OF THAT IS A WAR!*

I Prevail – Trauma

Let's find out if I Prevail's Trauma disappoints me so much I need professional therapy. Aside: I hate bragging, but that's an amazing lead off sentence.

https://youtube.com/playlist?list=PLBDi8oLoUF39lhHt_81JVuTQZxglGKyIX

Why even check it out? Well, I like the song Every Time You Leave. Every time I hear it though, I can't help but compare it to the Ben Burnley/Lacey Sturm duet Dear Agony. I know nothing else about either I Prevail or their guest vocalist Delaney Jane.

Ooof, you're gonna get from the Djentcore of Bow Down to Every Time You Leave with only 1 track in between? That does not instill confidence in consistency for the 10 tracks after that. Musically sure, I can hear the beauty and the beast duality, but, uh, your particular beast does not sound like even the minimum requirements of secretly boyfriend material.

That's certainly a track two. Some tropes are popping up here. First, whispering the bridge to the chorus is becoming almost mandatory in Metalcore, and I'm not thrilled. Second, this is straight up R&B Crossover. Ignore the fact that it's drop-tuned ElectroMetal, this is serious beatwork, guest vocals, samples, rap. I know I mentioned Metalcore evolved from Nu-metal, and you can't unhear it now, can you?

Why am I not just listening to a Tech N9ne or Hopsin album? Why am I not pulling out El-P's Cancer 4 Cure again? Don't misunderstand me, I enjoy this very much. What I'm wondering is why I have to endlessly search the underground for the dark and heavy intelligent Hip Hop, but be bombarded by the 20-something loser white guy metal version of it? The most obvious comparison for this album's sort of look at mental health is Kids See Ghosts. Sorry guys, Kanye and Cudi win.

Oh, I've heard Hurricane, but no I never would have guessed it's the same band as the last 4 tracks. It's just all over the place from Emo to Trap to Djent to Acoustic Alternative, to Death Metal and back. That *could* work if this was in any way a self-aware album, but it's not. It's just random genre hopping. It sounds like you were trying to make a mix tape, not a concept album.

"But Bottle, isn't that the point? Like, life is a deluge of terrible that messes you up."

No. If the intent is to silently call itself "damaging garbage" then it's even more worsely messed up than I'm giving it credit for. A self-hate variety album? Vomit. No, this is just throw crap at the wall and see what sticks. That crap happens to be topically related, but there are 3 different bands trying for hit singles on 3 different radio stations in 3 different cities. None of that is the topic of the album, none of that is even necessary. The various styles don't add a layer of complexity to any particular song's meaning, they don't play off each other like the cross-track themes from Kendrick Lamar's DAMN., for example, they don't even really represent the "code switching" I'm sure they are supposed to represent. There's no reason for any of it other than 4 of the 20 songs from this session were real potential radio singles and the other 9 were the best of the rest.

I put this right on par with Fire From the Gods. A few of these songs are great, but the album and their larger career are, in my opinion, completely forgettable.

Which is pretty crummy to be honest, because I think their wider intentions and message are great. That doesn't help me enjoy the album as a whole, but it does underscore the fact that the big show is not what these guys are really all about, and it just ends up feeling like they're trying to reach an audience that doesn't actually exist. They just end up feeling like the Metalcore version of 21 Pilots and it's not working for me.

Webern – Passacaglia

Oh, Webern. It's tempting to view the complete works through any number of socio-political and biographical lenses, but it's not fun. You know what is fun? Realizing that Webern begins with his graduation piece, his last student composition under Schoenberg, his last grandiose statement of Expressionistic Romanticism, the Passacaglia. Ignore its larger structure, its loose grasp on tonal comprehensibility, stop trying to hear it as a single movement symphony, it is really not much more than a set of variations above an ostinato.

That pizzicato ostinato is to my mind ominous, the dual climaxes tumultuous bordering on ferocious, the muted brass terrifying, the ponticello passages an almost forlorn reflection of its themes distorted by the ripples of the river in the moonlight. Moments of sweeping beauty underscored by the sounds of rats scampering in the shadows, soulful expressions punctuated by background giggles, love and terror, force and delicacy, sweetness and brutality, humor and ponderous sadness.

The crash of a society in motion gives way to the fragility of a single violin down a side alley. It builds and recedes, it reminisces while moving on, it is all of the colors and feelings and hopes and memories. It is born from the abstract, weaves its way forward, and trembles before its final exhale. It is a life filled with all the variety and wonder and confusion of complexity, and it is quite a beautiful thing to observe.

Hum – Inlet

I didn't give you much time to make suggestions for bandcamp payday, did I? I'm like that, sorry. Tonight's winner is a band that broke into the mid-90s alternative rock-osphere with their major label debut You'd Prefer An Astronaut. Not ringing a bell? I'm sure you've seen it in passing, it's the green album with a zebra on it. Can't find that one on vinyl, but you can get their 1998 album Downward is Heavenward and their 2020 album Inlet, so I did. We'll just enjoy the bandcamp version of Inlet while those relocate from Illinois to Iowa.

https://humband.bandcamp.com/album/inlet

Their drummer sadly died last July. Shoegaze is an interesting genre, mostly because it's named after the fact that you have to constantly look down at your feet to keep stomping on all those guitar effects pedals. Space Rock is not an interesting genre because it's boringly named after themes of outer space and science fiction. Fun to listen to, though. These are long, drawn out, but much more energetic than Stoner Rock deluges of crushing guitar riffs and synths and reverb. Chino Moreno said Hum was a major influence on Deftones' sound, and it's hard to disagree.

Some people compare them to a Shoegaze Helmet, but I think that's just dropped-d riffage, not an actual comparison. Hum is much more like Failure and Orange Goblin or Dinosaur Jr. than My Bloody Valentine or Jesus and Mary Chain. Crushingly loud, almost Doom to be honest, and there's genuine moments that might make you wonder if you didn't accidentally stumble into a Crowbar album, but then no screaming whatsoever takes place.

Goodness, Inlet just rocks. This really is like a blast from my teenage past. This is my Alternative Rock, the sound in my head when I'm mentally humming (pun intended).

There's really not much to say. Close your eyes, bang your head, never want it to stop. Obviously not as sonically complex as last night's Webern, but beautiful all the same.

Something about the vocals was really familiar, but I couldn't put my brain-finger on it. Then near the end of The Summoning I realized the vocals sound a lot like mid-career Meat Puppets. Arizona and Illinois are about as different as you can get, but the Too High To Die/No Joke flavors are definitely taking the foreground. To clarify, no this doesn't sound like Meat Puppets at all, but the flavor of that almost deadpan delivery and modal melodies is unmistakable once you get a taste for it. Delightful.

So, if you just want to air drum and head bang and put a giant sonic wall between you and the outside world, I highly recommend checking out Hum's surprise 2020 album Inlet. Think I'll unempty my beverage cup and give it yet another listen. It's quite excellent.

Heart Shaped Box (in 3 parts)

Part 1

I was gonna do a whole big thing about religious persecution, how I grew up without religion, the way it all ties into my larger project of trying to decipher the insanity of the Klein Bottle that is the Christian Right using historically Left rhetoric, but then I was like "nah, let's climb back up the umbilical noose and do a tediously intricate reading of Heart

Shaped Box instead. That'll ruin everybody's Friday night appetite."

I think any proper pop song analysis should start with considering the chorus in its isolated context, then observing what the verses do to it or require from it, and finally culminate with some coherent statement about the song as a whole.

> "Hey, wait, I've got a new complaint;
> Forever in debt to your priceless advice.
> Hate, Haight, I've got a new complaint;
> Forever in debt to your priceless advice.
> Hey, wait, I've got a new complaint;
> Forever in debt to your priceless advice."

So, the chorus is A-B-A with a repeated "advice" at the end. The B version is all about the puns, and the fact that you can't really hear any difference between them unless you over-enunciate or intentionally mispronounce them. In other words, all of the nuance is completely lost if you're just randomly yelling them. I think it's fair to extend that analysis to say you have to already understand the differences to understand the actual meaning, you're in on it or you're oblivious, or you're transitioning between those two states. If you already knew the words were different you might say "oh, I can't actually hear that difference." Conversely, you might say "oh, I had no idea he was saying different words each time."

Now, what do those words actually do? "Hey, wait" is of course a standard interjection, and the immediately understood surface interpretation of yelling words that sound like that. I think we all understand the statement of "hold on there, Mr. McPerson, I have some objecting to do before we proceed."

Now it gets kaleidoscopic. "Hate, Haight...." Haight of course referring to Haight/Ashbury, a kind of synecdoche for the more general 1960s hippy culture. That's a fun little progression, "hey, wait/complaint" transitioning to the general attitude of aggression and hate, then contrasted by the symbolic epitome of love and tolerance. It is of course a coin flip as to which hallway you use to approach it, but this chorus is really doing some stuff. All that's left is to add the actual refrain "forever in debt to your priceless advice." And there it is, the duality phrased as sarcasm. Smooth move, Exlax. Do you want a cookie to go with all that "milking it?" I'm hyperbolizing to point out the inherent sarcasm of "priceless advice" implying an insurmountable debt. What's more interesting is how we view the possessive implications of the two parts together. Culturally speaking it's obvious how this total sentiment works, but grammatically speaking there is no signifier of direction; is "forever in debt..." the complaint he is voicing, or is it the complaint he has received. Like I said, culturally we instinctively understand that he is issuing the complaint at some form of authority, be it either the hate or love side, but ultimately, we decide whether he is actually complaining at that authority, or whether he is the authority to whom this complaint has been presented.

Taking a step back, we can see that the chorus as a whole represents an objection in its most abstract form: stop, I don't want/like/need/care about/etc. this (whatever "this" turns out to be; that's what the verses are for, after all).

And some spectacularly imagistic verses these turn out to be. First, the highlights. We have that pun on Astrological Signs, sexual euphemisms, and the aforementioned heart-shaped box. Now we have to unpack all that stuff, so maybe grab the rolaids and/or dramamine cause things are about to get a little bit icky.

Is this song specifically about Courtney Love's vagina, like Courtney Love thinks it is? No, Simpsons did it, I mean there's a Carly Simon song for that. Sure, motherhood, vaginas, childbirth, it's all there, but whether or not it's personal or biographical or abstractly Oedipal, or anything else is completely up to the listener to construct. There is no clarifying communicative authority, no actual narrator, only an "I" and some contextual "self-victimization." That's how the verses and chorus seem to interact, he describes how he is the victim and objects to it. Who "he" is is anybody's guess; the not telling you who "he" is is the generalized artistic expression at work. We open a door to interpretation by removing personal omniscience, rather than closing the door by explicitly stating it.

I'm sure I'm going to regret it (I have a tendency to wander away and forget to rejoin the tour at the scheduled reboarding time), but we're gonna call this a to be continued. Hopefully part two materializes, but if not, at least you've got a head start on thinking deeper. 'Til then....

Part 2

Ok, I'm back after winning several rounds of Guess Who and getting a proper retaliatory stomping at Candyland. I am now disconcertingly sticky.

"She eyes me like a Pisces when I am weak."

I do not have any idea what that actually means. Do us February/Marches give a specific kind of look at people? Does "she" think of him the way people think of a Pisces at their most fragile? Is it just an elaboration on "fish eye?"

"I've been locked inside your heart-shaped box for weeks."

It's tempting to rag on rhyming weak with weeks, but we have the benefit of knowing that the needs of the homonym outweigh the needs of the rhyming acumen. Is "your" the same as "she?" If so, then we have a shift from third-person to first-person. If not, then we have an uncorroborated love triangle kind of situation. More meaningfully, however, we now clearly understand that he is a prisoner of whichever situation it is. He is "locked inside," he can't get out, he has no control of the situation. It's fairly intuitive to say that "heart-shaped box" simply means she loves him, but the connotation is that he is not an active participant. Rather, she has put him in a box, out of sight but still in her possession AS a mere possession to take out in the future whenever she wishes. He is merely a keepsake.

I should point out that these pronouns are non-deterministic. I say "he" in reference to Curt singing, "she" as a quotation, but gender roles or identities are in no way inherently meaningful, and in the larger context of Nirvana interestingly fluid. In this song there is no indication of the gender of the "paper speaker," so we revert to the known gender of the singer who voices "I" and "me," but it will eventually become extremely plausible that the speaker is a literal or metaphorical baby. That singer is not literal person Curt, but the middle ground character voiced by Curt.

"I've been drawn into your magnet, tar-pit trap."

Quick check up on the status of human understanding about magnetism... yep, I thought so, it's "prohibitively complex" to try to figure out why all the quantum thingies vibrate like they do, what with all those electrons doing whatever they feel like. Tar pits are much better understood, but also much more icky. Dunno why, but can't escape. Mysteries of the universe.

"I wish I could eat your cancer when you turn black."

Oh deity, I need a shower. That's the most gruesome sentence I've ever heard in my entire life, and the obvious pisces/cancer pun doesn't help me one little minuscule quark of an iota. I can only assume it's meant to be the most grotesque possible expression of thriving on someone else's misery. It makes sense, her love is his prison, her suffering his nourishment. If this song is about Courtney like she thinks it is, she might not want to be so proud of it. On the bright side, it's clearly not about her in any way, it's the dichotomies talking.

So, now we're at the chorus and we have to ask what is this advice? Is the advice to get married? Have children? Be famous? I think in the grander scheme of Nirvana it's most likely the Fame to which he's referring, but inside the song itself there's nothing. No advice has been presented in any way, shape, or charred rotting form. I'm grossed out, though, so that's a plus.

And now the moment of truth. Can Bottle survive the dreaded 2nd to be continued during which he sleeps it off? Tune in tomorrow for either the riveting conclusion or the equally riveting non-sequitur of doom!

Part 3

Holy moly, we actually made to part 3. Bacon and eggs and potatoes and coffee, we need our strength 'cause we're about to contemplate that second verse of Heart Shaped Box.

"Meat-eating orchids forgive no one just yet,
Cut myself on angel hair and baby's breath.
Broken hymen of your highness, I'm left black,
Throw down your umbilical noose so I can climb right back."

Wowzers, I maybe haven't had enough coffee yet. The orchids might forgive someone in the future? Hang himself with his own umbilical cord? Is this just the most grotesque possible way to describe a stillbirth? I don't think a botany lesson will help much; I think maybe we should just remember that opposites are really the driving force behind the whole song.

We should also take a moment to consider Bush because Summer is Winter and you always knew it's the little things that kill.

Ok, climbing back into the womb is a fairly common idiom for describing wishing to not be alive, safety as opposed to danger, etc., but it's a noose so we have to consider the similarities between after dying and before being born. Again, Samsara is probably not the actual operating theme, and tempting as it is there's no real karmic balance being equalized, it's a much simpler opposites kind of thing. I wasn't alive before I was born, I won't be alive after I'm dead.

Maybe the advice, just throwing it out there, is "get a life." It certainly matches the sarcastic tone of the song.

It's tempting to look at all the sexual innuendo that grows out of the astrological symbol for pisces (yin/yang, 69, you see what I'm saying), but I already know the punch line at the end of that hallway is Monty Python's "sit on my face and tell me that you love me...," so I'm not gonna do it. It's also interesting to add it all up to the feeling that life is pretty terrible if you're nothing more than an actual meat puppet. There's the larger connection to the album and the discography, parents/children, marriage/divorce, young/old, serious/ironic, nourishment/poison, and so on.

For this song, what stands out to me is that central opposition between priceless advice from authority (whatever form that authority takes) and the subjugating debt it places on the receiver. In a very real sense, that advice has no effect on the giver, but collapses the free will of the receiver into nothing more than a coin flip. Either the advice turns out good and we owe an unrepayable debt to authority, or it turns out bad and we have no way to escape the miserable life forced upon us by authority. Life, it seems, is never our own, and the only possible response is the sarcastic lashing out at everyone and everything else, giving if not an actual identity, at least a coherent voice to the feeling of victimization. But there too, always remember that you are making it up in your own mind as you go, deciding to play the victim and passing it on as your own priceless advice.

Does that say anything about our absurdist experiment in being a dysfunctionally backward experiment in being an idiotic country led by a perpetually bankrupt real-estate mogul? Yeah, I think so. The only war on religion happening right now is the concentrated effort of a small subset of Evangelical Christianity attempting to seize political power and enforce its own doctrine on the world. Conversion and rebirth are after all the central impulse of Evangelical Christianity, the world full of wretched, hell-bound heathens in need of teaching and salvation through the belief in Jesus's atonement as the salvation of all humanity. Contrary to popular belief among themselves, Evangelism is by far the majority of America's religious demographics, crossing nearly all denominational boundaries of Protestantism, and it has a long history of using its own propaganda to acquire as much politico-economic power as it possibly can to "protect" the way of life it believes it rightfully controls. America, for the Christian Right, is an unquestionably Protestant Christian nation prevented from exercising its rightful political and moral authority by Roman Catholicism, and the competing and even more dangerous man-made institutions of Science, Humanism, and secular governance.

Propaganda, by the way, is language and information that promotes any larger cause while omitting any consideration of opposition or criticism. Conversely, absolute rejection of a competing idea without consideration of its potential merits is also propaganda. It's a highly Borderline view of the world and reality. Nearly all political speech is propagandist in nature, regardless of the topic it addresses.

Did we solve anything? No probably not, but we did come to a relevant statement about the subjective nature of all of it. We looked at both sides of the coin, and sort of watched the Stockholm and Lima syndromes fluctuate back and forth. I probably sounded condescending at some point in there, but it's hard not to when our topic is competing for non-tangible fun and prizes. Still half a Saturday left, I say use it as thou wilt. Interesting grammar thingamabob, "thou" was originally the singular form of the plural "you." Y'all have fun now, and I'll see you when you're visible.

Epictetus and Stoicism

Epictetus has been popping up a lot lately, and Stoicism in general is an interesting topic. Like everything else, when you fire up the youtubulator or oscillate the wikiplunger, you get a thousand versions of an introductory synopsis, and they mostly don't do anything for you. The reality is you have to go read stuff for yourself, and you have to admit that you don't know anything until you do.

Epictetus is colloquially known as the loser's philosopher (not to be confused with Diogenes, the actual bum philosopher), and Stoicism is usually dismissed as the philosophy of prisoners and slaves (Epictetus being a slave, then freed from slavery, then exiled in the Great Roman Ban on Philosophers). But even that is too deep, because I'd bet money you think Stoicism is like Vulcan Logic, the complete suppression of emotion. That's just wrong, and the biggest problem we face with any philosophical study is that we imagine it's a lifelong dedication, a menu we select from and have to adhere to for the rest of our lives. That's stupid.

Philosophy is a garage full of tools, schools of thought are individual tools, you fill up your brain box with the things you need to go do stuff. You wouldn't try to tighten nuts and bolts with a tire inflator any more than you'd only use the green handled screwdriver on Thursdays. The choice of tools is based on knowledge, experience, and intention.

Stoicism is a philosophy of control; it won't help you pick out an appropriate birthday present for your cousin, it won't help you lower your golf score, it won't make pain and sadness evaporate. What it will do is help you keep a more objective perspective on what is or is not useful for living your life during the deluge of garbage people sometimes throw at you.

What can you control? Well, for the most part, you can control your thoughts, emotions, and actions. Not control the fact that you have or don't have them, but rather how and for what purpose you react to them. We like to pretend that we can't, we like to blame external forces for our internal misery, we love to identify legitimate disorders that prove we can't control our thoughts and actions, then deny their validity as a bizarre substitute for the control we have chosen to give up.

Fame, fortune, popularity, material wealth, all of these things lie outside of our control. Obviously, we can base our choices and thoughts on known strategies for obtaining those things, but ultimately their acquisition rests not upon ourselves, rather in the accumulative actions of others. These are things we receive from others, and therefore we have no control over their actual materialization or the quality of their acquisition.

We like to believe that a good choice is preferable to a bad choice, but again, do we have control over the distinction itself? To some extent yes, but many of our choices are defined by society at large and the burden of choice placed upon us rather than of our own devising. If one admits freedom of choice for others, one must equally relinquish control of the choosing: assembling alternative choices is itself the act of giving up control. If one can change the future by choice, then there is a future over which our own future selves have no control, and that is a paradox that renders the entire exercise absurd. We can of course control our choice of actions, but we have no control of their future value after failing or succeeding to accomplish them.

So, while we cannot control the experiences that engulf us in the future, we can control our perception of those experiences by choosing to experience them as fully as possible now. I don't mean ridiculous things like intentionally breaking your arm to know how much it hurts; I mean to be psychologically conscious of our experiences as they happen and apply that knowledge to their recurrence rather than avoiding them through delusion or intentional misinterpretation.

Strangely, this central notion of consciousness as the foundation of Stoicism is itself frequently misinterpreted as a delusion. So, for a rebuttal, we turn not to Zeno's "virtue is sufficient for happiness," but to the sage wisdom of John Candy's character in Cool Runnings: "A gold medal is a wonderful thing, but if you're not enough without it, you'll never be enough with it."

Where Are We, Bottle?

E: Where are we, Bottle?

B: Not sure, Skip. I told you it was dangerous to swim out past the leeward side of full albums, but that invisible conversation we had between whichever pages those were back there kind did a real number on the old cerebral gyroscope. We're definitely floating in the Philoso-sea, possibly somewhere between the US and UK Virgin Islands.

E: I was unaware there were British Virgin Islands.

B: Yeah, Turks & Caicos isn't an American territory.

E: Oh, ok, I guess that makes sense.

B: Does it? More importantly, you're not even going to ask?

E: Ask what?

B: You know, why they call them that.

E: Call them what?

B: The "Virgin Islands."

E: I don't want to know.

B: Horse hocky, you're just afraid to look naive and/or foolish.

E: Ok, fine, why?

B: Because Columbus was a tool.

E: What?

B: Remember? Columbus thought Eurasia was it as far as Earth was concerned, so he logically believed he had already circumnavigated this newly round globe thingy, ergo everywhere he landed must have been India. Finders namers, so he decided to name these beautiful islands after St. Ursula and her 11 (or possibly 11,000 martyred Christian virgins, history is not good with numbers and disturbingly unkind to women). That story, by the way, comes from a plaque on a building mentioning "Huns murdered virgins here in Cologne a long time ago."

E: So basically, none of that is even remotely helpful?

B: Well, it is remote, but no not helpful. We're still lost at sea. Why don't you try floating and I'll see which direction you drift?

E: Why don't you?

B: Interesting fact, the lower half of my body is not buoyant. Never has been, never will be. Mystery of the universe, that one.

E: Hhhhhhh, fine.

B: Ok, good enough, follow me for about 11,000 stokes and we'll do it again. Keep an eye out for driftwood or turtles or something.

E: Are we going to die?

B: Eventually. Oh, you mean soon? Probably not. The trouble with washing up on a deserted island is that you can't actually do it until you're delirious and about to drown. I'm still disconcertingly chipper, so we got a while. If it makes you feel any better, you'll probably pass out first and I'll reach exhaustion trying to drag you along. If we're lucky we'll be sipping drinks from a pineapple in a day or two.

E: What if we're unlucky?

B: Coconut water and a one-way trip up the volcano.

E: I wouldn't mind a few days stranded with Meg Ryan.

B: 1) I'm impressed, 2) I'm disturbed you actually know Joe Vs. The Volcano well enough to catch my drift, and 3) grab that passing volleyball from that other Tom Hanks movie where a fedex plane crashes. He's not gonna like how his plot line turns out anyway; we're practically doing him a favor.

Some amount of time later…

MEEP

B: Ahoy, there to you too.

Meep meep meep?

B: No, no, I'm always out of my depths. My flotation device might be a little worse for wear, but who knew Editors were so buoyant? Mind giving us a lift to the nearest island without a volcano?

Meep.

B: Thanks, little dudes. We'll just tie this around his ankles like so and I'll climb up first. Heave ho and junk. No sense wasting good rum and algae water, he'll be fine, just leave him in that fish hammock. Mind if I take a nap?

Meep meep.

B: Excellent. Wake me up when we get somewhere…

But Bottle did not get anywhere. Instead, he woke up with a terrible case of the Mondays, and an urge to hear something different....

Cigarettes For Breakfast – Alee Of 'Em

B: Ugh, I just had the worst dream.

C: The one where you're falling off a cliff?

B: No, I like that one, it's exhilarating.

S: The one where you're in a shopping cart on a rollercoaster?

B: No, I think that might have been a dream someone else told me about, not actually mine.

WHITE ROOM, BLACK CURTAINS?

B: Nah, that one's more annoying than bad. I dreamed it was Monday and tough actin' Skipactin and I were totally lost trying to steer this ship in some direction that gets us somewhere. Like 3 minutes after he passed out some nice pirate minions gave us a lift and brought us back.

C: What's so horrible about that?

B: Nothing. Literally nothing. Worst dream ever. Then I woke up and it really was Monday, and those are the worst. They taste like Cigarettes for Breakfast. Then out of nowhere Cigarettes for Breakfast appeared in my feed trough and I was like "hell yeah, we're gonna buy their whole digital discography and thoroughly enjoy some gloomy fuzzed out psychedelic shoegaze from Pennsylvania."

First up is their self-titled album from 2020. It's a deluge of brain-thumping low end and noise, just noise and reverb and good gracious it's delightful.

Then it's on to their later that year album Aphantasia. I personally have whatever the opposite of aphantasia is. I see cosmic spiderwebs and glitches in the matrix and the cogs of ideas rotating like clockwork, smell of sounds sort of nonsense. Hard to get any meaningful work done, really. Oh my, this is gorgeous. It is a lot like Hum, but with female vocals a mile away in a cavern in the woods. It's very Chelsea Wolfe if you need that comparison. A lot more electronic noise, though.

Then a live show and some other tracks. This is very much my Alternative Rock. It grooves, it floats and shimmers and banishes all coherent thought from your brain like a warm bath with the lights off. Tons of feedback and ill-advised pedal combinations that are more noise than actual tone.

Sertraline? Best specific drug reference since Greta van Fleet. You know it as Zoloft. It's an SSRI like Paxil or Prozac or Celexa like I took. Serotonin is a complicated thingy mostly involved with your GI tract and cell growth, but inhibiting its reuptake is one of many ways to treat depression, or cause worse depression if that wasn't the problem. They all seem to exacerbate dementia compared to people who never used them, so if you thought I was bad now....

Was I smarter before or after the antidepressants? That's a tough one. I mean, I didn't know I needed glasses until my 20s and my optometrist actually said "people as far sighted as you often don't graduate high-school."

"I am not completely like other people -eople -eople - eople..." is sort of how I responded.

Cigarettes for Breakfast is just fantastic. This goes right on the shelf next to Mirror Travel and Parts and Labor and those Hum records if they ever actually get here.

"What is the meaning of all this existence?" Like he said, to explore and find out together. I can't describe it; you just have to hear it for yourself. I do very much love it, though. You should all definitely check them out. Unless you just hate psychedelic noise rock from an underground cavern near a steel mill where everything smells sad. If that's the case then I'm not gonna be much help, am I?

cfbofficial.bandcamp.com

Meeting of the Album Club – Vaughan Williams – A Sea Symphony

B: I hereby call this meeting of Bottle's Album Club to order. First, will the secretary read the minutes of our previous meeting?

E: 17, 19, 44.

C: Hut!

B: is there a second?

S: 12 of them, to be precise. Oh sorry, I meant hut hut!

B: I definitely approve of those minutes as well. 37 was touch and go if I remember correctly, but we definitely pulled it together around 44. Any new business?

C: Well, I was rechecking the figures and I'm afraid we're out of options.

E: What are you talking about, there's hundreds of albums left in the stacks.

C: Yes, you are of course correct, many albums our Bottle has but hasn't reviewed. I'm afraid, however, you'll find the vast majority were composed by long dead white guys of the European persuasion, ranging backward from now to the bowels of barely double-digit centuries. I don't think I need remind any of you that the world has moved well along.

S: Yeah, hard to argue people aren't tired of pontificating from crusty old white dudes. Present company excluded.

B: Why? I totally resemble those remarks. I don't think I'm the worst by a long shot, but genetically speaking I'm just about as English as beans on toast. I'll make the motion. 781 random albums from all across the spectrum, I think we can safely wade into the swamp of Equal Tempered European Aristocratic Musics of the Common Practice Period ranging from roughly the year papa Bach died up to the 2nd Industrial Revolution (we're in the midst of the 3rd, by the way). All in favor?

Chorus: Mumble, mumble, mumble, I guess so....

B: Motion carried. Our friend Gerard mentioned he was listening to Vaughan Williams not too long ago, and I got one of them obsolete compacted vertebrae things featuring the BBC Symphony Orchestra and Chorus, so it's even got wordy words like all the other albums I like.
First Symphony's first. Old Rayfee's sea is not at all like Debussy's or even Anita Kerr's. Vaughn Williams studied with Ravel, and makes use of decidedly English Folk and Renaissance approaches to melody and texture. Less turmoil or terror or passion, more fanfare, gallantry, and sentimentality. It's not much like a symphony, for that matter. It feels a lot more like a Cantata played on the Mildy

Meandering River Raft Ride at Walt Whitman World. Very much like those big symphonic pastoral oil paintings our own French educated American composers liked so much, but with some chant and operatic writing thrown in.

At just shy of an hour and a half if you're breaking the speed limit, you might need a proper intermission between each movement. I certainly need at least one bathroom break in there somewhere, whether they stop playing or not. "Unprecedented in England?" That's ring-a-ding-dang-donculously long for anyone anywhere except Beethoven or Mahler or Wagner. It's good though, so that helps.

Like you might expect, there's nothing weird or strange about the BBC Symphony Orchestra. They're like the RP of orchestras: calm, articulate, generically understandable at all times. The instruments sound like instruments, the voices sound like highly trained vocalists with a proper amount of rehearsal time. That's usually a little dull in my book, but it's completely appropriate for Vaughan Williams, the prim and proper socialite who believed sharing music with the public was a just and worthy gift to society. Yawn. Not a condescending yawn, sorry if I mistakenly gave that impression. Even by my standards this is completely lovely. I've just had a rough week and this is a completely acceptable warm bath with fizzly stuff and smell good oil to get you through one more blizzardpocalypse day of it. Enjoy.

Snowpocalypse '22

As the next round of snow moves in, I'm proud to say I am already home and did all my running around so I don't even have to think about worrying about leaving tomorrow. Mrs. Bottle called me a functional adult and everything. I'm deeply offended, but there's nothing else to do except pour a plastic cup full of Admiral Cola and watch the Bottlemobile disappear from the ground up before tackling my super busy schedule.

You see, I was not looking forward to being Bottle the Classical Music Critic, so I foresightedly grabbed a few albums to pass the time. I also got confirmation that my two Hum records shipped, so we can enjoy those in a week or two. Plus, I have a B&N gift card from that Christmas thing we skated over a while back, so there's another episode "cheapest new records I can find, giftcardganza edition" in our future. Things are looking swell.

I am a bit conflicted, though, because on the one hand it is absolutely atrocious that Barney Fife shot and killed Eko, but it's also pretty terrible that the zoo is more concerned about suing the maintenance company for lost investment than anything. To be fair, that guy's job was to clean the gift shop, not pet/get mangled by a tiger, but I'm not sure sending him to federal prison for felony trespassing/3rd-degree endangered species murder will actually accomplish anything, or that a janitorial service is gonna do much for the financial future of a zoo. Then again, it's Florida, so I'm not sure why any of this is actually a surprise to anyone.

Bye bye, functional adult Bottle, hello UFO and ZZ Top and another attempt at liking Moody Blues, and those potentially wackadoodle solo albums from famous Rock drummers. My weekend's looking pretty exciting.

UFO – Obsession

Wowzers, it is really coming down, or should I say across, out there. Glad I'm in here.

Obsession is the last original run UFO album with Michael Schenker on Guitars. Michael is of course Rudolph's little brother. I'm not gonna play over/under rated with Scorpions and UFO like most people do, I'm just gonna point out NWBHM bands weren't dropping the name Scorpions in their "influenced by" sections.

Christgau didn't like this one, so I'm sure it will be great. He liked their earlier albums, but called this "exhibitionism." I assume he's referring to the macho late 70s when every early 70s Hard Rock band was forced to grow moustaches and give Disco an ill-advised whirl before breaking up.

I think we'll pair it with the Harland Williams classic Rocket Man and do this what we like to call "the right way." The chimp will steal my sleep pod and I'll be forced to stare at the wall for the entire trip to Mars, I mean playlipsis, and when everybody else wakes back up I'll get in trouble for whatever wacky shenanigans I got up to. No countdown, just blast off...

... oh yeah, guitar heaven. The solos are obnoxiously fantastic. The album is a bit of a triple-split personality between Hard Rock, Prog, and Heavy Metal. It's a bit disconcerting to jump back and forth that way, but as for what they actually do in each genre I've got no complaints at all. I'll explain, Hard Rock means catchy Pop Songs, Heavy Metal means chainsaws and power chord based riffage, Prog means random orchestral interludes, piano ballads and string sections, and actual melodies.

What's with the ball bearings? Well, it is a Hipgnosis design, so Stormy Storm the Pig Inflator, and Sleazy McCartilage are either involved or in the next office doing something much worse. Maybe they wanted it to look like some kind of Mercury based alien life-form infestation, I don't know.

What I do know is there isn't a dud on this thing. No, it doesn't add up to much in the way I tend to appreciate albums, but that is kinda what the late 70s were when you think about it. No rules, just Rock. It does rock, and you simply can't honestly tell me Schenker doesn't go out with a bang. His tone is absolutely disgusting, even the softer clean stuff and occasional acoustics play in counterpoint with a distorted part that sounds like 400 grit sandpaper on a fence post.

But back to my original point, which is that this is clearly meant to be a variety album, and in that regard it's incredible. Usually, a band doesn't quite get one of the styles right, but this is top notch across the board. So, final verdict, get the ball bearings out of your ears and check out the eclectic stylings of one of the top underappreciated transition bands from 70s Hard Rock to 80s British Heavy Metal.

Look at that, I behaved, didn't even use our food supply to paint a mural or nothin'.

By the way, best coincidence ever, the lyric "I turned around to the janitor, asked him 'just how long you been dead?'" Is totally hiding in there. You're welcome.

ZZ Top – Tres Hombres

Have mercy. Next up on our Snowpocalypse Staycation of Doom we have the soundtrack I wish I'd had back when Skip was waiting for the bus all day after getting lost. 2 dudes and a Rube playing Blues Rock in the fine Texas tradition, it's ZZ Top's 3rd album, Tres Hombres. Quite a few Classic Rock staples on this one, Bus, Chicago, La Grange. this is one of those "Boogie Woogie" albums critics liked to dismiss until the mainstream listener got a hold of Eliminator and put a stop to that nonsense.

I'm not gonna add much, if you don't adore ZZ Top then there's no helping you. There's a fair bit of not radio single material, but it's interesting. If you thought ZZ Top was all boogie all the time, Hot, Blue and Righteous will surprise you. Slow dance jam with vocal harmony in 6/8 that one, the good stuff.

You might not be accustomed to Dusty Hill's vocals, and it can throw you for a loop if all you've ever heard is Billy singing. You'll get over it, Dusty's just as good if not quite as distinctive. It's a bit like Canned Heat or Grateful Dead in that respect, you get locked into 1 vocalist and lose the larger picture.

This is another one of those variety albums, as clearly depicted in the borderline grotesque gatefold photo of every possible combination of meat, cheese, tortillas, and hot sauce that restaurant could sloppily pile on a plate. Garnish with enough pinch harmonics to heat-stroke a horse, wash it down with a rapidly approaching room temperature beer, that's a recipe for pretty tasty in my book.

The Moody Blues – On The Threshold Of A Dream

We finished out yesterday evening with Tres Hombres by ZZ Top. Today we're gonna give The Moody Blues another try with On The Threshold Of A Dream. This album has literally been to the moon.

So, Compy, do that thing you do and remind me of all the reasons they're fantastic but for some reason I don't enjoy listing to them.

Unrememberably SQUIRREL!, Folk when I'm not in the moody for it, extreme limitations in recording technology, mildly hard to follow plotlines, yep that all sounds like a smorgasbord of wasting away in Rum and Cola-ville, aka it's my own damned fault. Clearly, I'm confusing the band for Jimmy Buffet, and that seems like a completely unfair comparison.

So, first things second, we have to tackle this novella of prose and poetry, experimental fonts, bipolar critical response, you name it. Everybody has a thing or 5 to say. We might get to actually listening to it at some point, but this thing comes with a lot of prep work.

Believe it or not, I like every single part of that. For better or worse, this album is clearly intended to be a tactile experience. I gotta say, nobody half-assed their part of it. Sure, you could look at it through the pretentiousness prism, but why do all that thinking if you've already decided to hate it? You're wasting your own time and energy. Future alert, we'll look at a stellar example of wasting other peoples' time energy and money a few albums from now, with the amazingly coincidental contextual commonality of the word "moon."

Anywho, what's this thing about? My reading glasses are thankfully the same as my regular glasses, so we can just dive right in to the explanatory paragraph.

Hmmm, yes, indeed. Well, David Lymonds writes exactly like I do with an incredibly similar sense of humor, and it is not in any way helpful, so it's got that going for it.

Graeme Edge says this first poem is meant to encapsulate the themes of the whole album, so that's exactly like the concept he says it isn't. Cognitive dissonance appears to be on the menu. K, so, humorous reworking of Descartes, we are the ink that runs the Establishment's giant computer printer, smile and nod and don't let them see you not pay any attention to their machinations. Sure yeah, think for yourself, question authority. I'll of course point out that those roles can be easily reversed and I am completely capable of questioning the questioning of authority when authority turns out to mostly agree with my own assessment of things. If you're demanding I be dumb, I'm gonna morph into a brick wall.

Here's the real-world problem. Should the current administration have the power to mandate vaccinations? No, absolutely not. Are people like Ben Shapiro or Tucker Carlson or whoever justified in cheering the Supreme Court's decision like their sports team won? No, because their argument completely misconstrues both the issue at hand, and the mechanisms necessary to produce it. These self-proclaimed champions of liberty and "freedom" ironically limit the very freedoms and liberties they say they champion. We don't live in the 1890s anymore, those notions of tyranny and freedom and power and whatnot are completely inadequate to deal with the kinds of geopolitical problems our federal government has no choice but to deal with in this bizarro reality where a single person trying to live a relatively uneventful life is legally identical to a corporate entity like Microsoft or ExxonMobil or Portland, Oregon.

    This is tough, I know, but stick with me. Here in 2022, America is a business. Each successive President since Eisenhower has been forced to increasingly treat the country like a business, and Trump (whether you like it or not) was the breaking point. America is now a really terrible corporation making it real tough to get anything accomplished outside of its jurisdiction because the leading world economies conduct their business in U.S. dollars. We won the Cold War, now we're Minnesota Fats in that Twilight Zone episode. America is a Capitalist. Not a capitalist economy, or a capitalist country, an actual imaginary human being who owns the product of its citizens' labor and conducts global competitive business for profit. Whose fault is that? It's the fault of privately owned but publicly traded corporations demanding increasing legal protection for refusing to fulfill their own trade deals and contracts in good faith. It's the fault of everyone who chooses antagonistic/competitive rather than cooperative negotiations. Governors believe they are the CEOs of State corporations, the President is the CEO of Corporate America. There are only 2 ways out of that situation. One is we just glide all the way to the scene of the plane crash; the other is we pay off that outstanding debt against the wishes of the rest of the world.

    The SBA's best guess at the failure rate of startups is around 90%. There are currently 195 countries. When we apply logic to the concept that Countries are businesses measured by their GDP, we cannot help but come to the conclusion that the whole world in fact depends on or feeds off the 20 most productive national economies.

Obviously, that data could change, and the logic of the situation would change with it, but we do have to return to Marx to get a grip on the situation as it stands.

Overdetermination encompasses this situation. The proportion of failure to success in terms of business is structurally identical to the proportion of top-tier to subordinate economies because they operate under the same rule system. Having these two data sets not match up would be an incredibly shocking reality.

The interconnectivity of national economies is determined by their resources and mode of exchange, and the geography of resources has always been the primary factor of all political decision-making. But what happens when that geographical foundation disappears through technological advancement? The answer is that privately controlled economic states begin to supersede geographic states and will continue to do so until their actual resources are depleted. We'll keep burning oil until we run out. We'll keep planting field corn and soy beans and spraying artificial fertilizers until the country is a barren, inarable wasteland. We'll keep wasting millions of tons of everything until there's more plastic garbage than wildflowers, then pave it over with concrete and forget about it. I sound particularly curmudgeonly today, don't I?

I'm actually not, I'm simply trying to point out that the harder you bash people over the head defending what amounts to intentionally stubborn ignorance, the less productive anyone actually is and the more dependent they become on the authority you're arguing against. People don't have a choice in that matter.

Those ultra-conservative pundits are not arguing for change that benefits you the demographic. They are arguing that right now, everything exactly the way it is, major corporations making whatever choices they want without any responsibility to you is as good as it could possibly be, and any attempt to change that is an act of war against the supremacy of uncompromising individuality. They wanted GM and Ford to go bankrupt and not get bailed out leaving hundreds of thousands of people unemployed, they want people fighting in the street about their supposed god given rights, they were unhappy back when the Trade Titans got caught in their own pyramid schemes and wail about the loss of their right to gamble with employee pensions, they want force and violence to be the determining factor underlying social interaction, they want people to get sick and die from completely preventable diseases because that is how they make a profit; that money gets absorbed back up the metaphorical economic food chain. Winning lawsuits really is their favorite sporting event right up until they themselves get caught on the losing side of their own loopholes. I'm thinking of Governor Reynolds who appears to be politically hedging her bets by being super happy that her administration now has 1.2 billion of discretionary tax income and is desperately trying to push through massive tax cuts to hamstring the next Governor should she happen to lose. When and if those cuts are ratified, she will immediately set about allocating as much of that surplus as possible to her own political and commercial allies to prevent it from being reinjected into general (unregulated) circulation.

 Again, I know this is a gargantuan problem to try to hold in your brain, but you have to understand which side of the equation you actually stand on at any given moment. You the real person are actually 2 different legal entities from the perspective of governance: you are a consumer of goods and services *and* a producer of goods and services. The government measures economic activity in terms of payroll and sales; how much you earn vs how much you buy. Collective you not individual you.

An interesting phenomenon occurs when you do that. The city of Fort Dodge for example neither manages its water treatment facility, nor pays an in-state company to do it. Instead, the water treatment plant is managed by Florida based US Water Services Corp. Presumably there is a clear economic reason for that, but the tradeoff is that the state and city have no choice but to monitor the outgoing expense of that contract with the incoming wages that return as salaries for local employees. In that sense the state economies of Iowa and Florida are interconnected, as are the economies of every other state in which USW operates. That's not inherently bad at all (in fact it is presumably a good thing given USW's significantly larger access to national resources), but it does require monitoring as interstate trade because the city manages the exchange between individual consumers and the company that actually maintains and operates the facility. We have to ask the question, is this state sponsored monopoly better or worse than the potential reality of continuously changing local competitive ownership of the facility? It's not a simple matter of quality or popularity, municipal water supply is not a competitive market because it must operate outside the realm of traditional economic scarcity. 100% supply of drinkable tap water to all residents is the mandatory minimum standard of operation, whether practically achievable or not. Competition in this case comes instead from the choice between the public utility itself vs private commercial water treatment. I think we can all recognize that a city completely reliant on private wells, storage tanks, and commercial distribution would be extremely impractical in terms of infrastructure, highly volatile in terms of selective scarcity, health, and economic stability, as well as unpredictably wasteful. Keep in mind, someone like me out in the country on a deep well hundreds of feet down in an aquifer trades the cost of water services for the cost of electricity necessary to pump that water, i.e., my water supply is dependent on my electricity rather than the gravity systems used in most municipalities. You certainly wouldn't want to have to worry about your tank level every time you took a shower any more than our forefamilies enjoyed carrying buckets of water home from the nearest stream. Bottled water or delivery is exponentially more expensive by comparison.

Ironically, the more we go around this grumpy-go-round, the tighter we weave our economy into the tapestry of fiduciary insurance, all money being spent not to facilitate productive trade, but hoarded for future legal defense and recuperation; profit by natural or artificial disaster, I'll emerge the richer when it all crumbles to dust! Bah humbug.

What dream are we on the threshold of having? The band say "we don't know, it just sounded like a compelling title." Holy cow, we did finally make it to the listening to find out. I was starting to wonder. 3, 2, 1...

I can tell you this, I like Side A a whole lot better than any of their other albums. It's still a bit scattered, but that's the point. These are all random inner monologues, people just thinking about their experience. It's hard to tell what's critical or not, but I think the underlying theme is that everybody is running around all stressed out and desperate for material wealth and order and pushing people around, but wouldn't it be better if we actually loved each other instead? It's definitely The Moody Blues, but it's also a completely normal Rock album for 1969, albeit with flutes and sinister sounding synths and an undercurrent of deep skepticism. On to Side B then.

Oh yeah, no mistaking it here. I don't know how to break this to you, so I'm just gonna say it like I always do: this Bourgeois life of work weeks and Sunday afternoons is total crap. Side B is like your own personal A Christmas Carol. This is a terrifying dream. Waste your life away working for nothing or take life back and live in the now instead of a future that will never actually materialize.

Then Lionel Bart (whoever he is) gives us the least coherent epilogue I've ever read while the runoff grove endlessly cycles that creepy ode to the vacuum of space. He writes nothing like I do. I'm joking, Lionel Bart is pretty famous for writing the musical Oliver! and selling all his publishing rights to pay off his debts. The value of his creative output for the next 6 years went from the 300k he received for it up to about 2-million for someone else. That's why selling out is bad. You can't predict actually hitting it big, but you can be assured that you don't get any money at all if you no longer own the rights to your own work. I have the opposite problem, nobody's offering me diddly squat when 300k British pounds would solve every problem I could imagine and then some.

How in the world are you still reading this? Ok, so yeah, we found a Blue Mood Group album I really like. It reminds me of Blows Against The Empire, The Association, all that great stuff from the year the feces hit the fan. This, according to Bart, is a fantastic beginning from some professional beginners, and the whole thing is a "once upon a time...."

So, is space really the place with the helpful hardware? I suppose if all the rich people really do go there and leave us plebes alone to be perfectly happy eating food from trees and loving each other then yeah, get the hell out of here as quickly as possible. Let 'em go Florida up the universe, long as I don't have to listen to people argue about it anymore.

Also, yes if you mean Marx's actual idea of spreading people back out, giving them the ability and opportunity to be meaningfully self-sufficient rather than compete for artificial fame and fortune. Why is government so big? Because the titans of industry are absolutely terrible at running the accumulated economy. If they weren't terrible at it, they wouldn't spend 90% of their time and energy suing each other for profit. They'd actually help eliminate poverty instead of creating more of it, help people meet the needs of their own communities instead of exploiting their labor to pay for unrelated bad investments.

So, long story longer, I think I'm getting the knack of this understanding the universe, so later tonight we'll listen to Get The Knack, and tackle a double bass drum of solo albums from Keith Moon and Carmine Appice tomorrow. Unless I change my mind, which is totally a thing I'm capable of doing. You should get an award for reading this far, it literally took me 9 hours to write it, compared to the less than 1 it takes to listen to it. Enjoy, like I actually did for a change.

The Knack – Get The Knack

Do The Knack hate women the way critics mansplain how much they like this album in spite of its misogyny? That's an interesting question. I don't remember My Sharona being that bad, Good Girls Don't is a little more iffy, ooh the track list is not doing you guys any favors, is it? No reason not to listen to it, though, so here we go.

- Let me out of this relationship.
- Lamenting his inability to hit on passing strangers?
- Oh Tara, you're totally right to be terrified.
- How selfish is she? This song is refreshingly vulgar, but not in an appropriate way.
- I know why, you're a douche bag.
- Good girls don't. No, of course not, and you're a grade a jerk for pretending she was winkingly saying "but I do." She didn't.

Whoo-ee that's a Side A.

- My Sharona isn't quite so bad because he's actually singing it to her. He's literally telling her she's driving him crazy, and that's totally fine, she's an active participant in this song for a change.

- This isn't bad either, she kissed him. Totally normal not psychopathic psychology at all. 2 for 8.

- Wowzers, another vulgar one. Very little actually offends me, but Siamese Twins probably has a dedicated FCC fine or a mandatory minimum sentence or something. You definitely couldn't play this on the radio, even at 1:42 am on a Thursday morning.

- I have a hard time believing Lucinda is as bad a heart breaker as you're implying. Your track record with women is sketchier than sidewalk chalk drawings in front of a day care.

- Little girls should not be doing anything to you, you're a grown-up college dropout creeping on high schoolers. She'll break your ego then your heart? In that order? You sure about that?

- Frustrated? This album is like the soundtrack on eternal repeat in a date-rapist's Camaro. My brain needs a shower like Ace Ventura after finding out Einhorn is Finkel. That's probably offensive too, but it's Ace Ventura's homophobic overreaction that's the funny part.

Ok, now that that's over, you know how in all those 80s John Hughes movies the girls like the jerks and ignore their awkward platonic male friends? The Knack are simultaneously both of those stereotypes at the same time, only the platonic friend is just a shy version of the date-rapey frat guys. So exactly like the subtext of a John Hughes movie.

I get what the critics are saying, though. This is a really great album to listen to. If you replaced all the lyrics with anything else, a Cracker Barrel menu, the text of a missing dog photo, even most bathroom graffiti is less offensive than these actual lyrics, then yeah it would be amazing.

The two hit singles and Heartbeat are fine. Like I said, describing how what she actually does makes you feel is totally acceptable, even if it's not exactly polite conversation. However, half these songs are you making up things she definitely didn't do or say, and at least two of them are you just elaborately calling her a bitch for not putting out IN YOUR OWN IMAGINATION! Absolutely horrible. Get The Knack sounds more like contracting an STD than something I ever want to do again.

That said, damnit it's catchy and fun. If you can listen to it with a skewed sense of humor then it's not so jarring, but at face value it's a bit much. So is their almost farcical overnight success. Nobody wanted their demos, period. They however kept playing shows and developed a huge sellout following on the club circuit. When they finally did get it released it went Gold in 2 weeks and Platinum in a couple months. Faster than even Beatles albums at the height of their popularity. Everybody was a bit critical of them, but they don't suck. The mentality most of their lyrics come from is horrible, but we're gonna listen to Keith Moon's debacle of a solo album tomorrow, so adjust your perspectives accordingly.

Two Sides of the Rock Drummer Solo Album

Part 1 – Keith Moon – Two Sides Of The Moon

Keith Moon is a lot of things, but I suspect prolific waster of other peoples' money is pretty close to the top of the list. Bad for investors, great for anyone who made their living cleaning up the debris left in the wake of his Tasmanian Devil like rampage through life.

The story goes that in between a bunch of John Lennon produced album and the filming of Tommy, Moon convinced everyone to help him make a solo album so he could pretend to be a Beach Boy. He barely plays drums on his own record, instead just singing and taking tons of drugs and threatening to take a pick axe to the record exec's desk if he didn't pay for the elaborate cut-out cover concept. I've chosen to be delicate and not show the other side of the moon with an actual moon in the form of presumably that lady's butt sticking up in the air. Ringo Starr gets credit for naming this album. There's really no way this can't be terrible, so let's just dive right in.

Crazy Like A Fox is perfectly lovely old-school Rock and Roll with Piano and backup singers.

Solid Gold is terrible. He's doing that funny voice like McCartney does on Uncle Albert and such.

Don't Worry Baby is equally terrible. It's almost like an Edith Massey or William Shatner version than anything.

One Night Stand is one of the selections from part of the sessions where he wanted to do a bunch of Country songs, but everyone else said "hell no, knock that crap off."

I zoned out and looked at side b, this thing ends with some sure to be enthralling "rap" from Ringo, so we got that trainwreck to look forward to. Right now, we have to get through this slower and significantly less enjoyable version of classic Power-Pop Who's The Kids Are All Right with a god awful Animalesque drum solo for no reason.

Side B really isn't that bad, except for In My Life, that's objectively horrible. There's definitely a conceptual problem here. This is supposed to be ridiculous, raucous, raunchy, crazy, loony, hysterical....

No, it's not. No part of this sounds like it was fun, everybody loses. Oh god, Together is like a Conga line at a Ministry of Silly Walks convention. That interlude of sub-Dad joke level banter leaves everything to be desired, and the best part of the whole thing is it's over.

This is not wacky, or over the top, or scandalous. If you randomly inserted a track or two in any rock and roll playlist no one would even guess in a million years that it's Keith Moon, or care, or think anything is out of the ordinary other than that these are random covers and this is a randomly uninteresting cover album like everybody else was making at the time.

A couple songs are legit stinkers with no redeeming quality, but mostly it's just "meh." Seems like the two sides of the moon are just dumb and dumberer. I wonder if the drummer from Vanilla Fudge can do a better job....

Part 2 – Carmine Appice

... well, Carmine Appice actually cowrote most of the songs, and the couple covers are instrumental arrangements, so it certainly seems like he's intentionally making a solo album instead of dicking around and getting high like Keith. That's already a much better start. Calling the band "The Rockers" is a little cheesy, but I've got no complaints if they actually do.

I will say this, it's the straight-ahead, apartment rock 80s approximation of Carnivale with a couple tablespoons of slightly less than authentic Noir thrown in. As far as mental images go it's about as menacing as Beverly Hills Cop or Police Academy. I hear how it's supposed to appear menacing and sinister, but my disbelief is not in any way suspended. You didn't actually rush past a dozen mugging victims to get to the studio after a sideways drug deal behind a cargo container at an unbelievably unsecured dockyard. You woke up in your hotel room and put on your best Tuesday headband, had a cup of coffee, taped your knuckles, and four-on-the-floored for a few hours after lunch. I'm not really here to judge, though, except in the sense of whether or not I believe you. Yeah, I believe you, this is what you were going for, it does rock within the confines of its context. I promise this is not an insult, it sounds like a Pat Benatar album.

Unlike Two Sides of the Moon, this is a masterclass in workhorse radio-friendly rock drumming, 4-bar phrases with an infinite variety of drum and guitar fills, about as vanilla rock as it gets for 80/81. Carmine is not the most compelling lyricist or vocalist, but none of this is bad enough to change the station.

We're all so conditioned to think generic and mediocre are bad. Why is that? I have a theory or 12. Mainly what it boils down to is this strange notion of me, I'm the center of the universe, I decide, and only the most amazingly mind-blowing awesomeness is worthy of my attention. I don't like that, and I'll tell you why: it's boring. Absolutely, the 5 best people can just do everything while the rest of us stare at the ceiling and wait to die. 10 more people can compete for top 5, sure, but what are the rest of us supposed to do? Compete for the opportunity to compete for the privilege of buying a lottery ticket?

Even I have that problem. Having to slog through it all to try to impress a couple people isn't fun, and the results become a standard thing that nobody really cares about after 10 minutes. More and more I find myself increasingly frustrated about all the meaningful things I can't do today because they jeopardize all the meaningless crap I have to do for someone else tomorrow while listening to people alternatingly rawr-rawr-rawr about productivity and how inconvenient it is to have to go to a store to buy things and how waiting for it to get delivered is even worse. You know who complains about capitalism the most? Business owners. I don't mean to offend anyone personally by saying that, but us regular people working crap jobs just to buy food have mostly all given up.

And that brings us around to the music business. I'll pick on ASCAP because I know their structure. We have this basic notion that ASCAP collects performance royalties and distributes them to producers. Yes, that's what they do. ASCAP operates as a non-profit, operating on approximately 10% of revenue, 90% being distributed to its members. The fiddly paperwork part is where it gets tricky because it's not as simple as them writing you a check for 90% of the royalties collected from your actual individual music. Top selling artists get a larger share of revenue inside that payout, obscure artists and publishers get a smaller percentage. They break it down into 5 or 6 weighted calculations to make sure moneys are fairly distributed, for example it wouldn't be particularly fair for the producers of background soundtracks in TV shows to get paid from revenue generated by streaming broadcast of live performances, and vice versa and sideways, but yeah Drake is technically going to earn some amount of money generated by a fluke good week for an obscure singer/songwriter in Idaho. That stuff is all spelled out in the contracts, I have no real care. The part that irks me is the monopolization of royalty distribution by the small oligopoly of major PROs.

    Historically, these unions (that's what they really are) grew out of the bad-faith exploitation of all those old school labels who simply stole their own artists' rights and royalties. It helped for quite a long time, artists still made their daily money as the house band, touring, etc., with royalties being a nice side income helping them get through the valleys between successful projects. But, as all those independent labels gradually tucked themselves under the umbrella of the big 4, the proportions shrank accordingly. The supply of available licenses is theoretically infinite, the number of buyers accounting for the majority of royalty revenue is countable on fingers and toes. Long gone are the days when an enterprising person can start a studio and negotiate enough to both keep it running and distribute it just because they like the music. 90% of bands simply aren't going to generate enough royalty revenue to fund the next one themselves, or even break even, it still takes about a decade to really connect with a proper fan base. Chucking it in a PRO's database as a self-publisher and hoping it pays off in a decade is really all you can do in terms of long-range financial planning. All a label does is buy the rights to your music and try to reach a large enough audience to make its own royalties profitable. It manages the finances of a whole group of bands who can't effectively or consistently do it all themselves, exactly the same way ASCAP is doing. It's objectively better for as many artists as possible, but it's only worthwhile if you are already fielding offers from people who want to pay to use it for something and need help keeping track of it all and/or making sure you aren't getting ripped off behind your back. It's insurance for already successful artists, not a viable income for most people.

 The downside is that a blanket licensing system is a zillion times easier and consistently cheaper for license purchasers, so it becomes a standard cost of operation and you aren't even going to get a meeting with a mid-level A&R person unless you're already on their radar. They will choose something they already have the rights to use: kids and cousins of already established artists, bulk license auctions to ad agencies and subsidiary holdings, let the janitor make an album during downtime, sign a band that doesn't realize they're already about to step up or just to prevent someone else from potentially signing them.

 The problem is actually a psychological problem. Once you achieve an apparent level of success/reward, that becomes the new subjective standard, and people equalize their lives based on sustained income, i.e., they naturally live within their means until it becomes obvious that they are no longer being paid an observably fair price. It's not so much greed or envy of your neighbors, it's the equivalence between what you have done, currently do, and want to do in the future. A 70/30 deal can look good on the way up, but terrible if you find yourself scraping by on 3 out of every 10 dollars you generate 20 years later. It looks a lot different when you see your label pocket 70k while you get to keep 30k, doesn't it? 7-mil vs 3-mil stretches the tangible imagination a bit, but the point is you make less than half the profit from your own work and the nature of the business prevents you from renegotiating that relationship unless you made sure you retain full rights to nullification.

Take this album, Appice was already generating revenue for half a dozen labels, he cowrote Do Ya Think I'm Sexy, so someone was gonna publish this whether it made money or not. It's dedicated to John Bonham, and even Led Zeppelin wasn't crazy enough to not list Vanilla Fudge as one of their biggest influences.

Man, I've given this a couple relistens and I take back most of my earlier reservations. This really is a masterclass in great Rock drumming and a completely serviceable album of songs. I'm so accustomed to weird vocals I wasn't fully appreciating his consistency and clarity. I know I don't say this very often, but this album is much better on vinyl than digital.

Critics say they can hear how much fun these sessions must have been, but I can hear the thoroughly enjoyable sounds of actually playing instruments that sound like instruments rather than triggered samples. The stuttering background vocals on Be My Baby are absolutely terrible, but they are definitely doing it on purpose so I can't really fault them for it much.

All in all, it's perfectly lovely. This particular listen I thought I might have to take back my statements about mediocrity/excellence and call this boringly exceptional, but I think my original sentiment holds. This is not a top ten best seller kind of album; it really is a thing he had the opportunity to do so he did it kind of album. It's not going to blow anyone's mind, but it's definitely more valuable than a "for die-hard fans only" production. You're always gonna hear it in its context as Carmine Appice's first solo album, but it definitely proves he had the goods to deserve to make one and it certainly doesn't sound like it was a chore to make. Very nice, I consider myself serviceably rocked and not at all sad I listened to it 3 times to really come to terms with what I was hearing.

Oh, Monday

Hello, universe. Whatcha got in store for us this week? Ask and ye shall receive. I was doing some research on the recent global oil kerfuffles so I could randomly throw that into this insanity I keep making, and it quickly dawned on me that absolutely no one understands the structure of pretty much anything anymore. Where would I even start? You can't just jump right in to the creation and dissolution of OPEC+ because nobody understands what OPEC actually is or why it can't not exist or why it controls 44% of known global oil reserves, they can't understand how that happened without understanding the oil crisis in the early 70s that led to the collapse of the 7 Sisters (just as much a cartel as OPEC, but one we happened to have a say in), they can't understand that without reaching back to busting up the Standard Oil monopoly, and so on. But even that's not really approachable because A) nobody's had a proper economics class in 40 years so we have to talk about the two completely different ways of thinking about markets to really pin down why "oligopoly" and "cartel" are synonyms and the logical evolution of Capitalism, 2nd) everybody has this bizarre notion that the commodities markets represent real tangible objects, and Barnabas Collins III) like somehow Chuck at the gas station down the street has the phone number of the Angolan Energy Secretary in his recent contacts on his cell phone?

Why am I the guy who has to explain the global benchmarks in crude oil pricing, or how a civil war erupts in

South America because Russia didn't raise or lower its production rate by 0.3% the third Tuesday in March, so Chuck over in Columbus has to raise the price on the sign 3 cents a gallon?

I don't wanna! It's too big. People say "free market" when they obviously mean "black market," they think trading retail stocks 20 times a day is super awesome until they wake up tomorrow to the tax bill that they can't afford to pay on those capital gains or to find out that company divested and their holdings are actually worth half of what they thought.

I mean, sure I can do it, but I don't wanna. I wanna just listen to The Carpenters. I love The Carpenters. Yep, that's what I'm gonna do instead. Buggerit.

Ok, Fine, I Will

Ok, OPEC. What is it? It's an intergovernmental organization (oligopoly) that currently manages 13 oil exporting nations in the Middle East, Africa, and South America. Malaysia chose to leave OPEC in 2016. Qatar and Ecuador did too in the last couple years.

What is its goal? To stabilize oil prices among its constituent nations in order to help underdeveloped nations grow their national economies. In other words, OPEC wants to stabilize the value of global oil trade so that its member nations can effectively reinvest profits from the sale of oil back into their own economies.

Where is OPEC's headquarters? Vienna, Austria. It was originally founded in Baghdad, but quickly decided that housing its headquarters in a neutral state was the most beneficial way to ease diplomatic tensions. Switzerland said GTFO, but Vienna said "ok, we don't care."

What does OPEC actually do? It analyzes the global oil trade, publishes that analysis, and regulates the oil production of its member states in order to stabilize the actual delivery of oil to global customers and ensure economic reliability to its member nations.

Why is that a thing? Well, capital markets are a zero-sum game. If for whatever reason the value of say ExxonMobil's particular source of petroleum rises, the value of everyone else's' oil declines by an equal amount. OPEC's actual mission is trying to determine all of those values in order to correlate actual supply with actual demand. Extracting oil when you don't need to is wasteful, not extracting oil when it's needed means you have nothing to sell. Either way you're losing value.

Isn't that price fixing? No, not really. It's value stabilization. Value and price are completely different things. Saudi Arabia can supposedly ramp up extraction for around $3 a barrel compared to Russia's $30+, so Saudi Arabia's oil is more valuable in the face of a demand surge. Saudi Arabia the Capitalist wants that reflected in the price tag, Russia the Capitalist does not. That's the supposed "price war" between OPEC and Russia that led to Russia leaving OPEC+.

From what I've read, OPEC politely asked Russia to help them stabilize prices, Russia decreased its production accordingly but warned that decreasing production too much would make the reuptake worse, OPEC decided it didn't like Russia's advice and HOLY SHIT CHINA NEEDS HOW MUCH OIL THIS MORNING?!?!

So, all of us top 7 economies released an appropriate amount of our own reserves to mitigate the physical damage and get the actual oil shuffling around for as little price increase as possible because Saudi Arabia said they would be more than happy to oblige for a shitload of profits. You might have read different things than me, so feel free to jump in wherever.

Remember though, that's not really what OPEC cares about. Guessing exactly when the market will shift is impossible for anyone, OPEC cares about maintaining the comparative values of its member states in relation to non-member states because they all tend to fire missiles at each other when things get out of whack. Everybody is still reading OPEC's reports as the basis for their own decisions because OPEC is doing the vast majority of the research and controls nearly half of all the oil anyone knows exists in a place drills can reach.

We, by the way, are not innocent bystanders. We raised our hands and said "hey everybody, we found a bunch of garbage shale oil up near Canada. Canada and us wouldn't dare use it for anything, but we'd be happy to sell it real cheap if you're capable of making some usable product from it. We'll even pump it straight out to the Gulf of Mexico, if you'd like." Biden thankfully shut that down.

Are OPEC's rules and advisements good or not? Dunno, remember that OPEC replaced our own cartel because gigantic multi-national oil companies already influence global market prices. ExxonMobil or Shell or BP directly affect the economies of entire countries with relatively small decisions. Pretty sure Nigeria wants to be its own country, not a subsidiary of ConocoPhillips.

Ok, that part's out of the way, but I feel like we need a refresher on the difference between market value and real-world objects because I don't think anyone really understands just how many degrees of Kevin Bacon get us from those oil derricks of my youthful memories to the decades-long presence of our military in the Middle East, especially when Palestine and Israel are involved. Not tonight, though, this was a lot of work.

We Interrupt This Story To Tell You A Different Story

B: Well guys, I've got good news and bad news and worse news. The good news is my copies of Hum's Downward is Heavenward and Inlet arrived to day, and a whole batch of insanity should arrive tomorrow. The bad news is that I didn't get an unrelated thing I feel like I deserve, and that is the definition of demotivating. The worse news is I can't bring myself to crack open those Hum albums. I blame attempting to write about price verses value.

S: What are you talking about?

B: Not important. Let's just say there will probably be a different type of day shift in my near future, because why bother?

E: What does that mean for us?

B: Nothing. Business as usual down here.

C: Um.

B: Yes, Compy? Is there something on your mind?

C: Are you feeling ok?

B: Not at all, but when has that ever stopped me?

E: Sandra, I'm scared.

S: Perfectly normal reaction. One way or another, I have a feeling there's a lot of work ahead of us.

C: Uh oh.

B: Welp, I've got some proper thinking to do. Might be a day or two before I'm back to an agreeable headspace. Carry on, I'll be back...

... and with that foreboding exuant, the remaining cast of players blinked at each other until the sounds of Bottle's footsteps disappeared into B-space. You and I know he'll be back eventually, but even Gladys is avoiding eye contact, so something is definitely on an edge, or fulcruming, or something. I'm not much concerned, if that helps. We're all alright, we've had a few dress rehearsals, things will sort themselves into some sort of order. Tomorrow is a day, after all.

To be continued....

Part 2

Bottle wandered aimlessly. It may not look like it from the outside, but us omniscient narrators are, shall we say, in on it. Most people leave you alone if you look like you know exactly what you're doing. The down side, of course, is that they tend to also think you actually do know what you're doing, and that leads to all sorts of unrelated problems.

This particular meander through the endless corridor is particularly interesting. Every once in a while, a door opens and a trembling bony hand extends holding a record for Bottle's inspection. He looks it up and down, flips it over, occasionally nibbles on a corner and wrinkles his nose a bit. Sometimes he hands them back with a slow shake of his head, sometimes he appears to somehow magically shove them in his pocket and waves goodbye. Occasionally a minion will run up to him and the scene repeats itself with a lot more bending and hand gestures and general conversating. Oh, he's turning back around and walking with actual purpose. Sandra might be right, work might happen to anyone foolish enough to cross paths with the Bottler, Keeper of Brain Thoughts, Devolver of Conundrums, The Bearded Incredulator, he invented a lot of those titles, so don't take it too serious. Knowing we listened to Mr. Bungle this day last year is a tad ominous, but it's not like we get much say in the proceedings, so maybe have those helmets on standby...

B: Shut it, Bridbrad! I'm trying to think down here.

BB: Sorry, Bottle. I'll hand it back over to you then.

B: Much obliged. On second thought, this really is more like a preamble. Seems wrong to elide it with the album review. Maybe do like a news at 11 thing so's I can do a proper story time, or something.

BB: Sure thing.

See, I told you I wasn't worried, what the upstairs don't know about the downstairs is our own problem. It might take another day, but he's got the rubber mallet out so he'll be bopping us like little bunny foo foo in no time. Exciting. Until then then, I suspect this will be a special batch of something.

Gunpowder Gray

B: Ok, I'm back.

C: Is that a batch of records in your pocket?

B: Among other things, but yes of course.

S: How much are we going to suffer?

B: Possibly a lot, but who knows? We'll start off tonight super easy. Have you ever wished there was an alternate dimension in which fat sweaty Axl Rose was actually a skinny guy with long curly hair from Atlanta and Guns 'n Roses was slightly more of a Stoner Metal band?

E: I can't say that I have, no.

B: Well great news, I have the self-titled debut of Gunpowder Gray and the lead off track is also called that. Really nice cover art on this one, don't you think?

S: Oh, well, yes actually. That's pretty cool. How are they going to ruin it?

B: So judgy, jeez. Who said anything about ruining anything? I got 6 brand spanking new albums for 60ish dollars and only 10ish of those dollars were mine, thanks to my sister-in-law of not in any way doom. Discogs tells me crazy people have paid upwards of more than they actually cost for several of them. We'll get back to that, for now we're just gonna listen to it...

... well?

E: That was good, right? I feel like that was actually good.

S: That was great, actually. It is like G'n'R meets The Sword.

B: I know, the best part is the lyrics get better as the album progresses. The first few songs are awkward, but the playing is pretty phenomenal. It's honest to goodness trashy rock and roll that actually sounds good, no wonder nobody cares. Well, I care. This is great. Sure, if you're demanding the vocals be better than prime time Axl you might find it a tad annoying, but once you agree to let it go, I guarantee this will be totally enjoyable.

E: I mean, truth be told, I do want to hear it again.

B: See? And you guys thought I was gonna torture you with aleatoric noiseprovisation right off the bat. I very much will torture you with it, but I'll also even it out with more palatable things for the unpalated. I may be a condescending know it all, but I'm not a complete monster. Sure, I'm probably going to act like a complete monster at some point, but that's not the same as being one. Give Gunpowder Gray's self-titled EP a try, there's every possibility you just might like it. They aren't really as sleazy as the hype sticker wants you to believe.

Robocop/Detroit – Dead Language/Foreign Bodies

Today we go for Grind. I'd repeat the full conversation, but it's mostly unintelligible gargling and agonized screaming, not unlike tonight's album. That's not completely fair, you can actually understand the majority of words on this album. Be warned, it does not sound nearly as pretty as last night's Gunpowder Gray.

A really fun thing about Grindcore is the microsong, a kind of uber-minimalist approach to encapsulating a complete idea and its execution using a much energy and as little actual musical material as possible. Napalm Death still holds the record with the single grunt that is You Suffer, but tonight's album has some really good attempts. It's the Robocop/Detroit Split "Dead Language, Foreign Bodies," and it will peel the paint off your brain walls.

A lot of people don't like the more extreme side of metal, but as I keep pointing out, I'm not a lot of people on the outside. Granted, a lot of the people on my inside hate this, but I am Bottle, hear me sit quietly and enjoy this deluge of distortion, screaming, and intellectual experimentation.

Honest to goodness, the Robocop side struck me as somehow sarcastic, so I had to go see for myself. Here is the full description from their bandcamp page:

"This was written in the context of what we saw as a world spinning out of control. Paranoia, conspiracy theories, the structure of media, information control, etc. I was pretty keen on incorporating this into our imagery/lyrics without extensive commentary, The assumption was that people listening to this would let that wash over them, and get a sense of what was bubbling up from below the surface in our culture. This all reads very differently, now that far-right ideological extremism has become part of mainstream culture. The things we were "portraying" on this album should not be perceived as an endorsement of those ideas. I really wanted to give these things air to warn people about where things were going, it's hard to get people to remember how naive the majority of the population was before this album. This was before the capital insurrection, before Trump, before gamergate, before Snowden, etc. It was written as a small band in northern Maine. I have tried to clarify this whenever possible, but it's there's no way to preserve this in the environment in which it was formed.

I wrote about and sampled the things I did, because I wanted to make music to show what it was like in the deepest recesses of the net. Now that this monster has crawled out its hole, I want to make it clear: none of these songs was written from my perspective. In fact, none of the Robocop songs were ever written from my perspective. I thought of these more as experimental films, or some of the more extreme J.G. Ballard novels. I wanted our music to be a sort of "atrocity exhibition" where the worst parts of our culture could be grafted together. The fact that every topic covered here had essentially been grist for the mill in the genre's we were invested in, fit into the equation as well.

Regardless, I want to be completely clear: I wrote the lyrics as someone invested in far-left labor politics, (non-exclusionary) feminism, anti-racism, and LGBTQ rights. My commitment was/is more expansive than that, but I want to make that clear, because, even I feel repulsed by some of what's included. It was meant to repulse, do not read anything else into it.

    Nazi Punks Fuck Off.
    - RP"

    Cool dudes. Yep, this is exactly what the real-world sounds like if you listen with your face pressed up against it. To be clear, I absolutely love this albumstrocity of audiomalevolence, but you probably won't. It very much does sound awful on purpose. Two thumbs up.

Oak & Bone

    I have one more already opened record from this batch, the self-titled LP from Oak & Bone. The opener is called Oakener, so you should just expect pushing Hardcore Punk as close to the edge of Stoner Death Doom as possible.
    Aspirin and alcohol aren't the most exciting drugs in music, but I think we can at least give proper credit for specificity.
    I'm somewhat known for being really hard on lyrics, especially when they are terrible. These aren't. It might not be your cup of caffeinated beverage, but these are legitimate free verse poems delivered with what must be the world's strongest uvula. As screaming goes, this is appropriately mucus-laden while still maintaining a modicum of intelligibility. Many many many bands are much much worse and more famous. I might be totally biased by the particular bands from there that attract my attention, but Syracuse, NY does not come across as a particularly enjoyable place to live. In fact, that entire I90 run from Buffalo to Albany just seems totally depressed and miserable. Google maps research on that one? Of course, I go all out for these things. $100 real dollars if

you can guess one of the songs from my discography about a crush I had on a girl from Utica 9 lifetimes ago.

You're gonna say "whaaaaa?" like you always do when I'm imagineering your reactions, but this album is like Monster Magnet meets Crowbar on Quaaluuds. It's sludgy, but it grooves. There're a couple brief moments of super drippy surf reverb, soggy chorused cleans, some indescribably nasty leads through at least 3 stacked fuzz pedals, and the vocals are just putrid. Fantastic.

And that brings us to a really great story I've never told anyone. Once in one of my past lives I took a trip with my friend Vinh to visit his and my families in New York. I don't want you to get the wrong idea, I want you to understand the real mind-bending realities of life. A guy apologizing profusely for having to run off to the bathroom to shoot up, skating behind a grocery store where cops couldn't see you from the street, a death metal backyard graduation party with peoples' grandmas clapping between songs, friends frustrated with other friends for ruining their DnD game by breaking out the LSD, but nobody actually screaming or beating the crap out of each other, just some of the genuinely nicest drug addicts and fringe members of society I've ever met going about their day.

Downtown Albany seemed like a place I never want to visit again, but OKC's crime rates have always been tangibly higher and I don't recall ever personally getting mugged or murdered. I mean, if you're walking down dark alleys at 3am pretty much anywhere, you're probably going to stumble upon a few crime rate statistics in progress; that's reality. When I moved to Iowa, I frequently found myself explaining to people the concept of going three blocks out of your way because that particular light turned red and you DO NOT want to be stopped at that intersection, the surprising amount your friend's head bleeds when someone bashes it with a mag light, drive by shootings at the frat house. I saw a guy get shot in broad daylight walking down the sidewalk. I did not hang around to give my eyewitness report to the police, I kept on driving like a person who didn't want any part of that. I have a theory that people don't actually pay attention to real life because it is just too traumatic to handle. I pay attention. To quote Rutger Hauer, "I've seen things you people wouldn't believe."

I don't think that story is supposed to do or mean anything, it's just what bubbles to the surface while listening to this album. It's a fairly accurate aural depiction of wishing you were anywhere but smack dab in the middle of the bottom of the barrel and no longer having the ability to sugarcoat it. I don't have that reaction to say Lamb of God or Messhuggah or Black Dahlia Murder. There must be a terroir or zeitgeist or psychic nexus at work here with Oak & Bone. It connects.

Mean Creek – The Sky (Or The Underground)

I suppose you could call Mean Creek Power Pop or Indie Rock. They certainly wouldn't be completely out of place on a playlist with Wilco, or The War On Drugs, or Gin Blossoms, or even The Lumineers and The New Pornographers. It's much more downtempo Alternative Rock with crunchy guitars, a pinch of noise rock, and way more borderline falsetto than any of them, but that same kind of vibe of having no idea how you're actually supposed to be trying to figure out how to fit into the world. Nowhere near as Adult Contemporary as Train or The Wallflowers, so that's good.

Maybe we should just call it Rock. At first, I didn't hear the "Boston-ness," but it backhanded me across the face on track 6, Not To Dream, and now I can't unhear it.

If nothing else, The Sky (Or The Underground) is a thoroughly enjoyable listen from start to finish. It's not really challenging or experimental, definitely not energetic in a dance around the room way, but your head will definitely be bobbing up and down and whatever you're actually doing while listening to it will progress appropriately. One possible soundtrack for doing something; probably not the most rave review, but there's definitely something complimentary I'm trying to express. Pleasantly unsurprising? That'll do, pig? I don't know, it's lovely; I'm never good at elaborating upon that. Maybe it's just the kind of folk-tinged Alternative rock you enjoy by yourself. A common experience, not so much a shared one.

Anastasia Max Present The Haunt

I don't think I really need to tell you how bad a state of affairs it is when a Bottle such as myself can't even bring himself to open the freakin' record. Absolutely atrocious. It's a slippery slope, next I'll be trying to sell them for more than I paid to other people. It's true though, I totally wish I could wake up in the morning and turn on the open sign of my own record store. We'd do things the old-school way, invest directly in albums and split profits with the artists who make them, sponsor shows, hold signings, the works. It's probably a silly dream, but dream big I say.

Anywho, next up is a fun little debut EP from the brother and sister duo The Haunt, nee Anastasia Max (their last name is Haunt). I have hand-numbered 40/100 on black splatter. It's funny 'cause that long dead news flash about the White Stripes not being siblings is in heavy rotation on my feed lately. How is stuff that happened 20 or 30 years ago that we all knew about breaking news right now?

I suppose it is Alternative Rock, but it runs the gamut from Punk to Post-Punk to whatever you want to call the kind of dark psychological horror music often found in more mainstream Emo and Industrial Rock. Almost Dark Pop. Whatever you want to call it, it's phenomenal.

Like all brother/sister bands, it has a tendency to be super creepy if you forget and start taking it metaphorical. You have to remember they are brother and sister with a fairly large age difference.

We start with the super catchy almost Pop Punk Brat, then move to the even more catchy loser arena bass jam Dirty. Light and dark is a pretty good way to start your EP, the rest should fill in that wide open space. Then we get the cool down depressing ballad Bullet, with electronics and synths and timpani. The 3-spot is perfect for it, and it would be the perfect time to flip the album over if I weren't so damned reluctant to break the factory seal on this magically delicious album.

Get Back gives us some equally dark Blues Rock influence. Streets and Lies gives us the classic fuzzed bass creepy skeleton surfing Frankenstein feel with a super catchy chorus. And we end with All Went Black, an almost Poltergeist-like thriller on the dark side of suburbia.

This is gorgeous, a real musical masterpiece. I want to put it on repeat for days until I can listen to it in my mind whenever I feel like it. Yeah, it's that good. Everything they do so far is great. They have a very distinct sound and it lets them play around with any genre they want, scraps of dance, trance, blues, trap, top 40, all through sinister tinted glasses. None of it's vapid or cliched, and they can write some singalong worthy choruses, let me tell you.

Two thumbs up. If I were to open it, it would definitely get played to death.

Damsel – Distressed

I woke up with Rush's Time Stands still on the old brainbox of doom, so that can only mean 2 things. One, it's Sunday and we have to wrap up this adventure. Desmond

Tutu) it's always about money and new exciting ways to take it away from people. So, as the innocence slips away, we'll listen to the complete noise chaos that is Damsel. Liz Phair?

S: I suppose that is fair, the last two albums were really enjoyable and very mainstream. But how are we supposed to actually do it?

B: All sorts of ways. We could answer Maynard's rhetorical question how can this mean anything to me when I really don't feel a thing at all? Then again, overthinking, overanalyzing separates the body from the mind. I'm totally fine with that, but most people are not. Let's define our experience. It's only 4 tracks.

E: But that means they are super long.

B: Yes, but there are only 4 of them. Plus, there's a guy from Wilco here, so it's not like we're in a room full of strangers. Compy, give us the official album explanation.

C: Ok, gimme a sec.

"For the past few years, Avant-jazz legend Nels Cline (Wilco, Thurston Moore, The Geraldine Fibbers) and omnipresent beat freak Zach Hill (Hella, The Ladies, Team Sleep) have been waiting for an opportunity to spend a few hours making noise. When Cline joined Wilco full-time and Hill started The Ladies with Pinback's Rob Crow, the dream seemed increasingly unlikely. And by the time Hill's full-time gig as half of Hella saw him touring arenas with modern rock staples like System of a Down, the dream seemed dead. But through a bit of careful planning and a whole lot of serendipity, Wilco had a day off in Chicago the same day that Hill was in town. Recorded and mixed in one day at

Semaphore Studios in Chicago, IL, the four pieces on 'Distressed' are entirely improvised, with a little post-production editing courtesy of Cline's former Geraldine Fibbers partner, Carla Bozulich. Sitting somewhere between the most abstract freak-outs of Wilco's more recent material and the looser, more minimalist moments of Hella, Damsel exhibits a surprising amount of control over its chaos."

B: K, so made in a day, total improvisation with the titles giving us some conceptual framework. Take them or leave them, but I think it often helps to imagine they had that title in mind as they started playing. It also helps to remember that they aren't just standing in separate isolation booths playing whatever the Brownian motion of their seizure-fingers happened to produce. No, they see each other, they hear each other, they respond, they vie for psychic control of the lumbering ship that is the ensemble, they push forward then lean back, and the result is a product of pure doing, an artifact of an irreproducible moment in the universe. You might like it, you might hate it, it might inspire, it might make you cry, it might make you wish we could go anywhere except a future where 99% of us grind away at pointlessly meaningless tasks just so 3 guys can be trillionaires and their combined 7 friends run the universe, 'cause that's the actual structure of capitalism. Remember, you are not a capitalist you are a person leasing everything in your life from a capitalist. You get to keep the change. No matter how much change that is, it's still a fraction of the value you generate: you did thousand-dollar work for $47 and the only thing you can do is recruit more minions on the gamble that it'll work for you too.

Track one is Enduring Freedom. Does that mean "freedom that stands the test of time," or does it mean "trying to just get through it so you can go home and sleep?" Choose your own adventure.

Fork-Fed is much more jaunty at the start. Like you were looking forward to the meal, but those tines keep getting sharper and it's way too much food and what actually determines the end of "all-you-can-eat?" The concept of physically being able to not eat anymore is quite a lot terrifying, to be honest.

I don't need to guide you through it, listen and do it yourself. What's really going on?

It's quite simple, really. Is work and the product of that work more or less valuable than owning and controlling the mechanisms by which those commodities are distributed? One side says ownership and management are vastly more important, the other side says the work and its utility are more valuable. The owner side raises its value but putting up ever increasing barriers to entry and finding people to buy in on the promise of financial gain from selling the promise of that financial gain.

You'd look at this album and think "clearly the label and the studio and the pressing plant and their respectively successful bands and the stores that sell the record are more important and valuable than the 4 guys who spent one day playing gibberish on their instruments. Plus, I don't even like it."

That's certainly one way to look at it. It's not my way of looking at it, I'm using it as an example of the complexity of value. I suppose it's as valuable as any other record I could be listening to while I write this, I suppose it's as worthless as any other piece of plastic junk in my house. I suppose if you offered me $50 for it, I'd make that trade. Personally, I much prefer thinking about the accumulated chaos that led to me even holding it in my hand. They wanted to do it, but things kept preventing them until a brief coincidental moment in 2010 when they had the opportunity to be in the same place at the same time.

They weren't worrying about how to buy food or pay for car parts or send their kids to school or breaking their ankles but not getting to see a doctor because the hospital is full of people sick with a highly contagious respiratory virus. They weren't trying to steal someone's television or jewelry, they weren't robbing a bank or mugging a pizza delivery driver, or more horrible things. No, they were standing in a room and attempting to express some fundamental physical activity while some other people attempted to capture it so that anybody could hear it happen, hear that it happened, let it inside their brain to wreak whatever havoc it wreaks. They made it, I listened to it, and now it exists for me to use as I wish. I suppose you could spend all your time and energy trying to put a price tag on that convergence of chaos, but that seems to me to be much less valuable than most anything else you could be doing. Conversely, what possible value could you justifiably assign to my random statement to Barnes & Noble when that statement amounts to "send me the most amount of actual albums for the least amount of money." That whole process seems incredibly unfulfilling and stupid. That's probably not fair, but it is honest.

 One way of thinking says I got a whole lot of milage out of this $11 record (or whatever it actually cost, point was it was cheap), but move to the left a little and the whole sculpture changes. Now I'm noticing that maybe one or 2 of those dollars represents money the band got to use for something like gas and food. It cost me $9 to give you 2, or maybe it cost you $9 to get me to hand you 11. Either way, that's a lot of work for 2 dollars.

 Another step or two and now it looks like it would be way better for both of us if we just agreed on an up-front price and you send me the results of what you can do with it. Some people say that's worse though, so who knows? Am I the one doing Deathwatch On The American Empire or am I the one killing it? Yay sports team?

Handling frustration. Controlling anger. There are times, however, when you simply cannot have something you want. It may be Damsel.

E: I feel kind of nauseous.

B: Yeah, albums like this tend to make you seasick. Dramamine?

E: Yes, please.

B: Anybody else need some? No? Ok. Welp, this run is by the board. All hands on deck! Batten down the hatches and trim the sails! We got a Monday a-brewin' starboard.

Yay, Ranty Time!

S: Just out of morbid curiosity, what would you call this record store?

B: Bottle's Music.

C: That's not exactly an exciting name.

B: I'm not exactly an exciting guy. Records and a coffee pot, what more do you actually need? I suppose customers, but who the hell knows where to find them? Forbes said albums were dead 4 years ago. Me and my friends are dinosaurs in the micro-machine age. You could probably make 9 or 12 fortunes if you could find a mechanism for snorting music or injecting it between your toes or smoking it, but what kind of sales pitch is "if you buy it now and don't open it for 20 years it might be worth $20 more than you paid for it?" I suppose I'd have to sell stereo equipment and replacement cartridges and cleaning brushes and who knows what else.

E: But you'd need employees and an accountant and...

B: Why? I sell records, you buy them. Tell me what you want, enjoy a show twice or thrice a month, help Mr. Sandos carry groceries up 3 flights of stairs for 10% off Thursday, support what you like. None of this 8:30 to 5 garbage. 2 to 10 and weekends, you know, when people can actually shop there. DIY recording room in a closet, buy something or be cool, musicians and DJs stopping by to hang out and meet other musicians. Obscure stuff, not boring crap you can find anywhere. You hungry? I got snacks.

Why do down towns turn to shit? Because A) all the supposedly good people went home, and A^2) us night owls got no place awesome to go. Sorry if you own a bar, but bars suck because they're full of drunk people. Sorry if you're a drug dealer, but this is my block. We'll pick up trash and politely ask passing strangers to stop throwing that trash on the sidewalk. Bottle's Music helps little old ladies cross the street, Bottle's Music donates books and pencils to schools and libraries, Bottle's Music will drive you to your dentist appointment, Bottle's music will tutor you and your kid in algebra. I'm being ridiculous on purpose; the point is stop being terrible to each other.

S: I see your vision, though. I get it.

B: I feel like it's too nostalgic and sappy. There were still independent record stores when I was a kid, but I couldn't afford records and I watched them all die. Everything became a dumb corporate branded box store, and they suck. I want a butcher shop and a farm stand and kids riding skateboards and bikes in the middle of the street and ice cream trucks driven by guys who aren't creepy as hell like when I was a kid (I mean they weren't creepy when I was a kid). Was it all just a facade? A fake world of fantasticness where you could just run around outside all day and night, hang out at the arcade, go to the 24hr gym to work out? Was it really a world of grift and extortion and bribery and insurance fraud?

I mean, yeah, I listened to the economy die but no one actually realize it on my car radio in Denton, TX in 2008, paying $4 a gallon to drive back and forth between my apartment and my home in Moore, OK, watching the town get big as the people got less and less and reassuring the almost certainly meth dealers across the street that no I wasn't the one who called the police after we could all hear him screaming at his wife in their front yard, and pointing out to the traveling alarm system salesman that no I don't want a perpetual security system bill and if my house gets broken into 3 months from now his business card will be handed directly to the investigating detectives. I would sit on my front porch and draw during the Summer, made The Slumlord EP in the garage my dad and I converted ourselves just because I had nothing better to do in 100-degree temps with 90% humidity.

A new Wal-Mart opens and magically the other 3 nice grocery stores in town immediately decline. People scamming for gas in a Lowes parking lot, huge new movie theater I never went to. When I was as kid my dad would take us to the high school tennis courts until they tore those down for a softball field. I used to skate and bike and play basketball at the elementary school across the street until they locked those fences up tight.

That's not upper-middle Bourgeois extravagance I'm remembering, that's people trying really hard to take care of themselves and not burden their equally working-class neighbors. The world I knew just up and died in the late 2000s. I really am a 9,000-year-old curmudgeon on the inside, but maybe not the kind you're used to. People don't start out bad, you make them turn out that way by selling them cheap substitutes for things they once did for themselves and each other.

Which brings me to my real dilemma. I don't really care what job it is I'm supposed to be doing, but somebody has to pay to do it, and the money has to come from the community. The community at large has to support individual people when they need it, not the other way around. 100 people can help 1, 1 can't help 100 all at the same time. Do I want to be "warehouse manager" for an infant giraffe of a company trying to learn how to use its corporate legs before the lion attacks? No, not particularly, but hiring someone else above me is a pretty garbage move on their part and it puts us all in a real bind in the sense that I officially don't care anymore.

Are they spying on my facebook page? Don't care. Are they mistakenly mad about something I wrote in a book? Don't care. What good does it do to train a new guy on receiving and stocking if you immediately put him in a truck so he can't help me do all of it? If I have to filter and edit and double check every ticket and explain logistics every day, how long before I start complaining that everyone else is a moron? I'm on the phone 3 times a day correcting some other branch's mis-shipments compared to maybe once every other week of my own for which I apologize and correct immediately. I'm the bad guy for pointing out peoples' mistakes, I'm the bad guy if I ignore them. Guess what, don't care. I show up, I work all day, I go home. Pay me or fire me, don't care. It's trivial work anyone can do but nobody else does. Sorry for ranting, it's not your fault. Cheers.

The Warehouseman's Aria

I've have a secret libretto for the opera of my life. Here's the warehouseman's aria (and yes, the swearing is vital to character development):
(Recit.) ... sometimes people ask me what I do for a living. From this moment forward here's the answer I'll be giving....

> Oh I, Pick shit up and I move it over there. Sometimes I use a forklift, sometimes I use the stairs.
> Sometimes I just stand next to the dumpster and smoke, 'cause being an adult is a goddamned joke.
> I pick shit up and I move it over there, sometimes I climb the shelving cause the product's way up there.
> We may or may not have the thing you need today in stock, but if we do, I'll pull it for you and I'll leave it on the dock.
> I pick shit up and I move it over there. Sometimes I use a forklift, sometimes I use the stairs.
> Sometimes I just stand next to the dumpster and smoke, 'cause being an adult is a goddamned joke.

Ideologies Are Bad, M'kay?

I suppose we could revisit Zager and Evans, ideologies are bad, m'kay?
Why are they bad? Because they usually become lampoonishly infallible dogma that fallibly fails to accomplish anything except abject horribleness.

Does that mean your particular religion, your party, your ideals, your wants and needs? No, of course not. Unless it leads to killing people, then boo to that.

What's the deal with Ukraine? I guess Russia doesn't want Ukraine to join NATO? The invasion of Crimea back in 2014 was predicated on the dispute about who owns it. Is it part of Ukraine or is it part of Russia? The Russians who live there supposedly say Russia. The narrative has always been first-world America vs second-world Russia in an economic grudge match for the championship belt. That's dumb.

Before we all get confused, I'm not talking about human rights violations, war, shirtless horseback rides across the tundra, any of that stuff. I'm talking about the kind of "our sports team is better than yours and we'll light this car on fire to prove it" garbage blasted from all directions into our poor, fragile central nervous systems.

We're dealing with second and third generation connotations here. "Welfare State" doesn't refer to food stamps and social security and unemployment insurance, those are merely three poorly constructed manifestations of a huge variety of possible systems that represent a government attempting to assist rather than dictate the lives of its citizens.

I would argue that nation-states are simply Capitalism in is most extreme, belligerent form. What differentiates a President from a King or a Despot? Certainly not the structure of hierarchical bureaucracy, that is their commonality. There is no structural difference between a constitution, a list of commandments, a book of proverbs; they are the structure of ideology itself. In themselves they represent not the path to a goal, but the conservation of privilege for their most devout evangelists.

Liberty and freedom, then, are not some state of being bestowed upon us by some benevolent being, but the result of our own refusal to infringe upon the liberty and freedom of others, to refuse to make choices in our own interest for a common good, to in fact reject the ideologies we most admire and desire. Liberty can only be given away, not seized or conserved. Russia does not want to give Ukraine any liberty at all, and there's a real possibility they have a war about it.

This is of course the radical Leftist in me talking, but an elected king is still a king, the cabinet and congress are still the king's court, the rival kings are still rivals in this game of thrones. A king who does nothing of consequence is absurd.

I am certainly not the first or only person to claim that Marxism is the worship of Marx as Christianity is the worship of Christ, nor am I the only person pointing out that America has never had a non-authoritarian President. How could it?

The rude thing Biden said into a live microphone is no different than any other President, because the President is still merely a person. Rather than some supposed sign of hypocrisy, we must recognize it for what it really was: a window overlooking honesty built into a mansion of dishonesty. That honesty may not bear resemblance to your own, but the underlying/overdetermining dishonesty is not of the President's, or government's, or Constitution's making (the Russian Federation is now a Constitutional Republic, after all), it is instead the result of the collective psyche's refusal to accept the consequences of choice. I propose that that refusal of acceptance is in fact the pride of ideology itself. The winner must win, the slighted achieve justice, the good be rewarded, the bad be punished, immortality by any means necessary.

Our notion of Capitalism makes no such guarantee. In fact, it is predicated on the equality of failure. Not only must institutions fail no matter their size or intent, the more agreeable or popular their mission the more painful their failure must be. Those aren't my rules, this isn't my game, but they are the rules of the game nonetheless. The freest of laissez-faire black markets is the tyranny of the majority, it will make whatever choice it makes without hesitation and be replaced by another after it has reached saturation.

The will of the people is not some magical teleological consensus, it is 3-million disparate voices screaming for a few moments of silence during the daily deluge of disastrophe. The rallying cry is, after all, give me liberty. The irony of course is that we confuse giving for taking, a fortune for fortune, freedom for the better of bad choices (which aren't really choices at all).

There is immense sadness in the doing of good deeds, and that sadness arises from the recognition that for that brief moment in time that good deed is the exception, an abnormality. That brief moment of kindness, help, decency, call it what you will, that brief moment of trivial grace is an oasis in the desert of misery that forms the fabric of existence. That deep, inexpressible gratitude in the eyes of a fellow human breaks my heart, shatters my soul, and tells me there is so much more mountain to climb than I even imagined.

These have been brain thoughts with Bottle. No warranty expressed or implied. May cause dandruff. I have no idea why Polyvinyl records included this blue-raspberry flavored airheads with my Hum records, but I am definitely not complaining. Mysteries of life.

Machines Of Loving Grace – Gilt (Revisited)

I feel bent like a reed in the wind, so we're revisiting Machines of Loving Grace. I want to unpack Gilt in as much stultifying pedantry as possible, you know like I do with everything all the time. We got a poem and the title and the artwork and the lyrics which include "supply and demand" and everyone's favorite Jim Jones quote in a song called Serpico, and even though the allmusic review implies it's just the same song over and over, it's a damned good song with a lot of great heavy guitars and some bleep bloops. What a jerk, there's tons of variety.

I of course like all types of music, but Industrial Rock is like the core of my being. Supposedly their first two albums are much more synth heavy. I don't know, like I said, this album is a committed piece of art not a random throwaway stab at fame or selling bottles of colored sand or moving your cult to an epithetic socialist commune in South America. It's like ogres and onions and chickens, you know? Layers.

Gilt means covered in a thin veneer of gold. Looks all pretty on the surface, cheap junk underneath.

The photo is a recreation of the 1947 Robert Wiles photograph of Evelyn McHale 4 minutes after she jumped from the 86th floor of the Empire State Building. She did not survive that particular suicide, and the note in her purse was surprisingly terse and matter-of-fact.

The album predates the movie Suicide Kings by several years so I can't really justify a Christopher Walken impression. Maybe they are referencing Charlemagne, but I think it's probably a simpler metaphor of drug addiction, since the other character repeatedly referenced is "the richest junkie still alive."

Slaughterhouse five is definitely a reference to the Vonnegut novel, but how that reference actually works in the song is a bit lost on me.

The "discipline of flowers" is probably not Ikebana.

Isadora Duncan was a pretty famous dancer strangled to death when her enormous scarf got tangled around the hubcap of the car she was driving.

Those are some of the highlights, but Serpico is the real masterpiece. Frank Serpico was a NYC detective famous for whistleblowing NYPD corruption in the 60s/70s. Add to that the sentiments of "sick of it all" and "something has gone wrong" from an old man whose "insides spilled out" and the narrator concluding "he'd been dying or dead for years and this was just his way of saying let them hear it in the night" the way Jim Jones said "let them hear it in the night" in his tirade about the assassinations of MLK and JFK and how hatred of the US government was his primary motivation to amass weapons and fight like Mao told him to do. So, suicide is the ultimate stance against the corruption of power? It loses something in translation to Bottle-speak, I think. You can't do it justice by summarizing, you just have to hold the whole thing in your head as the culmination of the process of just completely and belligerently destroying yourself.

So, is the band's identity sarcastic? Does GREGORY like turtles? The thing about that Richard Brautigan poem is that it exists inside the very peculiar socio-political environment of taking the technological nightmare that was the Cold War and reclaiming it in the Ken Kesey/Merry Pranksters/Acid Test Hippy/Stewart Brand context of using technology to let us return to nature as the mammals we really are, those machines of loving grace preserving the earth for us rather than helping us annihilate it. That idea got Florida-ed up real good all over Al Gore's internet, didn't it?

The real heart of the album, though, is that unidentifiable moment where we switch from naive casual users to full on rotting-corpse junkies. Why can't we recognize the moment we go too far before it happens? That's obviously a rhetorical stupid question, but we can't remember from the remembering side either, so it's all fun and games until it isn't fun and games anymore but hell if we know where the dividing line is. One moment we're people doing things, the next we're dead and by definition not doing them anymore. Some of us, come hell or high water....

Do we need to understand the album as directly growing out of writing Golgotha Tenement Blues for The Crow? I suppose it gives some additional context for the religious metaphors at play (hello, Jesus and Mary Magdalene), but sinners and saints and the religious component of 12-step programs and power dynamics are already at play here.

What I'm trying to say is there's a lot going on on this album that you aren't going to get from a casual listen or two. Every song is a research project or dissertation in its own right, and that's what makes it one of the best albums of not just the 90s, but all time. It's like its own little hyper-real post-modern apocalypse in a jewel case. Plus, I love Industrial Rock anyway, Sylvia Massey made it sound amazing, and those riffs are so freakin' good.

Berlioz – Symphonie Fantastique

Why are we listening to Symphonie Fantastique? I just have the urge to hear it, I'm sure there's some subconscious reason we'll find out at some point.

At first, I was trying to work up a joke about some malformed breakfast cereal (Cheerios my ass, those are Barely-Os), but that's beneath me. So, I dug a little deeper and thought "ok, what is it really?"

Well, I'll tell me so you can find out. This is like a large-scale autobiography in the making about Berlioz driving himself crazy crushing on a girl, Irish actress Harriet Smithson.

Movement 1 is all about how sensitive an artist he is, filled with passion for Beethoven and Shakespeare and Harriet.

Then he's at a Ball and she's not paying any attention to him. Of course not, Harriet didn't attend the premier (and those who did didn't like it very much). So, he learned how to write fugues and won a big fugue writing contest. He won (like I just said) and used the prize money to study in Italy, where he tried to make this symphonic diorama of his tortured artistic soul less crappy.

He's terribly depressed that she doesn't love him, so he takes a bunch of opium and dreams that they send him to the guillotine. Turns out he does not get to keep his head at the end of that adventure.

So, all the monsters in Satan's army attend his funeral and it's a fugue, because mastering the Fugue to win a competition was a hellish amount of effort just to get your head chopped off afterward.

Luckily for Berlioz, nobody much cared for Harriet's acting anymore, so she had plenty of free time to attend a free concert when tickets showed up.

Everybody liked this second premier, even Harriet, so Berlioz got to woo her by apparently actually ingesting a crap ton of opium to guilt trip her into marrying him so he could Indiana Jones the antidote from his pocket. That lasted all the way up to their divorce, but he still financially supported her afterward.

I suspect permanganate of potassium or possibly atropine were the "antidote," but Berlioz isn't really trying to win my drug specificity award that I know of, and I might be the tiniest bit skeptical about fatal opioid overdoses being a serious player move, even in the roaring mid-19th-century fever dream that is Romanticism. It's a bit fantastic, and not in the "totally awesome" sense that we use that word today.

Drugs and chicks in financial desperation, I guess that is about as rock-star as it gets. It's not a total quack story, he did start out studying to be a doctor like his dad before deciding to disappoint everyone by being a musician. Some people thought he was a genius, some thought he sucked, lawyer/diarist George Templeton Strong called his music flatulent, rubbish, and the work of a tipsy chimpanzee. I'm not sure GEETS is even worthy of the nickname I just gave him, let alone critical authority. Sounds like music to me, the tubas aren't oom-pah-ing the whole time and he resolves most of his leading tones eventually. Why can't low brass play melodies?

I'll give you the fact that this is more of a concept album than a Symphony per se, but the thing about Beethoven was that he said convention be damned when it fails to express the ideas I have in mind. I have to assume this is what Hector was trying to do, and it's totally lovely. Melodramatic, sure, but also fun. You could learn a lot from a dummy. Buckle your safety belt.

Downward Is Heavenward, But how we got there I don't know

      C: I think you should talk about the corporate takeover of artists catalogs.

      B: I don't disagree, but that's a tough one to tackle because both sides have legitimate arguments, and neither choice is a good choice.

      C: What do you mean?

      B: How could I possibly say Bob Dylan or Stevie Nicks are wrong for choosing to cash in their chips and settle for the current monetary value of their music? They aren't wrong, it's their music and their choice. You can't afford to buy Bob Dylan's publishing rights, can you?

      C: Well, no.

      B: Whoever inherits them is just gonna sell them anyway. Regular people don't have the education and experience to make sound investment decisions as a legal business. At least this way they don't get tricked or robbed out of those future royalties. Now, I don't for one second believe Bob Dylan wants his music selling cars or funding the pet investments of UMG execs, but what other choice does he really have? You and I can't buy Bob Dylan's catalogue from

Bob Dylan. His songs are his capital and he decided to cash in their current market value rather than continue to use them as collateral to fund the next project he isn't going to make. It sounds morbid, but Bob Dylan is going to die soon.

Conversely, what does the giant grab for total rights from the aging demographic of rock stars do to the larger music economy? A few potentially possible goodish things if UMG wants to act like a proper steward of his legacy, but a whole lot of not good things for everybody not mentioned in Bob Dylan's will.

They are investing their money in old music at the expense of new music for the profit of UMG. Will any of that trickle down? Will the royalties from 10 million Bob Dylan streams be used to fund the next record from that band you like, or will they use it as leverage to jack license fees higher, sue independent labels into their own control, or shut down artist access to streaming platforms all together? Will they just pull all his music and we'll never hear it again? Will they reissue some of those albums? Will they upload 'em to the highest bidding database as a simple value swap? Flagging videos on youtube and dictating which platforms consumers must use to access it?

This isn't an exploitation problem so much as a question of UMG's larger economic intentions. It matters what they actually do with the music as an asset. The problem is what they aren't paying for, they aren't paying younger generations to make more music, they aren't searching for the new voices of new markets, they aren't supporting arts education or supporting retail, they are instead aggressively buying up the assets of artists who will soon die in order to profit from the capital gains when they do. The result is a bigger lottery economy at the mercy of huge corporations. It's a bit like wanting to be a baseball player, but getting traded to a new team every other year.

My lament is obviously the loss of record stores, but there are two sides to that coin. Heads, there is the inherent fluctuation of recorded music as a form of entertainment. That's just life. Tails, no one can afford to buy in to the old-school distribution system demanded by the physical media. You and I can't afford to open a wholesale account with The Orchard or The Beggar's Group, or any of them because that investment is well above any reasonably practical foot traffic (physical or internet based). That's the same problem facing agriculture. You can't afford a quarter million-dollar tractor, patented seed, and the land lease. Same problem with cars and houses. All the honest farmers I talk to will tell you, at the end of the ledger you're looking at living your life on the same 20-40k as everyone else no matter how many millions your harvest or crop insurance actually generated. It's not magic or a fluke of nature, the total economy tends toward equilibrium based on the per capita national debt (aka money supply). It's a zero-sum game, meaning all pluses have corresponding minuses in the real world. Every loophole has an equal and opposite gotcha.

The basic problem with all the flavors of capitalism is that they require infinite growth, an endless supply of new labor and an equivalent amount of money to pay for it. To use the familiar idiom, the interactive birth and death rate of consumers determines the amplitude of market volatility, but there is no actual net gain. All profits are equivalent losses. All Dylan did was take a fair exchange for the value of his assets. That's what you do every time you file an insurance claim or withdraw money from savings. That's completely different from Jesus and Mary Chain or Chevelle or any other band who took out a confusingly worded business loan at highway robbery interest rates.

As I implied, the scenario can go any direction UMG decides to go. The troublesome part is that UMG decides that, not the artists. It's not a certainty that this will happen, but as these high-profile catalogs get increasingly taken over by large corporations there is a real possibility that they then attack the fundamental concepts of copyright and public domain. UMG could decide that they do in fact have enough liquidity and market share to electively liquidate all assets, take the money and run. That would be an even nastier blow to the economy as a whole. That doesn't mean "go out of business" like you might think, it means that all revenue is allocated in a static internal flow under the control of UMG. The same way the government can be interpreted to threaten the private sector by printing new money UMG can dictate supply and logistics based not on consumer choice, but on advertiser preference. It's not what you want that matters, it what we can sell.

We can't answer these economic questions. These questions can be easily answered, the data very much exists, but it exists inside the impenetrable force field of UMG the private Firm. That's where it gets political. UMG knows exactly what their holdings have been paying for, they know exactly what they think any particular asset is worth and whether it's over or under valued and how they intend to manipulate and reassign those revenues. The real question is whether or not they are in fact intentionally running a Ponzi scheme.

The Ponzi scheme is often misapplied to any dividend-based payout, legitimate or not. The defining characteristic is not generically using new investments to pay off older investors (the common complaint against social security), the scheme is not actually investing any money in anything at all; meaning you aren't actually doing what your business plan says you are doing. You're just signing up new investors, handing that money to older investors, and fabricating your internal portfolio of activities because very few people actually look at or understand their financial statements. They see a plus sign and are perfectly happy. Back to social security. Our current system of social security managed at the federal level did not grow to its current proportions as some nefarious plot, it grew out of increasing failures of scale: from Civil War pensions, to company pensions covering about 15% of the labor force but barely paying 5% of them because they couldn't find a good reason to deny them, to state pensions that failed because they simply didn't implement them, to the current Social Security Administration which does actually implement the system with the occasional hiccup and rapidly changing eligibility requirements. Ancient Greece had an olive oil-based welfare system, for contrast.

So, the real question is what happens when the music business itself cuts out new music altogether? Investors are using the back catalogs of famous artists to buy more back catalogs of famous artists to pay for what? We don't know because they aren't reinvesting those profits into new music, so you end up paying your manager until he has enough to generously hand you back your own money? He loans you money so that you loan him money to buy what he already manages for you? You can see how this logic eats its own tail, the money comes from no source and disappears into nowhere.

We end up owing more future money than we can feasibly generate, but lack the ability to back down. For artists, however, they never really get those rights back because they were forced to transfer those rights to their publisher in the first place.

From an investment perspective it makes total sense. People like the music they grew up with more than anything happening right now. They just do. I'm not people, I like new stuff and when I do want something old school, I'm perfectly happy to buy a scratchy $4 used copy. I actually enjoy that more than a brand-new copy most of the time. I still haven't opened those Hum records or even the stuff I wrote about 2 weeks ago. Their potential commodity value got to me and I'm working up the adrenaline necessary to let Sandra's boots do the persuading. But nope, here I am listening to it on youtube instead. I don't feel guilty for doing that because I bought a copy. I've supported what I like in the way I'm allowed to, but I feel a deep sense of terribleness when I think about just letting it sit on the shelf until I can turn a profit from it. I don't like how it feels to be a capitalist in that respect, I can't do anything to help the guys from Hum other than tell you all how much I enjoy listening to their music. I enjoy it very much.

Still, a part of me wants to be real, a part of me desperately wants to turn my love of music into influence for profit that I'll turn around and hand to my friends in the form of funding their projects with only the brick wall of student loan debt standing in my way. Such is the conundrum of existence, I'm afraid. I can't crack it, only shrug and walk in a different direction. Anybody want to buy a hand-made copy of a p(nmi)t EP? I've got a theoretically infinite supply of those.

Excerpt From The Diary Of A Bridbrad

E: Copy and paste, copy and paste, at first, I really hated it, but now it suits my taste...

To say that everyone was incredibly confused by overhearing Skip's spontaneous burst into Editor: The Musical is a bit of an understatement. Sandra sat up on her beanbag chair and tilted her head in amusement. Compy kept looking over his shoulder with a mildly agitated nose crinkle, Gladys rocked a little faster in her rocking chair, Bottle hummed some experimental counterpoint underneath, and the whole thing was occasionally punctuated by a far-off screech and thud of a door as GREGORY moved from closet to closet. A different kind of Saturday, but not without its own bit of charm. I suppose you could say that for once the rooms weren't rearranging themselves, but rather the occupants had found different ways of inhabiting them. "What's the plan, Bottle," I heard myself call down through the floorboards. "No plans, the best plan of all," came the reply.

No argues from me, I suppose. Too cold to go check the mail, and I'm not much in the mood for excitement anyway. The last few weeks were a terrifying carnival ride of emotion, so there's a lot to be said for just enjoying the lack of inevitability about anything. Bottle's probably right, tomorrow reverts to being a day. The cynic in me says it will all turn sideways at some point, but for now, this day, the lack of a future, as Bottle often asserts, smells refreshing. As always, thanks for being my diary.

PS. Now I think I'll give one of those naps Bottle is always raving about a try. It has every potential possibility of in fact being fun.

Stop The Presses!!!!

This town needs an enema, no sorry, this book needs a proper Bottlean conclusion, not some wishy-washy "Bottle's probably right." A few more albums and a proper send off, that's what you deserve.

Helmet – Aftertaste

Ok, ok, I can't end it the way I was about to end it for the book version, the aftertaste is terrible. Luckily, I heard Exactly What You Wanted and I haven't reviewed the 3rd Helmet album, Aftertaste. I'm certain me picking a fight with Erlewine is exactly what you wanted, so let's do it.

He calls it bland, numbing, and a downright shame for such an intriguing 90s alternative metal band. His narrative is that they made the awesomeness that is Meantime, pushed too far to the experimental side with Betty, and failed to return to the grandeur of their original immediate and visceral hooky riffs and stuff. Disheartening.

You know what Stephanie? Thom Yorke says it best, we hope that you choke. I guess if it helps you sleep at night, we'll pretend like we care. See, although the sonic onslaught is indeed loud and cacophonous, the harmonic language is insane to the point that it's actually impressive most of these songs have an identifiable, dare I say, demonstrable tonic considering whether he's driving somewhere slow or nowhere fast, United Arab Emirates still keep the gas in his car. Also, he'd rather be insulted by you than someone he respects, so that works.

To be fair, I didn't like it that much for a long time either. It's a very acquired aftertaste. Like it or not, it's Post-Metal. I won't coma you with much of that, other than to say "post-" is kind of the catch-all term for using a type of music as a texture on top of which you do whatever thing you do. It's a bit like the floating head of David Bowie music I'm known for not being fond of. For this album, it's really just super noisy guitars playing extended harmonies over John Stanier's drumcophony while the bass does all sorts of weird stuff and Page sings little snippets of Alternative Pop songs. You really do have to put your brain back in 1997 mode because we're drowning out the madness with 10 times the madness.

Long story short for a change, whereas Erlewine gives it the predictable D for disappointment, I give it an A for accuracy. 17-year-old Bottle just nods his head and says "yep, that's exactly what it sounds like out there, glad my brain is melting inside this helmet." Interesting fact, it went out of print way back in 2006 of all places, so I better take extra special care of my OG CD copy.

And that, as they say, well, that's all folks. Porky Pig-ed it out of the park. Look for new and excitingly different things from Bottle of Beef some time that is later than now.

Skip's got some typos to wrangle, and Compy's got that appendicitis look in his eyes. Sandra of course took the liberty of already showing you the cover, so that cat's out of the box with the subatomic quantum thingy that might or might not have happened. Only one way to find out what's in the box, Mr. Pitt. Take a look, it's in a book, possibly one I've written, but you don't have to take my word for it. Space cadets, stand down. Que sera sriracha. Catch you on the flip side. Bottle out.

Badflower - This Is How The World Ends

Nooooooooo! I was done. I had it all finished. Then I didn't like it so I added the third Helmet album so it would end with the end of an era. All I had to do was edit it, and upload it, and pay the people, and tell you about it, but no, of course not. Way off down a hallway some little voice said I should really do the whole audio book, like seriously 47 hours of me actually reading these things, and then another voice was like "you should totally ask your friends to voice the characters," and everyone else golf clapped, and I was like "noooooooo!," but totally yes I am definitely going to start doing that right after I feed the dogs, and then somebody was humming Badflower's Don't Hate Me, and I said "what could it hurt?," and it hurts a lot because This Is How The World Ends is fantastic, so of course I have to review it, but I'm stuck in this Faulknerian epic of a run-on sentence, and damnit I'm exhausted, but it's Imbolc and we did have buttered potatoes as the bowl that holds dinner, and I tripped over a groundhog so there's 9,000 more months of work, but at least the teacher didn't take my socks away.

Stupid brain, making me do stuff. I give up, enjoy some delightfully downtrodden emoish hard rock. Coke and Ketamine, we have a serious drugs in music contender. It's funny, it's melodramatic, it's realistic, it's like if AWOL Nation hadn't plane crashed into we've lost our sense of humor ville.

And yes, the sarcasm is strong with this one. I think you'll be pleasantly surprised at how intellectually stimulating this album is. Highly recommended, and I will probably be seeing if their music is monetarily accessible in the very near future. Hopefully I don't forget. Enjoy.

Prince – Purple Rain

Dearly beloved. We are gathered here because we all know full well that I can't stop. We'll just pretend to not notice last night's album ended with us fantasizing our own funerals, and I just happened to need card stock and paper towels.

There are a few records mandatory for every record collection. I have quite a few, but I didn't have Purple Rain. Now I do. It's one of the specific albums Tipper Gore and the PMRC used to demand those important warning stickers. Darling Nikki is a bit of a freak. Golf claps all around for Tipper, how else would we know which albums to hide from the impressionable minds of our parents? It's also not lost on me that it's the soundtrack of Prince's movie about Prince's early days in the Minneapolis club scene and I had to unplug the USB cable from the mixer I'm using to record me reading my books about the things my ears heard over the last 3 years. The coincidences are astonishing.

You might be under the impression that it's Prince, just a totally normal dude in a purple suit singing love songs or that one about a fruit-colored hat. That's a big no, this is THE what the hell am I listening to album par excellence. The guitars are insane, the bleep bloops and noises and incredibly detuned synths are mind melting. Everyone says this was his most Pop album to date, but he's screaming, shredding, there tons of New Wave and Hard Rock hiding underneath.

This remastered at Paisley Park pressing on 180g from Target is spectacular, by the way. You should definitely pick it up if your Target has copies.

People often point out how often people forget how amazing a guitarist Prince was, but that's barely half of the amazingness. The songs themselves are masterpieces in their own right, his vocals and overdubs are totally crazy, this is real art.

Paranoid, Breakfast In America, Rumours, Purple Rain. You might have others, but if those 4 aren't there then I don't think you can really call it a collection at all.

Black Sabbath

Heavy Metal. I believe the lineage is pretty much Iron Butterfly's Heavy, Steppenwolf's "Born To Be Wild," Randy Holden's held up Population II, and then the official first publication of tonight's album, Black Sabbath. It sits comfortably on a bunch of great lists: self-titled debut, records recorded in a day (mixing on day 2), set list albums, albums that start with rainstorms and/or church bells, probably more.

Is the title track the primordial ooze from which Doom Metal lurched into existence? I dunno, but my goodness is it chock full of goodness, so we'll roll with it.

Is it really all that and a bag of chips? Yes. It's raw, it's awkward, Iommi's double-tracked solos sword fight each other through your brain matter, Geezer's bass sounds like an absolutely disgusting monster that crawled out of a tar pit to mumble at you, Ozzy sounds more like Ozzy than you even remember, they torture a rusty harmonica, it is glorious.

But perhaps more importantly, I think you can still hear how new and exciting and uncompromisingly critical of the horrors of the modern world it is even today. It's vibrantly gut wrenching, and completely unafraid of letting all the demons out to play.

It's also interesting to note how different people interpret the "satanic imagery." For the band and the album, it's a metaphor. The world at the time was "satanic." Us Americans, of course, received it through the coffee filter of Anton Lavey, the Church of Satan guy. I'm sure you will not be at all surprised to learn that I've read The Satanic Bible, and worshipping Satan isn't the point at all. The point of Laveyan Satanism is complete personal intellectual and physical freedom, no matter what form that takes. Theoretically, intentionally choosing to adhere to a life of Abstinent Catholicism is a completely lovely Satanic practice in its own right. It's a psychology of intention rather than obedience, and hedonism only works if you're actually a hedonist. The band was just trying to really drive home how horrible the Vietnam War was.

What this album really is is Blues Rock cranked up to 11 played by people who knew exactly how much they hated Birmingham, and led by a guitarist who actually had his fingertips chopped of in a sheet metal accident when he was 17. That's certainly a perspective.

King Crimson - In The Court Of The Crimson King

We could have a bit of a debate about the first Prog album. Most people would probably give that title to Days of Future Passed by The Moody Blues. Some would Argue In The Court of the Crimson King by King Crimson. I'm on the fence.

That Moody Blues album was literally a gift from the label: things are in a slump, why don't you guys try a pop album with orchestral interludes. The result is very much a concept album with a story, but it's really just a fairly standard Psych-Rock album of the time, no matter what anyone else says. You could definitely argue that it "created a new genre," but I don't think I can honestly believe it was written from that perspective.

In The Court Of The Crimson King, however, is very much Prog: the Rock band as ensemble, blending Rock, Jazz, Pop, and symphonic style composition into an eclectic amalgam that can't really be broken back down into its component parts. That's probably a needlessly fussy distinction. Ok fine, let's listen to the technically second Prog Rock as a definitive genre album, In The Court Of The Crimson King.

What a lovely album. Greg Lake can sing anything and I'll be happy. I never have much to say about lovely albums because they speak for themselves. I do wonder, though, which 3 lullabies in an ancient tongue he actually heard the choir softly sing. I suppose you could do the boring thing and interpret tracks 2, 3, and 4 as those lullabies the 21st-century schizoid man heard. I'm borderline not schizoid, so Imma go even weirder and pick from the actual list our buddy Gerard compiled for us.

Standing Stones, Third Eye, and The Storm are my choices this time around, but there's no reason you can't pick 3 of your own. Just head over to gerardsmith2 dot bandcamp dot com and flesh out the intertextuality on your own terms.

Resume The Presses!!!!

So, here it is, the final entry in the Ledger of Doom, Labor vs Utility and my final answer, Regis:
There is a remarkably common misconception about the Marxist Labor Theory of Value. It goes something along the lines of "the value of a commodity is determined by the amount of labor necessary for its production." The ensuing logic is that labor intensive commodities are more valuable and therefore cost more than easily produced commodities. This is simply false.

The Labor Theory of Value begins at the assumption that the value of labor is equivalent to the value of the product of that labor, and assigns comparative value to other commodities according to the comparative value of the product of their production. When one value is decided, the other is equivalent. An example will help, even if the values themselves are unrealistic.

Let's say it takes 9 hours to paint a house and 30 minutes to kill and butcher a chicken. The labor theory of value says that painting a house is equivalent to the butchering of 18 chickens. Note that the labor is equivalent, not the price (there is no price at the moment). We assume the cost of materials will be radically different based on the comparative values of the tools and materials needed to perform that labor. Let's say the paint and brushes and things cost $100, and the painter wants $15 an hour for his labor. 15×9=135. Therefore, the butchering of 18 chickens should be worth 135, so the cost of labor to butcher 1 chicken should be $7.50 + whatever the chicken cost to raise (a number derived from the inherited cost of raising them). Let's just pretend it's $5 (that's a guess based on my own fuzzy memory of the last time I actually calculated it 5 or 6 years ago).

So, we can say that having your house painted costs $235 whereas buying a chicken for dinner costs $12.50. Those specific numbers might seem wrong to you personally in real life, and that's totally fine, all we really care about is the relationship. Compared to each other, this relationship seems completely agreeable: the commodities themselves represent reasonable proportions, the equivalence between disparate labors is fair. If all of a sudden that guy who paints houses wants $400, you'll reply "I'd have to charge $22 per chicken, GTFO of here with that nonsense!"

Conversely, let's look at how the comparative value of painters works if the price stays the same. A painter who can do the same job in 7 hours will make more money in a year because they can do more gigs, a painter who takes 12 hours will earn much less. This isn't some nefarious scheme by the way, this is the chicken butcher's perception of value based on a day's work. So long as the painter is charging $135 for the labor of painting the house, plus or minus an hour is fairly irrelevant. Now, if you're painting the house in 5 hours and therefore charging me $27 an hour, we might need to renegotiate before I call shenanigans with a shotgun, and if you're painting the house in 12 hours at a measly 11-something an hour, then maybe house painting is not a productive use of your time and energy. But notice, the time factor is its own penalty. You can get ahead within reason, and you can grind away if necessary, but either way my house gets painted, so I don't really have to care.

You are intimately familiar with Marxist labor value if you have ever taken your car to a mechanic. It monetarily rewards the exceptional and punishes the lackadaisical, so long as they provide equivalent quality.

For contrast to the labor theory of value, we look to the Austrian School theory of Marginal Utility. If labor is the mindset of production, utility is the mindset of consumption. Keep in mind this is not the same as referring to demand-side or supply-side economics. This is about the psychology of the participants, not the analysts.

The theory says that the value of a commodity is determined by its most trivial usage. As supply increases, people find new and creative ways to use that commodity, resulting in higher steady demand and lowering the overall cost of production.

It's harder to give a good example, but we can look at corn. It is a labor-intensive staple that requires processing to be viably nutritious, but at high levels of production we use it to make corn syrup, animal feed, ethanol, etc. Mining silicon is another example. We use silicon for all sorts of ingenious things from potholders to microchips. These commodities, then, get their value in terms of their most trivial usage, their marginal value, and when we zoom out to the macro level, we can see that the result is a relatively stable commodity value over long periods of time. That phenomenon is the basis of sociopolitical systems like the "gold standard," and prioritizing investment over savings.

What we need to understand is that both theories exist at the same time, both theories are in essence true for their own descriptive values, but both theories fail to describe real world phenomena when they collide. That is the conflict between the US and OPEC, two capitalists arguing about the nature of value. Oil producing countries want an equivalent exchange of labor value, American consumers want cheap gasoline at the expense of its producers. The end result is a lot of war because neither side agrees about what is or isn't fair.

I think the source of this problem is the misinterpretation of the theories themselves as not simply descriptions of psychological states, but as ready-to-wear policy making decisions. They can't be. It is certainly true that people tend to respond to certain situations en masse, but no person is actually bound by any analytical construct. People tend to make what they think is the best choice for themselves, and that includes intentionally sabotaging their own goals and doing the opposite of what authority suggests. Any authority, a person, a book, conventional wisdom, mom and dad, etc. Policy has to equally address both sides of that coin.

So, to continue on from my previous explanation about the labor theory of value, we need to understand an important structural aspect of Marx's definition of Capitalism. Keep in mind that I'm not picking one side or the other to defend or bash, I'm simply describing the misconception.

In my example I showed where surplus value is created by performing the same job in less time, or what we would colloquially call "working hard." Marx is primarily concerned with where that surplus goes and how it is used.

Again with the caveats, but we have to use Marx's definition of Capitalism, not yours. If you call this structure something else, fine, but you are responsible for translating the terms for yourself. We are also using Bottle's reading of Marx, which is pointedly different from Lenin, Stalin, Mao, Bordiga, and on and on and on. If you haven't read my books or 3 years of facebook posts, you are at a bit of a disadvantage. I can't do anything about that except tell you to read my books (4th one coming out soon).

What is this surplus thingamabob that capitalists exploit? It's the additional value created by doing the same job faster and/or more efficient than another person producing identical results. Pretend most people can produce 40 a day (of whatever it is). Dudelady can produce 60 of equal quality in the same amount of time, but if you try to make everyone else do 60 the quality of their output decreases. Dudelady is generating surplus value. If Dudelady cuts corners to accomplish it, that's cheating and Dudelady gets demerits or slapped with a wet noodle or something, but in this essay, we'll say the situation is legitimate.

Capitalism is any system where someone other than Dudelady owns that surplus as profit. Communism as Marx vaguely describes it (not the political parties or the Soviet Union like you're thinking about), is the absence of that structure, so it does not actually exist in the real world. Communism is the afterparty after we all watch Capitalism eat its own tail.

Marxist Thought is a bunch of people trying to make the structure of Capitalism disappear, but Marx specifically says you can't make it disappear, you can only redistribute the surplus, and by the way the whole thing is stupid. That's Marx's assessment, and I happen to agree, much like Frank Zappa, that for the most part the whole thing is stupid. I don't think you're stupid, I think there are a lot of garbage ideas walking around in everyone's heads, and every so often we need to deposit them in the dumpster. That's my bias, and I'm sticking to it.

Now, most people would say that a significant portion of Dudelady's surplus should rightfully be redistributed back to Dudelady. Trouble is, Dudelady sold that surplus during the agreement to be an employee. Yes, even if Dudelady is a sole proprietor, Dudelady is 2 different legal entities and must account for the actions of both of them; you cannot spend the same dollar twice, even though it looks like that on paper. That's not my definition, that's Capitalism, and no one has ever proven that it isn't.

Now, some people will be tempted to argue that Marx's conception of Capitalism is wrong, but will almost inevitably use fundamental theories of Classical Economics to prove it. That's a problem because Marx's description of Capitalism is Classical Economics, so you end up rejecting your own argument. The inverse is also true, you might recognize it as the evolution from Structuralism to Post-Structuralism, or the Post-Modern Apocalypse. It's all the same extra-dimensional twist because economics is nothing more than a theoretical description of human behavior using counting. That's tough because we're bad at behaving and my goodness do we fight about it like Marx says we do.

To be clear, my official opinion is that we need to stop using abstract economics as the decision-making factor in our lives. It's a zero-sum game where both the winners and losers die having never received a trophy or a medal or even a "thanks for playing." It might be entertaining to watch on the weekend for some people, you might even make a career out of it, but I think you'll be hard-pressed to find anyone who can honestly say it's fun.

But back to compounding the problem. Marx advocates a Stateless global society, then quite confusingly seems to think that the State can be used to eliminate itself. We know that's not true, the state becomes a capitalist enterprise, and a lot of people end up selectively choosing who can or can't be a Capitalist. Same problematic twist there as well because you're arguing for taking away the private property of the people who you think are trying to take away your private property.

Property is another one of those problematic terms, because as I outlined above, if you think you own what you produce you are by your own definition Marxist. Yet again, I didn't make those rules, I'm just climbing up/down the Escherian staircase so you can see what it looks like.
As always, I both apologize and you're welcome?

Goo Goo Dolls – Dizzy Up The Girl

Great news! My 4 books are finished. I mean it, that's it, I'm not trying to write any more of them. From here on out we're just gonna let 'em be what they are as album reviews. Tonight it's the 6th Goo Goo Dolls album, Dizzy Up The Girl. The thing about the Goo Goo Dolls is that they are actually 3 different bands. You got John Rzeznik's Alt-Rock bangers, John Rzeznik's ballads, and Robby Takac's Punk sensibilities (he was the original lead singer back when they were a mildly shitty Punk band, and I think we all know how much I like mildly shitty Punk bands: quite a lot). Think Gin Blossoms/Soul Asylum, Goo Goo Dolls' biggest hits, and Alkaline Trio without the death humor for comparison, respectively. I like 2/3 of that, but the ballads are totally fine for what they are. This is a great album if you know that's exactly what you're getting into.

I have an interesting history with the Goo Goo Dolls. It's roughly 1) Long Way Down is an amazing song, 2) oh, I can't find a copy of A Boy Named Goo anywhere, 3) I cannot afford to buy albums anymore anyway, and 4) Iris? It's fine, I guess, but I definitely don't feel bad for not caring anymore if that's the direction their career is going. Let's unpack that.

John's summary of the Walmart problem goes like this:

"The name of the album is *A Boy Named Goo*. The picture is of a boy covered with goo. What part of this concept are they unclear on?"

See, people complained that they though that boy was covered in blood, like some kind of demon summoning ceremony in the forest or something. That's creatively stupid, I'll give you that, but stupid nonetheless. So, Walmart told Warner it was declining sales, which by the way is totally morally motivated market manipulation and groundless censorship, and stopped carrying it altogether. This was all part of that war on restless teenagers I hated living through, and also reminds me of that Rotary Connection Christmas album, but it wasn't a total career killer back then. They just switched gears and bumped the rudder to point toward a demographic that didn't offend the Waltons as much, and put out their 6th album to humongous commercial success. That demographic was teenage girls. See, nothing problematic here, she looks totally happy and intellectually stimulated, and that wall covering is très chic (ALT+232), not at all reminiscent of the padded walls of a psych ward. All dressed up and not allowed to go on a date, just the way Conservatives like it.

Yeah, I quite enjoy this. A bit of nostalgia never hurt nobody, and it's a proper 45-minute album showcasing the infinite variety of Alt Rock with weird noises thrown in. You could rag on John's moderately schlocky vocal fry, and change some of the lyrics like I'm silently doing in my head, but I don't feel the least bit embarrassed by enjoying any of it. Good solid all around alt rock of its time, which was also my time, so that's fun. Not particularly provocative, but I'm just as guilty as anyone of enjoying the blast from teenaged years past, when Alternative was Mainstream. Quite a lovely listen.

So, In Closing

There, it's done, I don't know if it's a million words, but I wouldn't be surprised if it's close after 3 years of me prattling on. Index this thing quick, Compy, before another one of those ideas puts on a puppet show with my talk-fingers. But before I go for real this time, you fans of real life chronology should know that I turned 42 a few days ago, Russia is invading Ukraine, Tears for Fears released a new album called The Tipping Point, and the whole world is basically a mess. What's new?

Until I can imagineer something else to occupy our time and brain cells, this is Cap'n Bottle signing off. Over and out.

P.S. Sorry to all the Steve's out there; I didn't mean you personally.

- Bottle 2/28/22

Andy Taylor, 50
Animal Slaves, 89
Architects, 118
Badflower, 257
Berlioz, 247
Billy Joel, 123
Black Sabbath, 259
Blood, Sweat & Tears, 70
Brian Setzer, 166
Buffalo Nichols, 62
Carmine Appice, 213
Cigarettes For Breakfast, 193
Cloudkicker, 14
CSN&Y, 132
Damsel, 233
Deerhunter, 84
Detroit, 226
doubleVee, 131, 147
Edgar Winter, 32
Feargal Sharkey, 76
Fleetwood Mac, 10
FM, 6
Frank Sinatra, 25
Ghost, 141
Goo Goo Dolls, 267
GREGORY, 24
Gunpowder Gray, 224
Helmet, 100, 255
Huey Lewis and the News, 5, 54
Hum, 178, 249
I Prevail, 175
Joe Bonamossa, 144

Judy Collins, 66
Keith Moon, 211
Kids See Ghosts, 30
King Crimson, 260
KMFDM, 16
Machines Of Loving Grace, 244
Marcy Playground, 14
Mastodon, 165
Mean Creek, 230
Ministry, 19
Nektar, 81
Nirvana, 91, 179
Oak & Bone, 228
Odyssey, 76
On! Air! Library!, 88
p(nmi)t, 24
Pearl Jam, 129
Prince, 258
Rage, 49
Ray Conniff, 170
Rest Repose, 93
Robocop, 226
Rolling Stones, 163
Runt, 55
Saosin, 21
Soundgarden, 136
Spandau Ballet, 43
Spirit, 12
Stone Temple Pilots, 13
The 4 Seasons, 57
The 5th Dimension, 128
The Association, 9
The Beatles, 72

The Bird And The Bee, 87
The Carpenters, 219
The Cars, 125
The Doors, 60
The Escape Club, 57
The Flaming Lips, 155
The Haunt, 231
The Knack, 209
The Lettermen, 105
The Moody Blues, 201
The Motors, 48
The Rascals, 77

The Reactionaries, 90
The Sandpipers, 64
UB40, 115, 126
UFO, 198
Uriah Heep, 5
Vaughan Williams, 195
Webern, 177
Weird Al, 146
White Zombie, 25
Zager and Evans, 241
ZZ Top, 200

www.ingramcontent.com/pod-product-compliance
Lightning Source LLC
Chambersburg PA
CBHW031238290426
44109CB00012B/350